Pro ASP.NET 4 CMS

Advanced Techniques for C# Developers Using the .NET 4 Framework

Alan Harris

Apress®

Pro ASP.NET 4 CMS: Advanced Techniques for C# Developers Using the .NET 4 Framework

ISBN-13 (pbk): 978-1-4302-2712-0

ISBN-13 (electronic): 978-1-4302-2713-7

Printed and bound in the United States of America 9 8 7 6 5 4 3 2 1

Trademarked names, logos, and images may appear in this book. Rather than use a trademark symbol with every occurrence of a trademarked name, logo, or image we use the names, logos, and images only in an editorial fashion and to the benefit of the trademark owner, with no intention of infringement of the trademark.

The use in this publication of trade names, trademarks, service marks, and similar terms, even if they are not identified as such, is not to be taken as an expression of opinion as to whether or not they are subject to proprietary rights.

Distributed to the book trade worldwide by Springer Science+Business Media, LLC., 233 Spring Street, 6th Floor, New York, NY 10013. Phone 1-800-SPRINGER, fax (201) 348-4505, e-mail orders-ny@springer-sbm.com, or visit www.springeronline.com.

For information on translations, please e-mail rights@apress.com, or visit www.apress.com.

Apress and friends of ED books may be purchased in bulk for academic, corporate, or promotional use. eBook versions and licenses are also available for most titles. For more information, reference our Special Bulk Sales–eBook Licensing web page at www.apress.com/info/bulksales.

The information in this book is distributed on an "as is" basis, without warranty. Although every precaution has been taken in the preparation of this work, neither the author(s) nor Apress shall have any liability to any person or entity with respect to any loss or damage caused or alleged to be caused directly or indirectly by the information contained in this work.

The source code for this book is available to readers at www.apress.com. You will need to answer questions pertaining to this book in order to successfully download the code.

*"What you leave behind is not what is engraved in stone monuments,
but what is woven into the lives of others."*

—Pericles

Contents at a Glance

Contents

About the Author

■ **Alan Harris** is the senior web developer for the Council of Better Business Bureaus. He also regularly contributes to the IBM developerWorks community where he writes "The Strange Tales of a Polyglot Developer." Alan has been developing software professionally for almost ten years and is responsible for the development of the CMS that now handles the high volume of users that the CBBB sees every day. He has experience at the desktop, firmware, and web levels, and in a past life he worked on naval safety equipment that made use of the Iridium and ORBCOMM satellite systems.

Alan is a Microsoft Certified Technology Specialist for ASP .NET 3.5 Web Applications. Outside of the IT realm, he is an accomplished Krav Maga and Brazilian Jiu Jitsu practictioner, as well as a musician.

He can be contacted regarding this book (or development in general) at dotnetalan@gmail.com. He is also available via Twitter at http://twitter.com/anachronistic and encourages discussion on his IBM blog at https://www.ibm.com/developerworks/mydeveloperworks/blogs/anachronistic/.

About the Technical Reviewer

■ **Jeff Sanders** is a published author and an accomplished technologist. He is currently employed with Avanade Federal Services in the capacity of a group manager/senior architect, as well as the manager of the Federal Office of Learning and Development. Jeff has 17+ years of professional experience in the field of IT and strategic business consulting, in roles ranging from leading sales to delivery efforts. He regularly contributes to certification and product roadmap development with Microsoft and speaks publicly on technology. With his roots in software development, Jeff's areas of expertise include operational intelligence, collaboration and content management solutions, distributed component-based application architectures, object-oriented analysis and design, and enterprise integration patterns and designs.

Jeff is also the CTO of DynamicShift, a client-focused organization specializing in Microsoft technologies, specifically Business Activity Monitoring, BizTalk Server, SharePoint Server, StreamInsight, Windows Azure, AppFabric, Commerce Server, and .NET. He is a Microsoft Certified Trainer and leads DynamicShift in both training and consulting efforts.

He can be reached at jeff.sanders@dynamicshift.com.

Acknowledgments

To my friends, family, and co-workers: thank you for sticking with me through another book as well as the development of the CMS. It's been a long process but a rewarding one; I hope I haven't been too unbearable along the way.

To the team at Apress: thank you for your help, invaluable suggestions, and continual patience while I developed an enterprise system and a book in lockstep. You gave me the freedom to make the system what it needed to be and to write a book that supports that vision.

To the great people at KravWorks: thank you for providing me with an environment where I can grow as both a fighter and a person. The experiences I've had within the walls of the school are unlike anything I've encountered anywhere else, and they've made me better than I was before. You will always have my respect.

To the readers of this book: my desire is that what you find in these pages serves to inspire you in some fashion as a developer. I had an absolute blast building the CMS; I can only hope that I have conveyed that sense of excitement within.

Introduction

I started down the road of building a content management system (CMS) as a direct result of the experiences I had working with another custom CMS in my day-to-day work. A handful of design decisions made at the conception of that system years ago greatly impacted the CMS from a development standpoint; some things worked exceptionally well, some things needed additional love and care to achieve the results we really wanted, and some things were outright broken.

As usual, hindsight is 20/20; although the system had carried us for years, the code base was so huge and so intertwined that rewriting it was the only cost-effective solution. Even simple maintenance tasks and feature development were increasingly resource-prohibitive. I set off on a skunkworks project to create the CMS while the remaining developers kept the existing one chugging along.

It's a truly difficult decision to throw away code. A lot of developers worked on the previous CMS over the years, and a completely new system brings with it a unique set of challenges. I wasn't only throwing the old code away; I was throwing away the applied project experience, the accumulated developer-hours spent working with it, and so on. It's the shortest path to incurring significant design debt that I can think of, and incur I most certainly did: the CMS was developed from the ground up over the course of approximately a year.

The end result is a CMS that the development team is happier working with, that management can trust will be stable and dependable, and that users find both responsive and fully featured. It's not perfect, but luckily, no system is. If there were such a thing, someone would've built it, and we'd all be out of jobs. What I've tried to do is build a system that met the evolving business needs of my organization and write a book to accompany it that acts as a guided tour of both the new .NET features and how they click together in the context of a CMS. It has proven to be a very interesting ride, indeed.

A tremendous benefit to the creation of both the system and the book was the early preview and beta of Visual Studio 2010 and .NET 4.0. Case in point: as you'll see, the new Managed Extensibility Framework makes up a significant part of the business logic in the CMS (and VS2010, which uses MEF for its add-on capabilities). Could the CMS have been built without .NET 4? Of course, it could have been, but I would venture to say that it would not be as robust or as feature-complete given the timeframe.

I can think of a dozen ways to accomplish any of the results shown by the CMS in this book. What I have attempted here is to demonstrate the methods that worked for me in a production environment, using a system that is concrete rather than theoretical, and with the newest technology Microsoft has to offer as the method of transportation.

About This Book

This book is fundamentally a companion text as much as it is an introduction. A content management system is a nontrivial piece of software with many "moving pieces." As such, it would be next to impossible to document the usage of each and every line of code in a meaningful way while still giving adequate coverage to the topics new to .NET 4.0.

In terms of structure, each chapter introduces a new topic of some sort, breaking down the core concepts quickly using small, straightforward examples. The remainder of the chapter is used to demonstrate how those concepts were applied to solving the challenges that building a CMS presents.

Along the way, I've tried to highlight useful bits of information (or pitfalls) that mark the way from design to implementation.

What You Need to Use This Book

This book assumes that you have a copy of Visual Studio 2010, .NET 4.0, and a web browser at your disposal. It also assumes that you have a copy of the source code to the CMS.

Code Samples

The source code for this book is available from the Apress website. The CMS core is licensed under a Creative Commons Attribution 3.0 Unported License; this means that you, the reader, are free to copy, distribute, and transmit the work as well as adapt it for use in your own projects if you so desire. This license does require attribution if you want to launch a CMS of your own based on the core; otherwise, it's yours to do with as you please.

Feedback

I'm happy to answer questions and discuss development topics; my email address is dotnetalan@gmail.com, and I'm also available on Twitter at http://twitter.com/anachronistic. As always, despite the eagle eyes of the reviewers, any errors or typos are my responsibility; Apress provides an errata form on its site for alerting you to these issues.

## CHAPTER 1

Visual Studio 2010 and .NET 4

"If the automobile had followed the same development cycle as the computer, a Rolls-Royce would today cost $100, get a million miles per gallon, and explode once a year, killing everyone inside."

—Robert X. Cringely

It has been eight years since Microsoft released the first version of the .NET Framework and Visual Studio to the world. In the interim, developers have found new and innovative ways to create tremendously powerful software with these tools, and Microsoft in turn has listened carefully to developer feedback, effectively putting the feature set and methodology into the hands of the people who will use it on a daily basis. The number and quality of tools in this latest version speak highly to that decision.

Now on version 4 of the .NET Framework, Microsoft has radically improved the developer experience while maintaining the core framework that so many have become comfortable with. As the framework has evolved over time, Microsoft has done an excellent job of preserving the functional core while adding impressive components on top, thereby reducing or eliminating breaking changes in most cases, which not only eases the upgrade process for developers but serves as an excellent bullet point for IT managers who must weigh the risks of infrastructure upgrade with the benefits of the newest versions of the framework.

■ **Note** The last release with potential breaking changes was version 2.0 of the framework; versions 1.0 and 1.1 of .NET were solid releases, but developer feedback resulted in several sweeping changes. That said, the breaking changes were limited, and since then components have been added, not removed or significantly modified.

Who This Book Is For

I assume that if you're reading this book, you've already got some experience with developing in a .NET language; the book uses primarily C#, with additional sections in IronPython for scripting purposes, jQuery for client-side JavaScript development, and so on. Ideally, before beginning, you should at least be comfortable with creating solutions, web sites, and class libraries, as well as comfortable with the general C# language syntax. Although the book will address the core concepts in a content management system as well as how to apply new .NET 4 features to its development, we'll be moving at a pace that assumes web development is already fairly natural for you.

Further, although we will be focusing mainly on C#, there are situations where C# is not the best language in which to express a solution to a particular problem, and there are so many great choices available in .NET 4 that it's almost criminal to ignore them. When a new language or tool is introduced, we'll take some time to cover its syntax and capabilities before applying it to the CMS, so you don't need to be a complete .NET polyglot expert before tackling those sections.

■ **Caution** I am using the Team System edition of Visual Studio 2010 for the writing of this book because there are components to the IDE that are made available only through that particular edition. If you're using Professional or Express versions of any of these tools, there will be certain components you won't be able to use. I will highlight these areas for you and do my best to make things functional for you even if you're not using the same version. The most notable difference is the lack of historical debugging in versions below Team System.

Who This Book Is Not For (or "Buy Me Now, Read Me Later")

If you have no experience in a .NET language (either C# or VB .NET) or no experience with the concepts behind web development (such as HTTP requests, the page life cycle, and so on), I would wager that you'll be in some conceptually deep water fairly quickly, and you probably won't enjoy the experience much. This book is aimed at the intermediate to advanced .NET developer who is interested in learning about the newest version of .NET and Visual Studio as well as the application of some of Microsoft's more interesting fringe projects that are in development at this time. You do need some familiarity with the tools and languages this book is based on; I recommend spending some time learning about C# and ASP.NET and then returning to see some examples of new Microsoft technology that makes the experience more enjoyable.

What's New in .NET 4

Before we jump into Visual Studio, let's take a look at the new features and tools that come with .NET 4. For now we'll take a quick look at each topic, effectively creating a preview of the contents of the rest of the book. Each topic will be covered in greater detail as we explore how to apply it to the design of the CMS (which you'll learn about at the end of this chapter).

Some of the tools and components I detail in this chapter are separate downloads from the core 4 framework; I have provided the current links and versions for your convenience.

■ **Note** The Common Language Runtime (CLR) is Microsoft's implementation of the Common Language Infrastructure (CLI). The CLI is an open standard that defines how different languages can compile to an intermediate bytecode for execution on virtual machines on various platforms. Essentially, C#, VB .NET, and other .NET languages compile to Common Intermediate Language (CIL) and are executed by the CLR. This means that any platform with an implementation of the CLR can execute your code with zero changes. This is a powerful new direction for software development and allows you an essentially platform-agnostic viewpoint as a developer; the exceptions are fringe cases involving pointers, unmanaged code, and types that deal with 32-bit versus 64-bit addresses, and the majority of the time you are unlikely to encounter them (unless unmanaged code is your thing, of course).

C# Optional and Named Parameters

We've all encountered development scenarios where a "one-method-fits-all" solution isn't quite right. Perhaps in one instance it makes sense to rely on some default value; an example might be hiding database connection details behind a GetConnection() class that uses the one and only connection string defined in your application. If you need to add more connection strings to the application, you could overload this method like in Listing 1–1.

Listing 1–1. *A Set of Database Connection Method Overloads*

```
/// <summary>
/// Returns a SQL connection object using the default connection string "CMS".
/// </summary>
public SqlConnection GetConnection()
{
    return new SqlConnection(ConfigurationManager.ConnectionStrings["CMS"].ConnectionString);
}

/// <summary>
/// Returns a SQL connection object using a supplied connection string.
/// </summary>
/// <param name="conStr">A connection string of type string</param>
public SqlConnection GetConnection(string conStr)
{
    return new
SqlConnection(ConfigurationManager.ConnectionStrings[conStr].ConnectionString);
}

var conn = GetConnection();
var conn2 = GetConnection("CMS2");
```

■ **Tip** Generally, it's a better practice to code to an interface, not a concrete class. By that I mean if you create a data layer entirely using `SqlConnection` and `SqlCommand` objects, you will have some work ahead of you if you decide to swap to Oracle or CouchDB. I typically use `IDbConnection` as the method type for this reason, but the example is less cluttered if I stick with the more familiar `SqlConnection` (which does implement `IDbConnection`), so I think breaking the rules in this case is justified. Throughout the book we'll be using the SQL Server-specific classes in all cases.

In my experience, major database shifts are not frequent occurrences, but your particular situation may benefit from additional flexibility.

That's a perfectly acceptable solution and a clean way to do things, but the code base is larger for it. With .NET 4, C# now supports optional and named parameters, providing a cleaner method for completing the same task (see Listing 1–2).

Listing 1–2. Handling the Connections in One Method with Optional Parameters

```
/// <summary>
/// Returns a SQL connection object using the default "CMS" connection if none is provided.
/// </summary>
public SqlConnection GetConnection(string conStr="CMS")
{
    return new
SqlConnection(ConfigurationManager.ConnectionStrings[conStr].ConnectionString);
}

SqlConnection conn = GetConnection(); // uses the default connection string
SqlConnection conn2 = GetConnection("CMS2"); // uses the optional parameter
```

■ **Note** You could accomplish the same task with a nonoptional string parameter and check its state within the method; however, I think you'll agree that the whole solution is simpler and more elegant with the optional parameter. A very large portion of software programming in most languages is devoted to "defensive programming": checking boundaries, value existence, and so on. Optional methods essentially remove lines of defensive code and thereby reduce the number of areas a bug can hide.

If you have a method that has multiple optional parameters, you can provide names for the parameters you do want to supply in the form (*name : value*), as shown in Listing 1–3.

Listing 1–3. A Method with Required and Optional Parameters

```
/// <summary>
/// Test method with optional parameters.
```

```
/// </summary>
/// <param name="id">an integer ID</param>
/// <param name="foo">a string value; defaults to "bar"</param>
/// <param name="initial">a character initial; defaults to 'a'</param>
public static void Test(int id, string foo="bar", char initial='a')
{
    Console.WriteLine("ID: {0}", id);
    Console.WriteLine("Foo: {0}", foo);
    Console.WriteLine("Initial: {0}", initial);
}

Test(1, initial : 'z');
```

As you can see in Figure 1–1, although a default value for Initial was supplied in the method signature, it is optional, and therefore a supplied value from a call will override it.

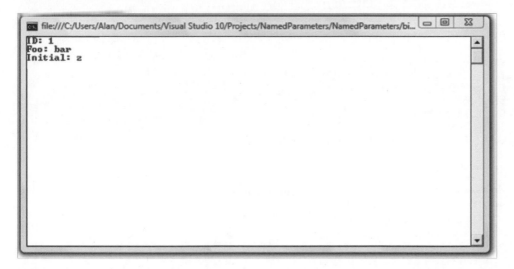

Figure 1–1. We supplied the required parameter and one of the optional ones using a name.

■ **Tip** Named parameters have to appear after required parameters in method calls; however, they can be provided in any order therein.

C#'s dynamic Keyword

Developers used to working with unmanaged code such as COM objects, C++ libraries, and so on, are likely very familiar with reflection in .NET. Reflection allows us to, at runtime, examine modules and assemblies and gather type information from them so that we may bind and call methods in these assemblies. A fairly common use case is to provide plug-in functionality to .NET applications; if an interface is defined that plug-ins must support, a developer can use reflection to gather type information from any assembly that implements that interface and act on it accordingly. It's certainly a powerful tool in the .NET arsenal, but .NET 4 opens new doors via the dynamic keyword.

Suppose we have a third-party library whose sole function is to reverse a string of text for us. We have to examine it first to learn what methods are available. Consider the example in Listing 1–4 and Figure 1–2.

■ **Note** This reflection example is adapted from a blog post by the excellent Scott Hanselman, the principal program manager at Microsoft and an all-around nice guy. You can find his blog post on the subject of the C# dynamic keyword at `http://www.hanselman.com/blog/C4AndTheDynamicKeywordWhirlwindTour` `AroundNET4AndVisualStudio2010Beta1.aspx`.

Listing 1–4. The Methods to Square Numbers Using an Outside Library

```
object reverseLib = InitReverseLib();
type reverseType = reverseLib.GetType();
object output = reverseType.InvokeMember(
    "FlipString",
    BindingFlags.InvokeMethod,
    null,
    new object[] { "No, sir, away! A papaya war is on!" });

Console.WriteLine(output.ToString());
```

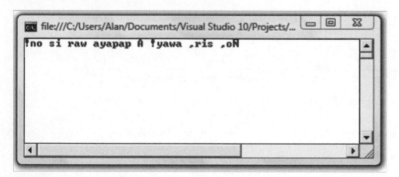

Figure 1–2. Flipped using reflection to get at the proper method

---

■ **Caution** Yes, I am nerdy enough to pick a palindrome to reverse. Back away slowly.

Reflection, although extremely functional, is really rather ugly. It's a lot of syntax to get at a simple notion: method A wants to call method B in some library somewhere. Watch how C# simplifies that work now in Listing 1–5.

Listing 1–5. *Using the* `dynamic` *Keyword to Accomplish the Same Thing*

```
dynamic reverseLib = InitReverseLib();
Console.WriteLine(reverseLib.FlipString("No, sir, away! A papaya war is on!"));
```

So, where's the magic here…what's happening under the hood? Let's see what Visual Studio has to say on the matter by hovering over the dynamic keyword (see Figure 1–3).

```
dynamic reverseLib = InitReverseLib();
```
dynamic
Represents an object whose operations will be resolved at runtime

Figure 1–3. *The Visual Studio tooltip gives a peek at what's really going on.*

Essentially, the dynamic type is actually *static*, but the actual resolution is performed at runtime. That's pretty cool stuff, eliminating a large amount of boilerplate code and letting your C# code talk to a wide variety of external code without concern about the guts of how to actually start the conversation. The application of this concept doesn't have to be so abstract; let's look at a more concrete example using strictly managed C# code.

Assume we have a abstract base class called `CustomFileType` that we use to expose common functionality across our application wherever files are involved. We'll create a `CMSFile` class that inherits from `CustomFileType`. A simple implementation might look like Listing 1–6.

Listing 1–6. *A* `CustomFileType` *Abstract Base Class*

```
public abstract class CustomFileType
{
    public string Filename { get; set; }
    public int Size { get; set; }
    public string Author { get; set; }
}

public class CMSFile : CustomFileType
{
    // …some fancy implementation details specific to CMSFile.
}
```

Now if we want to act on this information and display it to the screen, we can create a method that accepts a dynamic parameter, as shown in Listing 1–7.

Listing 1–7. *A Method to Display This Information That Accepts a Dynamic Type*

```
/// <summary>
/// Displays information about a CustomFileType.
/// </summary>
/// <param name="fileObject">a dynamic object to be resolved at runtime</param>
static void DisplayFileInformation(dynamic fileObject)
```

```
{
    Console.WriteLine("Filename: {0}", fileObject.Filename);
    Console.WriteLine("File Size: {0}", fileObject.Size);
    Console.WriteLine("Author: {0}", fileObject.Author);
    Console.ReadLine();
}
```

■ **Tip** Notice when using XML comments that Visual Studio treats dynamic parameters just like any other. Therefore, since the type is resolved at runtime, it's not a bad idea to indicate in the param tag that the object is dynamic so that you and others are aware of it when the method is used.

If we call this method providing a CMSFile object, the output is really quite interesting (see Listing 1–8 and Figure 1–4).

Listing 1–8. Calling Our Method with a Dynamic Object

```
static void Main(string[] args)
{
    DisplayFileInformation(new CMSFile{Filename="testfile.cms", Size=100, Author="Alan
Harris"});
}
```

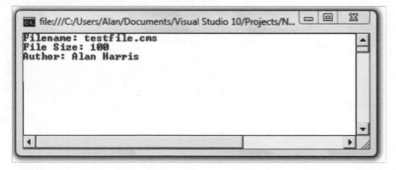

Figure 1–4. The results of a method accepting a dynamic type

■ **Note** This is really an application of *duck typing* to the stodgy, static language of C#, which I imagine will be appealing to developers used to Python and similar languages. For the uninitiated, duck typing means "If it looks like a duck and quacks like a duck, it must be a duck." It refers to the ability of dynamic languages to treat objects the same if they have the same method signatures. For example, if class A has methods Foo and Bar and class B has methods Foo and Bar, then class C can treat A and B identically since they "look" the same. This sort of thing gives developers used to traditionally static languages the heebie-jeebies.

The experienced developer at this point is shouting at the page, "You could accomplish the same thing with a method like static void DisplayFileInformation(CustomFileType fileObject)." This is true to a point; this falls apart once you begin to deal with classes that do not specifically inherit from CustomFileType but perhaps have the same properties and methods. The use of the dynamic keyword allows you to supply *any* object that has an appropriate footprint; were you to rely solely on the CustomFileType object in the method signature, you would be forced to either create multiple overloads for different object parameters or force all your classes to inherit from that singular abstract base class. The dynamic keyword lets you express more with less.

Consider Listing 1–9; assuming we have two classes, FileTypeOne and FileTypeTwo, that do not inherit from a common base class or interface, the DisplayFileInformation method that accepts a specific type (FileTypeOne) can operate only on the first file type class, despite that both classes have the same properties. The DisplayFileInformation method that accepts a dynamic type *can* operate on both classes interchangeably because they expose identical properties.

Listing 1–9. Demonstrating the Effectiveness of the Dynamic Keyword

```
public class FileTypeOne
{
    public string Filename { get; set; }
    public int Size { get; set; }
    public string Author { get; set; }
}

public class FileTypeTwo
{
    public string Filename { get; set; }
    public int Size { get; set; }
    public string Author { get; set; }
}

/// <summary>
/// Displays information about a file type without using the dynamic keyword.
/// </summary>
/// <param name="fileObject">a FileTypeOne object </param>
static void DisplayFileInformation(FileTypeOne fileObject)
{
    Console.WriteLine("Filename: {0}", fileObject.Filename);
    Console.WriteLine("File Size: {0}", fileObject.Size);
    Console.WriteLine("Author: {0}", fileObject.Author);
    Console.ReadLine();
}

/// <summary>
/// Displays information about a file type using the dynamic keyword.
/// </summary>
/// <param name="fileObject">a dynamic object to be resolved at runtime</param>
static void DisplayFileInformation(dynamic fileObject)
{
    Console.WriteLine("Filename: {0}", fileObject.Filename);
    Console.WriteLine("File Size: {0}", fileObject.Size);
    Console.WriteLine("Author: {0}", fileObject.Author);
    Console.ReadLine();
}
```

Dynamic and Functional Language Support

If you have any experience with Python, Ruby, Erlang, or Haskell, you will be pleasantly surprised with .NET 4. Microsoft has had support for dynamic and functional languages for some time; however, it has always been through separate add-ons that were in development quite separately from the core framework. First-class support is now available because the following languages are now included out of the box:

- IronPython
- IronRuby
- F#

■ **Note** Don't take this to mean that F# is a one-to-one equivalent of either Erlang or Haskell; indeed, F# is quite different from both of them. F# is simply the functional language of choice in the .NET ecosystem at the moment. We'll cover functional versus procedural and object-oriented programming later in the book.

IronPython and IronRuby execute on the Dynamic Language Runtime (DLR). The DLR has existed for some time but now comprises a core component of the .NET Framework; the result is that IronPython and IronRuby now stand alongside C# and VB .NET as full-fledged .NET languages for developers to take advantage of. Furthermore, if you have experience developing in Python or Ruby, the transition to .NET will be smooth because the language is fundamentally the same, with the addition of the powerful .NET Framework on top. Developers interested in working with functional programming languages will find F# to be a very capable entry into the .NET family; F# has been around for years and is able to handle some very complex processing tasks in an elegant fashion.

Parallel Processing

For several years now, it has been commonplace for even entry-level machines to have either multiple processors or multiple cores on the motherboard; this allows for more than one machine instruction to be executed at one time, increasing the processing ability of any particular machine. As we'll see, this hardware trend has not escaped the notice of the Microsoft .NET team, because a considerable amount of development effort has clearly gone into the creation of languages and language extensions that are devoted solely to making effective use of the concurrent programming possibilities that exist in these types of system environments.

■ **Caution** We'll cover parallel and concurrent computation in the chapters on data access and data mining, but don't fall into the easy trap of assuming that everything in your code will speed up if you perform a task in parallel. Although some tasks are "embarrassing parallel," meaning they are trivial to separate into discrete elements and process individually, some tasks do not benefit at all and in fact slow program execution considerably. The overhead involved in managing parallel elements can overshadow the performance benefit of splitting the task in the first place. Only through careful planning and testing can you properly evaluate the performance effect of parallelism.

Parallel LINQ (PLINQ)

Language Integrated Query (LINQ) was first introduced into the .NET Framework in version 3.5. LINQ adds a few modifications to the Base Class Library that facilitate type inference and a statement structure similar to SQL that allows strongly typed data and object queries within a .NET language.

■ **Note** The Base Class Library defines a variety of types and methods that allow common functionality to be exposed to all .NET languages; examples include file I/O and database access. True to form with the framework, the addition of LINQ classes to the BCL did not cause existing programs built with versions 2.0 or 3.0 to break, and PLINQ has been applied just as smoothly.

PLINQ queries implement the IParallelEnumerable<T> interface; as such, the runtime distributes the workload across available cores or processors. Listing 1–10 describes a typical LINQ query that uses the standard processing model.

Listing 1–10. A Simple LINQ Query in C#

```
return mySearch.Where(x => myCustomFilter(x));
```

Listing 1–11 shows the same query using the AsParallel() method to automatically split the processing load.

Listing 1–11. The Same LINQ Query Using the AsParallel() Method

```
return mySearch.AsParallel().Where(x => myCustomFilter(x));
```

PLINQ exposes a variety of methods and classes that facilitate easy access to the multicore development model that we will explore later in the book, as well as ways to test the performance effects that parallelism has on our applications in different scenarios.

Task Parallel Library (TPL)

Not content to only expose convenient parallelism to developers using LINQ, Microsoft has also created the Task Parallel Library (TPL). The TPL provides constructs familiar to developers, such as For and ForEach loops, but calls them via the parallel libraries. The runtime handles the rest for you, hiding the details behind the abstraction. Listing 1–12 describes a typical for loop using operations that are fairly expensive in tight loops.

Listing 1–12. A for Loop in C# That Performs a Computationally Expensive Set of Operations

```
// declares an array of integers with 10,000 elements
int[] myArray = new int[10000];

for(int index=0; index<10000; index++)
{
    // take the current index raised to the 3rd power and find the square root of it
    myArray[index] = Math.Sqrt(Math.Pow(myArray[index], 3));
}
```

Listing 1–13 shows the same query using the Parallel.For() method to automatically split the processing load.

Listing 1–13. The Same Loop Using TPL Methods

```
// declares an array of integers with 10,000 elements
int[] myArray = new int[10000];

Parallel.For(0; 10000; delegate(int index)
{
    // take the current index raised to the 3rd power and find the square root of it
    myArray[index] = Math.Sqrt(Math.Pow(myArray[index], 3));
});
```

Does this shift in techniques automatically convey a matching increase in performance? You should already know the answer: "it depends." Unfortunately, that's a very accurate answer. A little testing usually reveals the truth, and we'll learn how to do this shortly.

Axum

If you're used to typical object-oriented development (particularly with C#), Axum is going to turn your coding perception on its head. With a syntax and set of constructs very similar to C#, Axum is designed to help developers who want to write message-passing, concurrent code that is thread-safe and easy to work with and test.

■ **Caution** Axum remains a Microsoft incubation project; what this means is that support for it may be dropped at any time, plus any and all language features may change or be removed at any time. It's such a strong and interesting development in parallel languages that it is certainly worth coverage. More to the point, as an incubation project, it is strongly driven by developer feedback, so let Microsoft know what you think of it; with sufficient support, the language should survive and becomes a first-class citizen of the .NET Framework.

You won't find classes, structs, and many other C# entities in Axum. What you will find are agents that pass messages back and forth to one another. You can define millions of agents in a single application; they are designed to be extremely lightweight, much more so than typical threads. With Axum, you can create complex networks that communicate with one another asynchronously and in a highly scalable fashion, avoiding the overhead that comes with the traditional constructs of other languages. Axum is truly specialized to allow developers flexibility in creating massively scalable components and applications.

Axum has not yet been fully integrated into the .NET Framework but does plug directly into Visual Studio 2010 (and 2008 as well). It can be downloaded from the Microsoft DevLabs site at http://msdn.microsoft.com/en-us/devlabs/dd795202.aspx.

■ **Note** If you've ever worked in a language such as Erlang, the message-passing aspects and agents of Axum will be fairly familiar. Axum isn't quite functional programming in the traditional sense, but the similarities are more than passing.

Managed Extensibility Framework (MEF)

Until .NET 4, developers who wanted to create a plug-in model for their applications were left with the task of creating an implementation and infrastructure from the ground up; it's an attainable goal but potentially cost- and time-prohibitive. Microsoft's answer to this situation is the Managed Extensibility Framework (MEF).

■ **Note** Microsoft believes strongly in the MEF and in fact uses it under the hood of Visual Studio 2010 quite extensively. It introduces quite a bit of powerful add-on capability to the already extensible Visual Studio environment.

Fundamentally, MEF exposes ComposableParts, Imports, and Exports, which manage instances of extensions to your application. The MEF core provides methods to allow discovery of extensions and handles proper loading (as well as ensuring that extensions are loaded in the correct order). The nature of extensions is exposed via metadata and attributes, which should be very familiar territory to .NET developers and allows for a very consistent usage across .NET applications.

■ **Tip** The concepts of reflection and metadata come up frequently in discussions regarding extensibility. Reflection gets a bad rap for being slow; it indeed is slower than direct calls, but generally you pay only an appreciable penalty when using reflection in tight loops or in a critical set of methods that get called far more frequently than others. Reflection is used quite liberally throughout the .NET Framework, but in an intelligent fashion and only where needed. Don't write off a perfectly reasonable development solution because you've heard the worst of it; if nothing else, do a limited test, and use a profiler to get some hard numbers for your own edification.

Distributed Caching with Velocity

Ask any developer who has done serious work in a server farm where .NET sites are running behind load-balancers, and they'll tell you the same thing: although the in-memory .NET cache is both convenient and fast, the hit ratio is terribly low and not a viable solution in a multiserver situation. The largest sites in the world (Facebook, LiveJournal, MySpace, and others) all rely on distributed caching servers to maintain service availability in the face of ever-increasing user demand and data. Velocity is Microsoft's answer to that problem, allowing developers to set up distributed cache servers that hold data in-memory; objects stored in the cache do not have to be retrieved from potentially expensive database calls, resulting in greater availability and a better distribution of workload.

■ **Note** Hit ratio defines the number of times an object was successfully retrieved from the cache (a cache hit) versus how many times it could not be (a miss).

In a distributed environment, one or more caching servers sit separately from the web servers and database servers. The purpose of these servers is to provide extremely quick access to frequently used resources and data, reducing the load incurred by expensive database calls and operations. For example, once a user has logged in to your system, their personal information can be cached so that requests for that data do not need to be processed by the database; rather, they can be quickly looked up by key names and used by the application, eliminating one or more potentially costly database calls. Figure 1–5 shows the typical rough layout of a system involving distributed caching servers. Note that the caching server is a branch of the overall communication; the primary data store is still the database server, but the cache servers exist along this communication pathway as a potential source of the same information without the overhead of processing data to assemble it.

■ **Tip** Figure 1–5 should illustrate just why it's so important to have as high a hit ratio as possible: each time your code makes a request to the cache server and misses, your code has paid the performance penalty of the extra request without the benefit of returning with data and skipping the database call. Although it's nearly impossible to get a 100 percent hit ratio (excluding the rare cases where you can prefill the cache before client requests are executed), there are patterns to ensure that you maximize these cache requests as quickly as possible.

Listing 1–14 details a generally applicable pattern for working with caching. Please be aware that the purpose of this snippet is to demonstrate the pattern, not specific classes. We will cover the CMS caching classes later in the book. The basic pattern is to first determine whether a specific key exists in the cache and has a value. If it does not, we need to retrieve the appropriate data from whatever data source it would normally be found in and add that value to the cache using the key we were checking for with an optional expiration (in this example, defined in minutes). Finally, the value is returned, and program execution continues.

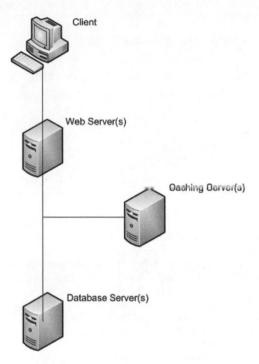

Figure 1–5. The typical architecture of a system with distributed caching

Listing 1–14. A Pattern for Working with a Distributed Cache

```
// attempt to retrieve the value for "myKey" in the cache
string myValue = CMSCache.Exists("myKey");

if (String.IsNullOrEmpty(myValue))
{
    // the key did not exist, so fetch it from the data tier…
    myValue = CMSData.SomeDataCall();

    // …and add it to the cache for retrieval next time with a 40 minute expiration.
    CMSCache.Add("myKey", myValue, 40);
}

return myValue;
```

■ **Tip** With situations such as distributed caching, it's a good idea to hide the implementation details of the cache behind a custom abstraction (in this case, `CMSCache`). If at some point you decide that `Velocity` is not for you and you would rather use `Memcached` or `NCache`, it's much easier to modify or extend your caching classes than to modify every area in your application where caching is used. Save yourself the headache, and hide the guts out of sight.

The current version of Velocity is Community Technology Preview 3, available from the Microsoft site at `http://www.microsoft.com/downloads/details.aspx?FamilyId=B24C3708-EEFF-4055-A867-19B5851E7CD2&displaylang=en`.

ASP.NET MVC

Microsoft, since the inception of ASP.NET, has essentially stuck to its WebForms model with a single form element on a page, ViewState fields, and so on. The MVC framework, which stands for Model View Controller, is a pretty radical departure in the opposite direction and certainly one that developers have been requesting for quite some time. To understand why MVC is so significant, we need to examine the evolution and purpose of the WebForms model.

The traditional WebForms model is meant to solve the problem of maintaining state on a web page. By definition, the HTTP standard is stateless; before the advent of real server-side architecture, web pages were static affairs that were limited to displaying content and permitted basically no real user interaction, short of clicking links to go to other static pages. The WebForms model has served developers well over the years, but it's not without warts and rough edges.

The most common complaint leveled at WebForms is that it is heavy and by no means optimized. Up until version 2.0 of the .NET Framework, the HTML output rendered by .NET controls (Buttons, GridViews, and so on) was in no way standards-compliant, and at the time the options were a bit limited in how to resolve these problems. In the years since, Microsoft has definitely cleaned the markup that standard .NET controls produce, but ViewState remains a critical component in the WebForms solution.

ViewState is Microsoft's primary way of preserving state information between page requests. It consists of one or more hidden input fields (typically one, but ViewState chunking allows separation of the field into multiple fields) that contain an encoded set of information about the state of any and all .NET controls on the page. Sounds great, so what's the problem?

■ **Tip** Most of the time you won't really need ViewState chunking; however, certain load balancers, reverse proxy, and firewall devices will choke on an HTML input field that is beyond a certain length. Chunking the field into some reasonable length usually resolves the problem immediately. You can experiment with different field lengths in the root `web.config` file of an application; an example would be `<pages maxPageStateFieldLength="2048">`, which will split the ViewState into an additional hidden input field at 2,048-byte divisions.

The problem with ViewState is that it can get tremendously large very quickly. Try placing several GridViews with paging inside ASP.NET AJAX UpdatePanels and view the source of your page as you navigate; it becomes obvious that the ViewState is significantly bloating the size of the page that the user receives. Worse, the ViewState appears at the top of the page, potentially putting a large roadblock between you and content that is search engine–friendly; search engines typically index only a particular number of characters in a page's content, and if 5,000 or more characters are wasted on content-less ViewState data, that's 5,000 fewer characters that a potential audience could see.

■ **Tip** Please don't fall into the trap of assuming that ViewState is encrypted. It is not. It is *encoded*, and the difference is significant. There exist several ViewState decoders that will readily show you the contents of any particular ViewState data, and writing your own from scratch is a very doable task as well. Repeat after me: ViewState is not for sensitive information.

Model View Controller is designed to solve all those problems and return to .NET developers clean, standardized markup using traditional HTML elements as well as the complete elimination of ViewState. The Model aspect refers to the data source of the application, which for our purposes will be a SQL database. The Controller is the brain of the operation, fetching the appropriate information from the Model and feeding it to the View, which is our user interface.

MVC and WebForms are both based on ASP.NET, but they place value and importance on different things; where WebForms aim to provide a very rich, stateful application, MVC aims to operate in a way that mirrors the HTTP specifications. In the MVC world, the page itself is quite dumb, capable of very little without being told. The View relies on being fed complete state information from the Controller and makes no decisions on its own. The result is a clean separation of concerns, a lightweight page model, and 100 percent control over the markup on your applications.

You're by no means limited to either MVC or the WebForms model; in fact, you're quite free to mix and match within the same application. The emphasis in .NET moving forward is on options and choices, freeing developers from constraints and allowing them to make the choices that are most appropriate for the application at hand.

■ **Tip** The technical name for the model used in WebForms is Model View Presenter (MVP), which does bear some similarity to MVC but with some critical fundamental differences. For the purposes of this conversation, the biggest difference is that in MVP, the UI is responsible for handling user input. In MVC, this is handled by the controller. Who exactly handles the input and decides what logic to execute in an application is actually a very big implementation decision.

A Tour of Visual Studio 2010

Visual Studio 2010 is a major overhaul of the VS environment, no doubt about it. Not just a shiny coat of paint, the 2010 editions are a ground-up improvement, and as mentioned earlier, Microsoft is using many of its own .NET 4 tools and components within the IDE itself. Let's take a 10,000-foot tour of the new 2010 IDE.

■ **Note** IDE is short for "integrated development environment." An IDE combines code editing, compilation, debugging, and more into one application. You are still free to perform many tasks via the command line if you choose (and many do), but the convenience of the IDE is quite impressive.

Windows Presentation Foundation

Windows Presentation Foundation (WPF) first arrived with .NET 3.0. Using Extensible Application Markup Language (XAML), WPF allowed developers to create rich application interfaces with a level of quality and visual polish previously reserved for developers working with Flash and similar tools. In Visual Studio 2010, WPF is the driving force between the new user interface spit-and-polish that you see from the moment you spin up an instance of the IDE. It's a powerful application of WPF to real-world development, and Visual Studio looks and feels like a very complete system with much attention paid to how the typical developer will use it. Figure 1–6 shows the IDE as it appears the first time you start it.

■ **Note** Microsoft Silverlight (or its Unix-based version, Moonlight) is a subset of WPF that is designed specifically to compete with Flash on the Web; before Silverlight, you could create web-facing applications in WPF, but the barrier to entry was higher. With .NET 3.0 installed, only Internet Explorer can run WPF web applications, and with 3.5, only Internet Explorer and Firefox support it. Silverlight has a much wider reach, comes with a smaller subset of the more mature WPF and .NET Frameworks, and is web-only. In general, for purely web applications, choose Silverlight over WPF.

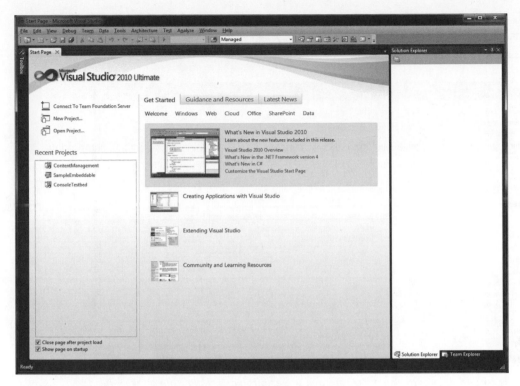

Figure 1–6. *The new and improved Visual Studio 2010 IDE*

Historical Debugging

Software development is generally a complex beast, even given the many tools and frameworks available to developers today. From thread management to distributed caching solutions, there are a lot of aspects in play at any given time, and getting everything to interact in such a fashion that the system runs correctly and efficiently requires a considerable effort.

Historical debugging allows you to set specific events in your application where the debugger will collect data that represents a snapshot of the current application state, effectively allowing you to replay the application execution and determine precisely what was happening. Alternatively, you can opt to retrieve debugging information at all method entry points in your program. The focus on the historical debugger has really been on providing an in-depth debugging ability that is familiar to developers who are comfortable working with the Visual Studio debugger.

Quite a few configuration options are available when working with the historical debugger, and the Visual Studio team has paid a lot of careful attention to the effect that data collection has on application performance, which is part of the reason so many granular levels of options exist.

The historical debugging information is presented primarily using the standard Visual Studio debugger (see Figure 1–7); since a smaller subset of data is collected, this is reflected in the information made available to you while working with the debugger. With that in mind, it is still one of the most powerful tools to make its way into Visual Studio in quite some time.

■ **Note** Historical debugging is available only in the Team System edition of Visual Studio.

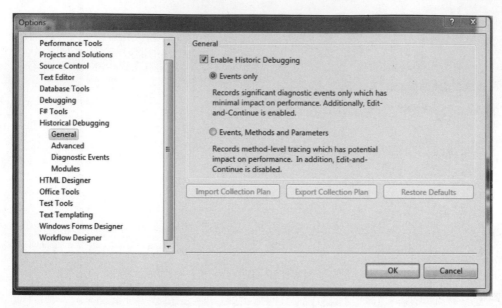

Figure 1–7. *Historical debugging can be configured in various ways depending on your needs.*

How critical is a good debugger and knowledge of how to use it effectively? Consider the following quote from a person far wiser than I:

"Debugging is twice as hard as writing code in the first place. Therefore, if you write the code as cleverly as possible, you are—by definition—not smart enough to debug it."

—Brian Kernighan, co-author of *The C Programming Language*

With historical debugging enabled, a debug history window opens to the right of the code panel when you run the application (Figure 1–8). Setting breakpoints allows you to drill deeper into the state of the application at each step. The Autos window and call stack are available as links, as well as information about the current thread, file being executed, and line that the recorded step was on. As you can imagine, this is quite the powerful tool for rolling back execution state in a complex application where interaction between different threads and modules can be difficult to reproduce any other way.

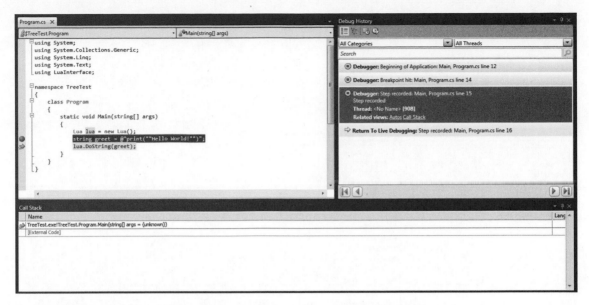

Figure 1–8. Historical debugging offers a step-by-step view of program execution.

■ **Note** If you're curious, the code in Figure 1–8 is using LuaInterface, available on Google Code at http://code.google.com/p/luainterface/. Lua is a very popular (and free) scripting language that has gained a lot of ground with developers in recent years.

Improved JavaScript IntelliSense

Working with client-side code is now significantly easier; those who are used to working with JavaScript IntelliSense in 2008 should rejoice. The IDE picks up JavaScript syntax quickly and properly, offering the same level of support that you'd find working with a server-side code in Visual Studio. See Figure 1–9 for an example of the JavaScript IntelliSense in action.

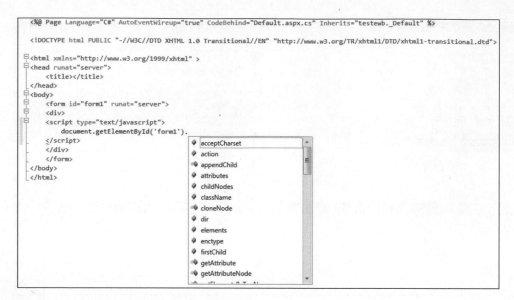

```
<%@ Page Language="C#" AutoEventWireup="true" CodeBehind="Default.aspx.cs" Inherits="testewb._Default" %>

<!DOCTYPE html PUBLIC "-//W3C//DTD XHTML 1.0 Transitional//EN" "http://www.w3.org/TR/xhtml1/DTD/xhtml1-transitional.dtd">

<html xmlns="http://www.w3.org/1999/xhtml" >
<head runat="server">
    <title></title>
</head>
<body>
    <form id="form1" runat="server">
    <div>
    <script type="text/javascript">
        document.getElementById('form1').
    </script>
    </div>
    </form>
</body>
</html>
```

acceptCharset
action
appendChild
attributes
childNodes
className
cloneNode
dir
elements
enctype
firstChild
getAttribute
getAttributeNode

Figure 1–9. JavaScript IntelliSense is fast and accurate.

jQuery Support

Not only did traditional JavaScript IntelliSense improve, but Microsoft has added full support for jQuery in its IntelliSense. jQuery is a freely available JavaScript library created by John Resig that has become quite powerful and popular in the developer community for its simplicity, ease of use, and cross-browser effectiveness. There is also a significant plug-in community as users find new and inventive ways to add some really startling client-side scripting elements to their applications via the jQuery environment.

■ **Note** How popular is jQuery? Well, ask Google, Digg, Mozilla, Dell, WordPress, Netflix, Bank of America, Major League Baseball, and many other big-name companies and organizations. They all make use of it on their production sites, and you can find many more supporters on the jQuery home page.

Compare the code in Listing 1–15 and Listing 1–16. The first demonstrates a simple JavaScript class change by locating an element with an ID of foo and using the setAttribute() method to modify the class attribute.

Listing 1–15. JavaScript Method of Locating an Element and Changing Its Class

```
<script type="text/javascript">
    var element = document.getElementById('foo');
    element.setAttribute('class', 'red');
</script>
```

Now take a look at how jQuery performs that task in a concise, clear manner.

Listing 1–16. jQuery Method of Performing the Same Task

```
<script type="text/javascript">
    $('#foo').setClass('red');
</script>
```

jQuery is really quite powerful in terms of the selection syntax it exposes to developers; consider that you want to find the third paragraph tag that has a class of storyText. jQuery makes the task trivially simple (Listing 1–17).

Listing 1–17. More Sophisticated Object Location Within the DOM

```
<script type="text/javascript">
    $('p.storyText:eq(2)').setClass('red'); // the position is a zero-based lookup
</script>
```

■ **Note** DOM is short for document object model, and it's a hierarchy tree of controls within any given web page. Navigating the DOM permits some rather sophisticated client-side modifications to be performed in your applications, and jQuery certainly makes elements conveniently accessible.

The library supports a variety of selectors; you can find elements by position in the page, ID, class, and so on. We'll look at creative ways to use jQuery to enhance our public-facing user experience later.

■ **Tip** Always consider the concept of *graceful degradation* when designing web applications where JavaScript is involved. Graceful degradation means that users with the most advanced or capable browsers can and should be presented with a pleasant and enhanced user experience, but users without such capabilities should be in any way restricted from using the site to its fullest. Basically, the bells and whistles can fall by the wayside so long as your app is functional. A user with JavaScript disabled is not going to find your accordion-style jQuery-animated navigation bar all that useful if it doesn't function with JavaScript disabled.

---

jQuery is now included by default when creating new web sites in Visual Studio 2010 and consists of a handful of .js files in the project solution. It is also capable of providing consistent client-side experiences in Internet Explorer, Firefox, Safari, Opera, and Chrome. The jQuery site (http://www.jquery.com) is an excellent resource for digging into the jQuery API as well as for exploring community contributions and plug-ins.

Building a CMS

Now that we have a better sense of what's new in the toolbox, it's time to consider what to build with it. For the purposes of this book, we'll be building a content management system (CMS) from the ground up.

The CMS detailed throughout this book is in fact a true production system used to serve tens of millions of pages per day. It was built for this book as an example of real-world application development, but also to fulfill business requirements learned over the life cycle of a previous CMS and deployed to a public-facing environment. As such, when examining the code, you will be working with an enterprise application that has been proven under a heavy load, providing high availability and a scalable architecture.

Because the CMS is a large application, it's not possible for me to cover and document every single line of it in this book. However, I have applied XML comments to every method and class in the system, and the overarching concepts of the system are covered in entirety in this book. So although I may not cover the specific function of every line in methods A, B, and C, I will certainly cover the motivation behind the creation of the code, and I believe the internal design patterns will be very clear. I highly recommend that you download the CMS from the Apress site and work with it as you progress through the book.

CMS Functional Requirements

Although I wouldn't go so far as to say we should define a complete design document, we should cover some ground on the requirements that the CMS is meant to fulfill. These are the core requirements:

- The system must support multiple sites.

- An administrative site must support end-to-end content creation (templates, pages, and styles).

- Whenever possible, the system should implement best practices (SEO, web standards, and so on).

- Scalability and availability should be primary concerns at all levels.

- Maintenance after deployment should be made as easy as possible (extensibility, plug-ins, and so on).

- Syndication, canonical links, RSS feeds, news, and so on, are necessary.

■ **Tip** Canonical links are custom links that can be inserted into the head tag of an HTML page that allow search engines to determine the preferred location of a piece of content. For more information, see Chapter 9, which focuses on search engine optimization.

A lot of technical considerations go into creating a complete content management system; put simply, it's a very difficult task. This difficulty and technical breadth make it an excellent choice for learning a new framework and how to apply powerful new languages. To successfully serve tens of millions of pages daily, there are some aspects of .NET that out of the box you may find simply don't perform under such a load.

For example, the ASP.NET AJAX UpdatePanel, although convenient in terms of usage, is a "heavy" control that if misused or abused can negatively impact performance of a page under load. I will highlight issues such as this as we work through the CMS, as well as solutions that have produced results in the actual production system.

We'll take advantage of power-user elements wherever possible; one example is via RSS feeds. It's common to create pages or user controls that output RSS feeds to users, but at the penalty of all the overhead of the complete page life cycle. We can use a generic handler instead, effectively simplifying the entire process and making the application more responsive. The framework (and ASP.NET in particular) does a great job of leaving the implementation choices up to the developer, but a lot of developers haven't made full use of these options. We'll cover many ways to keep the CMS speedy in the face of your users.

Creating the Application Framework

Let's set up some components of the application; the first thing I like to do when creating an application is define an overall solution that will house the individual projects within. I frequently keep most of my application's code in separate class libraries so that my web projects are as lean as possible.

1. Create a new project in Visual Studio; select Blank Solution from Other Project Types ➤ Visual Studio Solutions. Name the solution CMSParent, and click OK (see Figure 1–10). This solution will be used as a common location for the remaining CMS projects and libraries.

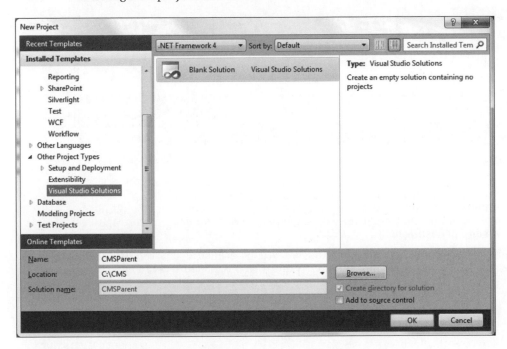

Figure 1–10. Creating the initial solution

2. Right-click the CMSParent solution in the Solution Explorer, and click Add New Project. Select Class Library from Visual C# ➤ Windows, and name it Business (see Figure 1–11). This class library will contain the business logic for our content management system.

Figure 1–11. Adding the business library

3. Repeat step 2 to create the CommonLibrary and Data class libraries. CommonLibrary will house classes and interfaces that are common to multiple tiers of the application, and Data will be focused on communicating with SQL Server and persisting data.

4. Right-click the solution, and select Add New Web Site. Ensure that web site is created below the CMSParent solution. Name it Web (see Figure 1–12), and click OK.

Figure 1–12. *Adding the web site*

5. Right-click the Web project, and click Set as StartUp Project. Your IDE should now look like Figure 1–13.

Figure 1–13. *The project solution in VS2010*

■ **Tip** Throughout the book, I'll assume that you've created your application at `C:\CMS`. Feel free to change the location if you prefer, but remember as you read that I'm placing things at this location.

Summary

Axum to Velocity, jQuery to MEF—the .NET developer could easily drown in buzzwords, code names, and acronyms. We covered the many new additions that come with .NET 4 as well as a variety of projects that integrate well with the newest framework. We examined C#'s new named and optional parameters, as well as the `dynamic` keyword and how it really functions behind the scenes. We also looked at Visual Studio 2010 and some of the new features that come with it, such as a new UI layer built on Windows Presentation Foundation and an extensibility layer created with the Managed Extensibility Framework. We discussed the overarching project of the book, a content management system, and created the skeleton architecture that will serve as the groundwork for the larger application components to come. Next, we'll begin to implement the foundation of the CMS and examine how the system will divide responsibilities across tiers.

## CHAPTER 2

CMS Architecture and Development

"Low-level programming is good for the programmer's soul."

—John Carmack

I think when id Software's programming front man made this comment, he wasn't referring to n-tier architecture and component-based development. That said, for a .NET developer working in a web environment, these concepts are sufficiently low-level enough to be the chicken soup he prescribed.

It's easy to fall into the trap of building software primarily using the WYSIWYG editor and the drag-and-drop components that .NET provides. The limitation is twofold: first, large-scale design tends to fall by the wayside when compared to the ease of use of these prebuilt components. Second, there typically is an unusually large amount of code and functionality present in the presentation areas of the application that really belongs elsewhere.

In this chapter, we'll take a look at the concepts of n-tier architecture and component-based development and begin work on the public side of our application. First we need to discuss the choice to build a CMS and why .NET is an excellent platform for its development.

Motivations for Building a CMS

There are plenty of content management systems on the market: Joomla!, Django, Umbraco, Drupal, and DotNetNuke are just some of the systems that spring to mind immediately. Many content management systems are free, some cost a pretty penny. Why even bother reinventing the wheel when so many off-the-shelf solutions exist?

The crux of the issue hinges on two points:

- First, the organization for which the system described in this book was created had very specific business requirements that were a direct by-product of the limitations that existed in the system it had been operating with previously.

- Second, as an instructional or demonstrational tool, a content management system touches on an expansive array of subjects and technologies. In short, it's a pretty useful learning tool, and it solves some real-world problems that international organizations have to consider.

At a basic level, a web-based content management system is essentially just responsible for storing and delivering HTML-based web pages. In practice, the typical CMS is now capable of handling much more, including workflow management, plug-in systems, and so on. As such, individual systems typically share some core values and focus the remainder of their energy on specific features that make them unique. Some focus heavily on providing content in XML form that is styled via XSLT; some focus on their extensibility model and ensuring that their plug-in capabilities are robust.

In the case of this book, the focus is heavily on building a system that can be expanded via plug-ins and that requires little to no modification of the core framework. For example, if I want to create a new component that displays advertisements on the right side of a page, I don't want to have to modify the CMS itself; the system should be fairly unaware of what specifically is running on a page and instead focus on the primary task of delivering content. We should be able to create our advertising module, place it in a convenient location, and have the system simply pick up its availability and use it when appropriate.

The CMS we will build together is not meant to be a replacement for Drupal or to oust DotNetNuke in some fashion. It is simply a demonstration of what has worked in production for a real organization on a day-to-day basis, as well as how new technology from Microsoft makes the job easier than it has been in the past. The code is available to you to modify, use, and reconfigure as you see fit without restriction from me.

Motivations for Using .NET

The other big question mark is (aside from the fact that I am a .NET developer by day) why does .NET make an attractive technology platform for building a content management system?

At a high level, the .NET Framework provides a great deal of features that make developing such a system fairly straightforward. The framework has built-in mechanisms for authorization and authentication, caching, rich server controls, and database access, just to name a few. Beyond the core framework, there are powerful languages such as C# and IronPython, tools like MEF, and the key fact that .NET is well-tested and known to be stable as a production system for some very large organizations. Having a mature platform that can be relied upon to perform at the level necessary to handle massive amounts of traffic is critical to the success of such a project, and .NET shines in each area. It's obviously feasible to build the same type of system in any number of other languages, but the .NET Framework makes things both convenient and (in many cases) easy.

Application Architecture

We know why we're building a CMS, and we know why we're using .NET to do it. Now we need to discuss the architecture of the application. We touched on the general concept of n-tier development in Chapter 1 when we discussed the architecture patterns Model-View-Controller and Model-View-Presenter. Technically speaking, these patterns are three-tier; each contains three distinct elements with a unique set of responsibilities.

■ **Tip** A *tier* denotes a physical separation, while a *layer* denotes a logical or abstract separation.

It is possible to have a one-tier architecture or a 100-tier architecture if desired. The most common separation is typically three-tier, and in fact when most people discuss n-tier architecture, the resulting output is a three-tier design. This is a common pattern because it conveniently separates responsibilities in a logical fashion, allowing for cleaner code that is easier to debug and maintain; for the purposes of this book, it is safe to assume that when I refer to n-tier architecture, I am speaking of at least a three-tier separation. Figure 2–1 shows the architecture and purpose of the tiers in a common enterprise application; the client is not included as a tier, and generally the data access tier and data storage tier are viewed as one entity.

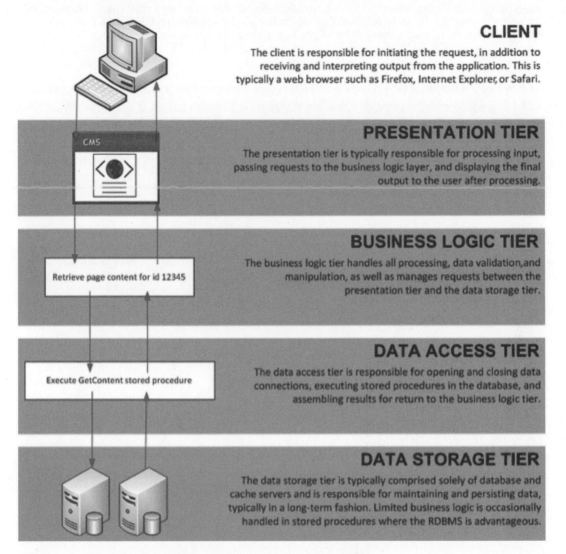

CLIENT

The client is responsible for initiating the request, in addition to receiving and interpreting output from the application. This is typically a web browser such as Firefox, Internet Explorer, or Safari.

PRESENTATION TIER

The presentation tier is typically responsible for processing input, passing requests to the business logic layer, and displaying the final output to the user after processing.

BUSINESS LOGIC TIER

The business logic tier handles all processing, data validation, and manipulation, as well as manages requests between the presentation tier and the data storage tier.

DATA ACCESS TIER

The data access tier is responsible for opening and closing data connections, executing stored procedures in the database, and assembling results for return to the business logic tier.

DATA STORAGE TIER

The data storage tier is typically comprised solely of database and cache servers and is responsible for maintaining and persisting data, typically in a long-term fashion. Limited business logic is occasionally handled in stored procedures where the RDBMS is advantageous.

Figure 2–1. A typical n-tier architecture separation of responsibility

Note the flow of communication between the tiers; the presentation tier never speaks directly to the data storage tier, and vice versa. All communication is routed through the business logic tier. The benefits to this design are varied. Should it become a necessity to support (or replace) your existing data storage with an entirely different system (such as moving from SQL Server to Oracle or from MySQL to CouchDB), the workload is reduced, and resulting bugs are easier to track down if code for data access is not liberally sprinkled throughout your web pages.

Furthermore, code in the business logic tier could theoretically be reused elsewhere if designed carefully and with modularity in mind from the beginning. Code written directly into a web page is considerably less accessible and also harder to perform unit and regression testing on.

■ **Note** Unit testing is a process where individual modules of code are tested with particular types of input to ensure that they are producing the expected output in a repeatable and reliable fashion; it is assumed by definition that a *unit* is the smallest testable component in the code. Regression testing is a method of testing code to ensure that as bug fixes and new features are added, previously resolved bugs are not allowed to occur again. Generally this is accomplished by creating tests that produce a known bug and running those tests frequently to ensure that the incorrect output is not generated. Combined, these testing methods are designed to reduce code fragility.

The CMS Application Tiers

In the context of the CMS, there are three distinct tiers to the application, along with some support modules that don't cleanly fall in the realm of the core three. The project is visualized in Figure 2–2.

- Presentation (the Web project)
- Business (the Business class library)
- Data (the Data class library)
- Data Transfer Objects (the CommonLibrary class library)
- Http Module (the GlobalModule class library)

Figure 2–2. The visual representation of the CMS project

We've covered the common three tiers already: presentation, business, and data. The remaining two libraries, CommonLibrary and GlobalModule, deserve some exploration to understand their purpose in an enterprise application where they function not as tiers but as support modules to the core three.

CommonLibrary: The Data Transfer Objects

Data transfer objects (DTOs) are essentially classes that do not have any specific behavior implemented within them; they are empty vessels for passing objects between tiers (which is why they're called data transfer objects). A project containing DTOs is also a good repository for common interfaces that multiple tiers rely on.

A logical question to ask is, why would such a construct be necessary? Consider the problem of dependency: later in the book we will create an interface called IEmbeddable, which will define the properties and methods for plug-ins that our CMS will be built around. This interface will potentially be required by (a minimum of) four distinct entities: the presentation tier, the business tier, the data tier, and any plug-ins we build (which will be required to implement it to be recognized by the other tiers).

■ **Tip** Dino Esposito offers great coverage on the pros and cons of DTOs in his August 2009 article on MSDN Magazine, located at http://msdn.microsoft.com/en-us/magazine/ee236638.aspx.

Let's look at a quick, concrete example. Listing 2–1 is the code that makes up IEmbeddable as it will be defined later in the book. Don't worry about the specifics of the code in this section; the important point is the concepts regarding where it lives.

Listing 2–1. The IEmbeddable Interface

```
using System;
using CommonLibrary.Permissions;

namespace CommonLibrary.Interfaces
{
    /// <summary>
    /// Interface that Embeddables are expected to implement.
    /// </summary>
    public interface IEmbeddable
    {
        Guid ContentID { get; set; }
        string EmbeddableName { get; }
        int EmbeddableID { get; }
        EmbeddablePermissions Permissions { get; set; }
    }
}
```

Note the namespace; it has been defined in the CommonLibrary project under the Interfaces folder. Now the CMS tiers and any plug-ins are free to use the interface without defining it themselves. Listing 2–2 shows a portion of the admin editor that restricts our plug-ins to specific sections of a page, and

Figure 2–3 shows that code in use; note that some of the namespaces and code have been trimmed for brevity.

Listing 2–2. Using the Library of DTOs in a Different Tier

```
using Business;
using CommonLibrary.Interfaces;
using CommonLibrary.Permissions;

public partial class admin_masters_controls_AddEmbeddableRow : System.Web.UI.UserControl
{
    protected void Page_Load(object sender, EventArgs e)
    {
        if (!Page.IsPostBack)
        {
            LoadEmbeddables();
        }
    }

    /// <summary>
    /// Loads the appropriate embeddables for this bucket.
    /// </summary>
    /// <param name="location">The string representation of the bucket.</param>
    private void LoadEmbeddables()
    {
        Business.Plugins manager = new Business.Plugins();
        foreach (IEmbeddable e in manager.GetEmbeddablePlugins())
        {
            bool validForThisSlot = false;

            switch (this.Parent.ID)
            {
                case "pnlHeaderEmbeddables":
                    if (e.Permissions.HasFlag(EmbeddablePermissions.AllowedInHeader))
                    {
                        validForThisSlot = true;
                    }
                    break;

                /* additional code snipped for brevity */
            }
        }
    }
}
```

Listing 2–2 demonstrates the benefits clearly; the Business.Plugins class relies on IEmbeddable to generate a generic list of plug-ins, and the presentation tier relies on it to filter a plug-in based on the permissions enum flags set within it.

DTOs permit us to define the structure of a particular object in a common location, and they allow any number of other classes in any number of separate projects to rely on a single definition for it. Without defining DTOs, we would need to define the interface in the multiple CMS tiers, as well as any plug-ins; should that interface change, we are left with a great deal of work ensuring that everything is kept in sync.

■ **Tip** If you find yourself performing the same task repeatedly in code (for example, opening database connections, finding an item in a tree, and so on), that's a reliable indicator that some refactoring is in order; look for opportunities to create less code, rather than more. Every line we write is a line we must test, debug, and maintain.

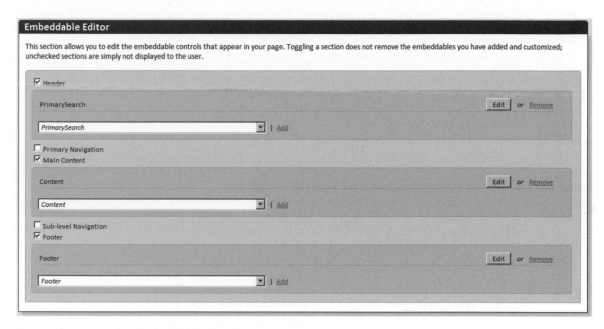

Figure 2–3. Using the IEmbeddable interface across tiers

GlobalModule: The HttpModule

One of the features of most modern content management systems is their ability to provide friendly URLs that permit users and search engines to access content without knowing arcane system details. In Chapter 9, we will explore in depth how to intercept incoming HTTP requests, parse them, and map them to specific data behind-the-scenes so that users can use URLs like http://oursite.com/contact-us/ instead of http://oursite.com/content.aspx?id=771a242e-19af-4dfc-a720-762491146acf.

Without delving into the specifics of mapping content, it's sufficient to say that a reliable method of performing this type of task is via the global.asax file, and more specifically by writing code within the Application_BeginRequest() method. Listing 2–3 demonstrates a very simplified version of this process.

■ **Caution** There is a lot more to mapping requests than Listing 2–3 will lead you to believe. Feel free to jump ahead to Chapter 9 briefly to get an idea of the types of tasks that must be performed for a page to be delivered correctly.

Listing 2–3. Intercepting HTTP Requests in global.asax

```
private void Application_BeginRequest(Object source, EventArgs e)
{
    var request = HttpContext.Current.Request.RawUrl.ToString().ToLower();
    string contentID = String.Empty;

    // ...code to hit the DB and fill contentID with the content GUID.

    if (!String.IsNullOrEmpty(contentID))
    {
        HttpContext.Current.RewritePath("/content.aspx?id=" + contentID, false);
    }
}
```

HttpModules are essentially portable versions of global.asax, contained within DLLs, that you can reuse in other applications if desired. As a result of this, they are generally preferable to writing code directly in global.asax. If desired, you could write one HttpModule specifically for rewriting "ugly" URLs to "friendly" ones, another for combining resource requests, and so on. These modules would not be tied to any one application and could solve the same problems across multiple applications.

A further benefit is a reduction in the size of any individual area of code; if a large number of complex tasks are to be performed, a single global.asax file can quickly become very bloated. HttpModules permit you to separate code in a clean fashion and accomplish the same result. The ability to unit test these discrete modules is also worth noting. In short, they're a significantly more flexible solution than the single file approach.

HttpModules inherit from the IHttpModule interface and implement a handful of methods; Listing 2–4 shows the code from Listing 2–3 placed within an HttpModule.

Listing 2–4. A Simple HttpModule Using the Code from Listing 2–3

```
namespace GlobalModule
{
    public class Global : IHttpModule
    {
        public Global() { }

        public string ModuleName
        {
            get { return "Global"; }
        }

        public void Init(HttpApplication application)
        {
            application.BeginRequest += (new EventHandler(this.Application_BeginRequest));
        }
```

```
    private void Application_BeginRequest(Object source, EventArgs e)
    {
        var request = HttpContext.Current.Request.RawUrl.ToString().ToLower();
        string contentID = String.Empty;

        // ...code to hit the DB and fill contentID with the content GUID.

        if (!String.IsNullOrEmpty(contentID))
        {
            HttpContext.Current.RewritePath("/content.aspx?id=" + contentID, false);
        }
    }

    public void Dispose() { }
    }
}
```

An additional step that must be taken with HttpModules is registration in the calling application's web.config file. Listing 2–5 shows how the CMS uses the GlobalModule via web.config.

Listing 2–5. Using the GlobalModule from the CMS via the web.config File

```
<system.web>
    <compilation debug="true" targetFramework="4"/>

    <httpModules>
        <!-- Registers the GlobalModule project to avoid reliance on global.asax -->
        <add name="GlobalModule.Global" type="GlobalModule.Global"/>
    </httpModules>

    <!-- additional elements snipped for brevity -->
</system.web>
```

Components of a CMS Page

At this point, we have a high-level conceptual overview of the physical nature of the CMS as a .NET project. Now we can address the lower-level aspects and explore what makes up a page within the system.

Every CMS approaches the concept of page creation differently, and some get very specific with their terminology and intentions. For example, Drupal users are probably familiar with modules, blocks, and taxonomies, while Joomla users work with tools such as categories, extensions, articles, and so on. In some cases, these are developer preferences, representing the actualized instances of conceptual desires. In the case of the CMS in this book, there are only two terms to become familiar with, and they are born as a result of limitations and problems presented by a previous version.

Buckets

Buckets represent the five major "zones" that make up a typical page on most systems; they do *not* indicate any sort of visual display or configuration (although for the purposes of discussion we'll use a graphical representation that is familiar to most developers). They are analogous to the WebPartZone controls that come with .NET, but they're specifically tailored to the nature of a particular type of page the system will deliver.

The concept of the buckets arose from some issues that existed in the CMS that this one was designed to replace. Certain controls were allowed in only certain sections of the page; for example, it probably doesn't make a lot of sense to have content for the footer appear in the middle of the content.

The implementation of this wound up being complex and unwieldy; zones were numbered, and the rules for coexistence were unclear and difficult to work with (not to mention repetitious). It wasn't a simple task to denote that a particular control could live in this zone and that zone, but not that zone over there. It also required developers to constantly look up which areas mapped to which numbers. In general, it was a headache on all fronts.

For this CMS, there are five major sections (or buckets) on any page; none is required, but each individual bucket can appear a maximum of one time. They permit very effective use of permissions using enum flags, which we'll discuss in a bit.

- Header

- Primary navigation

- Content

- Secondary navigation

- Footer

Although none of the buckets is required, controls are not allowed to live outside of them; there are reasons for this that we will discuss shortly.

Figure 2–4 displays these buckets visually. It's important to remember that buckets are essentially abstract containers for the controls that will be present on a page; as such, although Figure 2–4 demonstrates a typical organization of such content, it is simply one permutation and by no means the only way to lay out a page in the CMS.

Figure 2–4. *The CMS page has various buckets to contain the page controls.*

Embeddable Objects

Embeddable objects, or *embeddables* (as the CMS refers to them), are the meat and potatoes of any CMS page. They are server controls that inherit from the IEmbeddable interface and communicate in a very limited fashion with the core CMS itself. They can exist only within a bucket container; as such, they are somewhat analogous to the .NET WebParts.

■ **Note** Server controls were chosen over user controls to facilitate and encourage the reuse of components across multiple systems; in addition, they permitted an easier deployment process to production environments and could be stored off the browseable web.

Embeddables are responsible for their own data access, their own version control, establishing permissions regarding acceptable locations, and so on. The CMS knows only what is communicated via the IEmbeddable interface and otherwise is liberated from handling the low-level details of any individual component in the system.

Listing 2–6 demonstrates a simple CMS embeddable that displays a <div> with some text to a page. Although it's not critical to understand server controls or MEF yet (because both are covered in Chapter 4), the highlighted code in Listing 2–6 represents how embeddables handle bucket permissions, which we'll discuss next.

Listing 2–6. *A Simple Embeddable That Displays a Bit of Text to the Page*

```
using CommonLibrary.Interfaces;
using CommonLibrary.Permissions;

namespace Content
{
    [Export(typeof(IEmbeddable))]
    [DefaultProperty("Text")]
    [ToolboxData("<{0}:Content runat=server></{0}:Content>")]
    public class Content : WebControl, IEmbeddable
    {
        public Guid ContentID { get; set; }

        public EmbeddablePermissions Permissions
        {
            get
            {
                return (EmbeddablePermissions.AllowedInContent |
                        EmbeddablePermissions.AllowedInFooter |
                        EmbeddablePermissions.AllowedInHeader |
                        EmbeddablePermissions.AllowedInPrimaryNav |
                        EmbeddablePermissions.AllowedInSubNav);
            }
        }

        public string EmbeddableName
        {
            get { return "Content"; }
        }

        public int EmbeddableID
        {
            get { return 4; }
        }

        protected override void Render(HtmlTextWriter writer)
        {
            RenderContents(writer);
        }

        protected override void RenderContents(HtmlTextWriter output)
        {
            StringBuilder sb = new StringBuilder();
            sb.AppendLine("<div id=\"content\">");
            sb.AppendLine("[Sample text output - the Embeddable has loaded properly.]");
```

```
            sb.AppendLine("</div>");
            output.Write(sb.ToString());
        }
    }
}
```

Embeddable Permissions

It was decided during the development of the CMS that the restrictions on which embeddable objects were permissible in specific buckets would be maintained from the previous version of the CMS, although the implementation needed to be cleaned significantly.

The CommonLibrary project contains a folder called Permissions, which itself contains a class called EmeddablePermissions. This class, as shown in Listing 2–7, defines the flag enum that describes the permissions an embeddable can set.

Listing 2–7. The Permissions Available to an Embeddable

```
using System;

namespace CommonLibrary.Permissions
{
    /// <summary>
    /// Defines the possible bucket locations for an embeddable.
    /// </summary>
    [Flags]
    public enum EmbeddablePermissions
    {
        None = 0,
        AllowedInHeader = 2,
        AllowedInPrimaryNav = 4,
        AllowedInContent = 8,
        AllowedInSubNav = 16,
        AllowedInFooter = 32
    }
}
```

■ **Tip** The enum has been marked with the [Flags] attribute; this allows bitwise operations such as AND, OR, NOT, and XOR to be applied to the enumerated values. For more information on the topic, consult the MSDN C# Programming Guide at http://msdn.microsoft.com/en-us/library/cc138362.aspx.

Listing 2–6 described a simple CMS embeddable, which contained a property called Permissions. In the case of that embeddable, it was allowed to be present in all five buckets on a page. Restricting access to buckets is extremely easy; Listing 2–8 shows sample permissions for an embeddable that is only allowed in the primary-level and sublevel navigation buckets.

Listing 2–8. A Sample of More Restrictive Permissions

```
public EmbeddablePermissions Permissions
{
   get
   {
      return (EmbeddablePermissions.AllowedInPrimaryNav |
              EmbeddablePermissions.AllowedInSubNav);
   }
}
```

Besides being flexible, this approach removed the need for developers to memorize which areas were mapped to which integer value. Working on an embeddable is augmented by the IntelliSense the Visual Studio IDE provides, as shown in Figure 2–5.

Embeddable permissions in the CMS are an opt-in methodology; by default, an embeddable has no rights to live anywhere on any page. The developer must specify where a control is valid on a page.

This may seem to be an inversion of how things normally operate; it seems that it would make more sense to have a bucket define what sorts of things it can contain. In a way, that's true, but it requires that the CMS know more about the controls it will host. This approach places the control of determining valid locations in the hands of the developer creating the embeddable, while the CMS simply respects those wishes and dutifully allows or restricts as necessary.

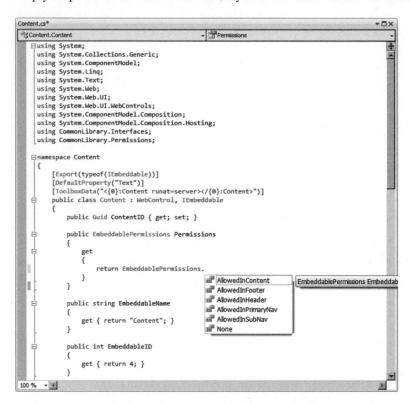

Figure 2–5. The permissions are easily accessed via IntelliSense.

Handling CMS Content

Now we've seen the overall architecture of the application and explored the lower-level details of what goes into a page's construction and the permissions applied within; at this stage, we can address the "content" portion of "content management system." Content within the system can be roughly broken down into two tables, Content and ContentVersion. We'll look at both individually.

The Content Table

The highest level of content in the system is the fairly bare-bones Content table. Shown in Figure 2–6, this is the first stop for the system when retrieving the materials that will assemble a final CMS page.

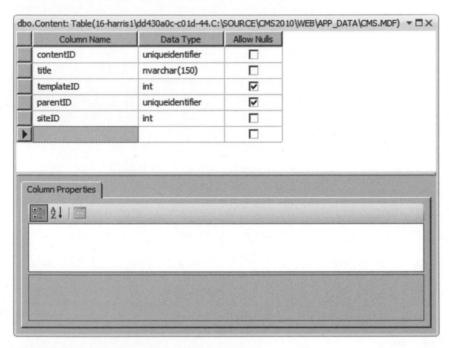

Figure 2–6. The structure of the Content table

Note that this table doesn't define whether you'll find a bucket or embeddable on the page; it only defines a GUID that uniquely identifies the page, a title for it, the ID for the site it lives in, and pointers to other elements in the site tree.

The ContentVersion Table

The second level of content in the system is the ContentVersion table. Shown in Figure 2–7, this is the second stop for the system while creating a page.

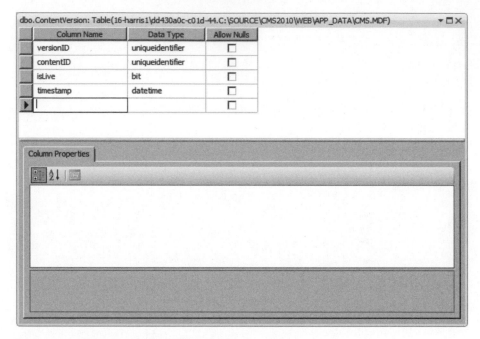

Figure 2–7. The structure of the ContentVersion table

Each time a user saves a revision of their page, this table will be updated. A unique identifier for the content is created, and a pointer is made to the entry in the Content table for this revision. The user can toggle any particular version as "live"; when the CMS is loading the data for a page, it will do so based on the revision that has the isLive field set to true. Finally, there is a timestamp field for denoting when the revision was created.

Assembling Content on Demand

The actual processing pipeline for assembling content is the CMS is fairly straightforward; it is enumerated with some fabricated data in Figure 2–8. Note that for the sake of space, the IDs are integers instead of GUIDs. In the actual CMS code, the identifiers are all GUIDs.

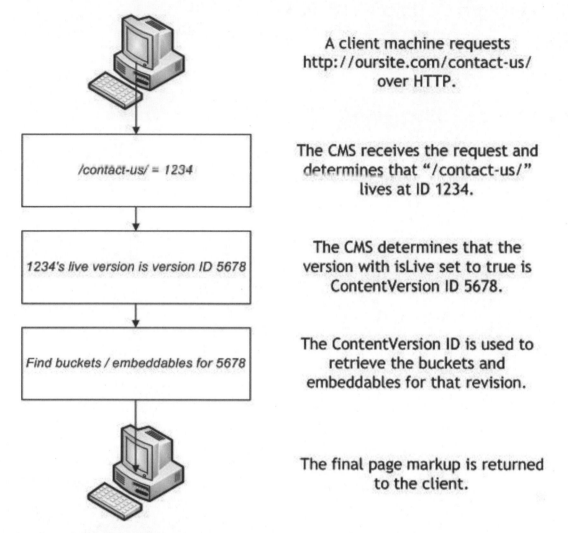

Figure 2–8. The processing of content in the CMS

The important point to take away from Figure 2–8 is that the value of the ContentVersion ID field is really the heart of content retrieval in the CMS. The Content table is used primarily to map friendly URLs to a piece of content, as well as to provide a parent container for different revisions of content. Once a piece of content has been identified, the ContentVersion ID is used through the remainder of the request to identify the particular revision that should be delivered to the client. This leads us naturally to the subject of how embeddable objects handle content versioning.

How Embeddable Objects Handle Versions

We saw earlier in the chapter that the IEmbeddable interface defines a contract the embeddable objects must abide by to be used in the CMS. Listing 2–9 describes that interface again.

Listing 2–9. The IEmbeddable Interface

```
using System;
using CommonLibrary.Permissions;

namespace CommonLibrary.Interfaces
{
    /// <summary>
    /// Interface that Embeddables are expected to implement.
    /// </summary>
    public interface IEmbeddable
    {
        Guid ContentID { get; set; }
        string EmbeddableName { get; }
        int EmbeddableID { get; }
        EmbeddablePermissions Permissions { get; set; }
    }
}
```

Note the ContentID property in bold; this is where the CMS will supply the ID for a particular version of content to the embeddable. As mentioned earlier, embeddables are responsible for their own version control, meaning that an embeddable can decide how (or if) it needs to store a revision of its own content.

Why wouldn't an embeddable store a revision? One simple example might be an embeddable that displays rotating ads that are defined in an XML file. When the user saves a page that has that embeddable on it, a new ContentVersion ID will be created and passed to the embeddable so that it can save a new revision. In the case of this embeddable, the content is unchanged; there is nothing to save.

How embeddables handle situations like this can be varied and distinct, which is the motivation behind handing such responsibilities off from the CMS core. The system will simply create the necessary data on its end and pass that information along to any components within. So long as each component is speaking the same language (meaning passing the same version ID between one another), the CMS operates knowing that the embeddable controls are handling their own responsibilities as necessary.

Summary

This chapter served as a springboard for the technical discussions to follow. We discussed the CMS architecture from a high-level perspective as a .NET app and then examined the lower-level implementation details and unique traits that differentiate this system from others. We closed with a discussion on content versioning in the CMS and demonstrated how the system handles a request, as well as the difference between content and a content revision. As we move forward into Chapter 3, we'll begin to explore the technical details individually and see how .NET 4 provides a lot of helpful tools that make developing the system an enjoyable (and productive) experience.

■ ■ ■

Parallelization

"Less than 10% of the code has to do with the ostensible purpose of the system; the rest deals with input-output, data validation, data structure maintenance, and other housekeeping."

—Mary Shaw

As time goes on, the processors in our computers have gotten increasingly smaller as well as increasingly powerful. There is a natural limit to this technology; physical restrictions have forced manufacturers to take different approaches to increasing computer power. A popular approach has been visualized through the commonplace nature of multicore processors; even baseline PCs can be found with them these days. In this chapter, we'll discuss key parallelization concepts and pitfalls, give you an overview of what .NET 4 has to offer us, and look at ways to exploit parallelization to our benefit in the CMS.

What Is Parallelization?

Strictly speaking, *parallelization* refers to the splitting of work across two or more individual cores. This is simply stated but not so simply executed. Even though .NET 4 makes the process easier, the task of identifying areas of code that are good candidates for parallelization remains a fairly difficult task and typically requires adequate testing coupled with intuition gained through trial and error with various types of data and scenarios.

It's also not a magic bullet. Parallelization carries with it overhead related to task management that may or may not be very significant, depending on the work being performed. It's not uncommon to segment work and discover that processing it sequentially is *faster* than in parallel; some tasks simply incur too much overhead for too little reward and operate slower in parallel.

Good Parallelization Candidates

There are a few common scenarios where code is likely to benefit from parallelization. At a process level, some examples include long-running processes ("Fetch me data from these 10 external web services and update me when you've done so") and types of data-mining operations ("From this list of English words, divide them into sections, and return every word that has the letter *I* in the third position").

From a code perspective, areas of code likely to benefit most from parallelization are self-contained, discrete blocks of code that don't rely on many external dependencies or share a lot of resources with other areas of code. There are specific considerations related to resources and dependencies that we will discuss in a moment.

■ **Note** We'll return to the topic of identifying good parallelization candidates in the "Amdahl's Law" section.

Differences from Multithreading

Parallelization and multithreading get lumped together occasionally in discussion, although there are some important distinctions.

Multithreading refers to the ability of the operating system or process to spawn individual threads and execute blocks of code within them. In this way, the operating system is effectively giving each thread a small slice of time in which to operate and then switching between those slices very quickly (called, appropriately enough, *time slicing*).

This is how single-core machines appear to run multiple applications at the same time; from a single-core machine, you can browse the Web, copy files, listen to music, and so on, while everything seems to happen at the same time. In reality, the applications are not truly executing at the same time; the operating system is simply switching between threads so quickly that it all appears to be simultaneous.

Code operating in parallel *is* truly executing at the same time as a totally different block of code on a different core. There is some conceptual overlap in the tasks and concerns between the two methods, and on a multicore machine threads *can* execute at the same time, but in general there is a concrete difference between parallel processing and multithreading.

■ **Tip** The .NET parallelization additions in framework version 4 are pretty intelligent and will execute even on single-core machines.

Parallel Pitfalls

The saying "there's no free lunch" is well-suited to parallel programming; Visual Studio 2010 and .NET 4 make the processes easier to develop and debug, but it still by no means "easy." Let's discuss some of the potential problem areas that we might encounter while developing parallel code.

■ **Note** These potential problems are also common to multithreaded applications, as mentioned previously.

Deadlocks

Deadlocks are the result of two or more sections of code that are waiting for the other to finish; the conditions prevent the sections from ending, effectively locking the application.

For example, code section A needs to access sensitive data from code section B and requests a lock so that no other code sections may modify that data while A is operating on it. Code section B needs to operate on sensitive data that code section A possesses and requests a lock on it. A's data is locked as it is waiting on a successful release by B, and B's data is locked as it is waiting on a successful release by A. This is demonstrated visually in Figure 3–1.

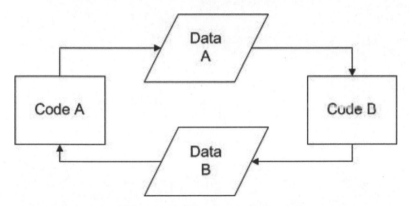

Figure 3–1. A deadlock occurs when A and B want mutually exclusive data.

By their very nature, deadlocks can be a bit tricky to cause outright. However, by using an unsafe method of locking resources coupled with a high number of iterations, we can cause the issue to happen more frequently.

Listing 3–1 iterates 100,000 times, creating instances of a class that locks resources poorly. The LockFoo() and LockBar() classes both acquire locks to shared objects in a different order. This implementation makes it impossible to guarantee that one lock will be released in time for another to be acquired. It's also impossible to guarantee that a deadlock will occur; however, it is fairly likely.

Listing 3–1. Poor Lock Utilization Can Set Up Code to Be Deadlocked

```
using System;
using System.Threading;

namespace Chapter3
{
    class Program
    {
        static void Main(string[] args)
        {
            for (int i = 0; i < 100000; i++)
            {
                Deadlock d = new Deadlock();
                d.Begin();
            }
        }
    }

    class Deadlock
    {
```

```csharp
string foo = "foo";
string bar = "bar";

public void Begin()
{
    Thread a = new Thread(new ThreadStart(LockFoo));
    Thread b = new Thread(new ThreadStart(LockBar));

    a.Start();
    b.Start();
}

public void LockFoo()
{
    lock (foo)
    {
        lock (bar)
        {
            bar = bar.ToUpper();
            Console.WriteLine(foo + bar);
        }
    }
}

public void LockBar()
{
    lock (bar)
    {
        lock (foo)
        {
            foo = foo.ToUpper();
            Console.WriteLine(foo + bar);
        }
    }
}
    }
}
```

Figure 3–2 shows the output of a sample execution. Notice that even while the application is running, there is no pattern to how the foo and bar variables have been modified. In some cases, the output is "fooBAR"; whereas in others it's "FOObar." Eventually the application stopped executing before completing the full 100,000 iterations. On several runs, the application did not even complete a full iteration before failing.

The intermittent nature of deadlocks coupled with their notable execution-ending effects makes them particularly nasty problems to have in code.

___

■ **Tip** One way to eliminate the deadlock issue in this sample is to acquire and release locks in the same order in both threads. Although there is still no synchronization and the output is not guaranteed correct, the program will complete its iterations as expected.

___

Figure 3–2. A deadlock occurred and execution halted.

Race Conditions

Race conditions occur when multiple threads or processes are attempting to access a single resource, resulting in unexpected behavior or security flaws when events occur out of sequence.

For example, consider the simple computation in Listing 3–2.

Listing 3–2. A Simple Loop to Update an Integer Value

```
using System;

namespace Chapter3
{
    class Program
    {
        static int x = 0;

        static void Main(string[] args)
        {
            for (int i = 0; i < 3; i++)
            {
                x++;
            }

            Console.WriteLine("{0}", x);
            Console.ReadLine();
        }
    }
}
```

When processed sequentially, the output is predictable; Figure 3–3 shows the correct answer of 3.

Figure 3–3. Processed sequentially, the result is correct.

If we modify the code from Listing 3–2 with a naïve thread implementation, we will get an entirely different result. Listing 3–3 shows the modified code. Note that we've given each thread a specific name; after we examine the output of the code, we'll see how Visual Studio's IDE can help us diagnose the situation.

■ **Note** If you already have threading or parallel programming experience, you're going to look at Listing 3–3 and know immediately why things aren't working properly. The example is supposed to demonstrate something that seems like it should work but has some conceptual flaws about how to access resources in a concurrent fashion.

Listing 3–3. A Naïve Threading Implementation with Unexpected Results

```
using System;
using System.Threading;

namespace Chapter3
{
    class Program
    {
        static int x = 0;

        static void Main(string[] args)
        {
            Thread thread = new Thread(new ThreadStart(Program.computeX1));
            thread.Name = "Thread One";

            Thread thread2 = new Thread(new ThreadStart(Program.computeX2));
            Thread2.Name = "Thread Two";

            Thread thread3 = new Thread(new ThreadStart(Program.computeX3));
            Thread3.Name = "Thread Three";

            thread.Start();
            thread2.Start();
            thread3.Start();

            Console.WriteLine("{0}", x);
```

```
        Console.ReadLine();
    }

    static void computeX1()
    {
        x++;
    }

    static void computeX2()
    {
        x++;
    }

    static void computeX3()
    {
        x++;
    }
}
}
```

Running this code produces entirely different output, as shown in Figure 3–4.

Figure 3–4. The result is different from what was expected.

The differences in output cannot even be guaranteed to be consistent across multiple executions. Running this application a second time resulted in the output shown in Figure 3–5.

Figure 3–5. The results aren't guaranteed to be consistent in terms of being wrong.

There are two important things happening in the code. There is no guarantee of the order in which the individual threads will access the shared resource (the integer variable x), nor is there any guarantee in this code that a particular thread was alive to actually access the resource. This is a cause of the output shown in Figures 3–4 and 3–5; the unpredictable nature of the implementation resulted in an unpredictable value being stored in the shared resource. This is illustrated in Figure 3–6.

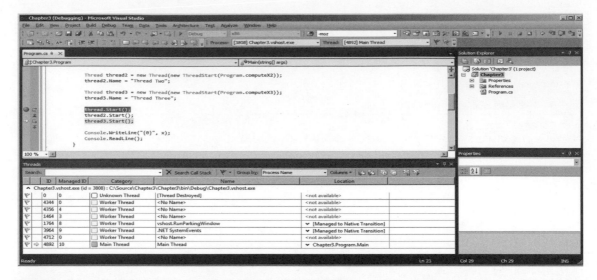

Figure 3–6. *The current threads, which don't necessarily match expectations*

Notice that although the breakpoint has halted execution on the start of thread3, the Threads window (accessible via Debug ➤ Windows ➤ Threads) indicates that none of our threads is currently running. When thread3 is about to begin, the others haven't yet started or have started and completed execution.

The approach demonstrated is indeed a naïve implementation of processing using a shared resource, but to developers not yet familiar with this type of condition, it *seems* like it should work by spawning three threads, having them all run and increment the variable x, and displaying the result afterward.

Thread Starvation

Thread starvation occurs when a process or set of processes creates too many threads, resulting in the system having insufficient resources to complete the tasks on the individual threads.

This in and of itself can trigger deadlocks and race conditions; for example, if code section A has insufficient time to complete its work and release any locks on data, code section B will never be able to acquire a lock and will be unable to complete its tasks, and so on.

Although thread starvation is less common as a result of the increase in system resources in modern computers, it's still possible to overload an individual core, particularly in high-load environments. Load testing and careful attention to resource management remains a significant consideration, even with the tools provided in .NET 4.

■ **Tip** Microsoft provides a free application called WCAT, short for Web Capacity Analysis Tool. WCAT is lightweight and can be very beneficial for testing the performance implications of heavy load on a web application; it supports multithreading and has a variety of other helpful features. We'll discuss the usage of this tool in Chapter 8

Amdahl's Law

At the beginning of the chapter, I mentioned briefly that there is overhead associated with parallel processing and that not all structures and operations are well-suited to being executed in parallel. Amdahl's Law does a nice job of summarizing the issue.

> *"In parallel computing, the resulting speedup of multiple processors is restricted by the areas of the program that are necessarily sequential."*

—Amdahl's Law

Consider the executions of Program A and Program B, diagrammed in Figure 3–7. Both programs have darker sections, representing areas of the code where parallelization would likely have a significant benefit. Program B has more opportunities that are of a substantial size, whereas program A has perhaps one segment worth the overhead of parallelization.

Figure 3–7. Program B has larger opportunities for parallel benefits.

In general, it is best to focus efforts on areas that will have the most benefit. Let's say that there are two sections identified as possible candidates for parallelization. The first takes up 2 percent of the total execution time of the process, and the second takes up 31 percent. The application of parallel techniques to either section results in a 1 percent speedup of their individual execution time, because of the areas of code that must execute sequentially.

Optimizing the first section is not worth the resulting 1 percent speedup created by that effort. An area that consumes 31 percent of your execution time will benefit much more from a 1 percent speedup and is a better option for improving application performance.

.NET 4 Parallelization Concepts

.NET 4 brings to the table some pretty significant new tools to ease the tasks that parallel programming requires. We won't use all of them in the CMS, but we will take a look at the big-ticket items so that we have a sense of what is now available to solve particular types of problems.

Task vs. Data Parallelism

The .NET 4 parallelism enhancements can be roughly broken down into two standard categories: task and data parallelism. The task enhancements emphasize the splitting of code into multiple sections that can be executed on multiple cores, while the data enhancements focus on splitting data into multiple sections and performing operations on it in parallel before reassembling and arriving at a result. Both types of parallel processing are provided via the new Task Parallel Library.

Task Parallel Library

Exposed via the System.Threading.Tasks namespace, the Task Parallel Library greatly simplifies thread and resource management for .NET 4 developers. The power of this addition is actualized via the task scheduler, which handles the low-level plumbing that previously needed to be worked out manually via threading.

Listing 3–4 demonstrates how to create two simple tasks to perform a unit of work. The StartNew() method accepts an Action delegate to a method and invokes that particular method immediately.

Listing 3–4. Creating New Tasks to Perform Work

```
using System;
using System.Threading.Tasks;

namespace Chapter3
{
    class Program
    {
        static void Main(string[] args)
        {
            Task foo = Task.Factory.StartNew(() => DoFooWork());
            Task bar = Task.Factory.StartNew(() => DoBarWork());

            Console.ReadLine();
        }

        static void DoFooWork()
        {
            Console.WriteLine("Inside the DoFooWork task");
        }
```

```
        static void DoBarWork()
        {
            Console.WriteLine("Inside the DoBarWork task");
        }
    }
}
```

The output of this code in Figure 3–8 demonstrates that the tasks have been performed as desired.

Figure 3–8. *The output of the spawned tasks*

Task.Wait()

Earlier in the chapter we discussed the issues around synchronization; specifically, we saw examples where we spawned threads to perform a unit of work and found inconsistent results. Sometimes thead one completed before thread two, sometimes it was the other way around, and sometimes a thread didn't complete at all.

TPL provides the Task.Wait() method as a way of ensuring order and synchronization. We can easily modify the code from Listing 3–1 to the way it appears in Listing 3–5, using the Wait() method to synchronize the tasks without having to place locks on any particular resource.

■ **Note** Given the concerns about thread starvation, it's a reasonable to ask if the scheduler creates new threads for every iteration. In some cases it will, and in others it will not. The scheduler is very flexible about how it allocates resources and threads and will attempt to choose the best method given the current conditions.

Listing 3–5. *Synchronizing Output via Wait()*

```
using System;
using System.Threading.Tasks;

namespace Chapter3
{
    class Program
    {
        static void Main(string[] args)
        {
```

```csharp
            for (int i = 0; i < 1000; i++)
            {
                Deadlock d = new Deadlock();
                d.Begin();
            }

            Console.ReadLine();
        }
    }

    class Deadlock
    {
        string foo = "foo";
        string bar = "bar";

        public void Begin()
        {
            Task a = new Task(() => LockFoo());
            Task b = new Task(() => LockBar());

            a.Start();
            a.Wait();

            b.Start();
            b.Wait();
        }

        public void LockFoo()
        {
            bar = bar.ToUpper();
            Console.WriteLine(foo + bar);
        }

        public void LockBar()
        {
            foo = foo.ToUpper();
            Console.WriteLine(foo + bar);
        }
    }
}
```

■ **Tip** You can also use Task.WaitAll(*task1…taskN*) and Task.WaitAny(*task1…taskN*) to achieve different effects. The WaitAll() method ensures that each task has completed before exiting, and WaitAny() ensures that at least one task has completed.

Figure 3–9 shows the output of this code; note that the text output is in the correct order, alternating between "fooBAR" and "FOOBAR" as each individual task is executed. The scheduler has appropriately synchronized the tasks based on the Wait() calls.

Figure 3–9. The output of the spawned tasks

Parallel.For() and Parallel.ForEach()

.NET 4 also introduces two new types of loops that can operate in parallel fashions: Parallel.For() and Parallel.ForEach(). Each operates in a similar fashion to their traditional sequential counterpart, although with a slightly different syntax as shown in Listing 3–6.

Listing 3–6. Using Parallel.For() and ForEach()

```
Parallel.For(0, myItems.Count, i =>
{
    PerformOperationOnIndex(myItems[i]);
});

Parallel.ForEach(set, itemInSet =>
{
    PerformOperation(itemInSet);
});
```

Parallel LINQ (aka PLINQ)

PLINQ is a powerful data parallelism enhancement in .NET 4. Objects that implement the IParallelEnumerable<T> interface can invoke the parallel execution engine, allowing data processing distribution across multiple cores. Although performance can vary depending on environment conditions, data being processed, and so on, PLINQ is simple to use and can greatly improve query performance on object collections.

■ **Tip** IParallelEnumerable<T> inherits from IEnumerable<T>, meaning that PLINQ acts as a layer of additional control to typical LINQ queries.

.AsParallel()

PLINQ makes executing a query in parallel a very simple action through the use of the AsParallel() method. For example, consider Listing 3–7, which operates on a set of 100,000 integers; this processing is currently done sequentially.

Listing 3–7. *Sequential Processing of a LINQ Query*

```
using System;
using System.Collections.Generic;
using System.Linq;
using System.Diagnostics;

namespace Ch3_PLINQ
{
    class Program
    {
        static void Main(string[] args)
        {
            List<int> set = CreateSet();

            Stopwatch sw = Stopwatch.StartNew();

            var query = from element in set
                        let result = element % 2
                        select result;

            Console.WriteLine("{0} seconds elapsed", sw.Elapsed.TotalSeconds);
            Console.ReadLine();
        }

        static List<int> CreateSet()
        {
            List<int> set = new List<int>();
            Random r = new Random();

            for (int i = 0; i < 100000; i++)
            {
                set.Add(r.Next());
            }

            return set;
        }
    }
}
```

Figure 3–10 shows the output of the sequential query; in this run, it took approximately 0.007 seconds to complete.

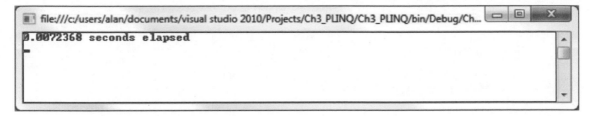

Figure 3–10. *The output of the sequential query processing*

Now the query can be modified as in Listing 3–8 to use `AsParallel()`, which automatically invokes the parallel processing engine.

Listing 3–8. *Modifying the Query to Use AsParallel()*

```
var query = from element in set.AsParallel()
                        let result = element % 2
                        select result;
```

Figure 3–11 shows the output of this adjustment. The query took approximately 0.003 seconds to complete, cutting .004 seconds from the processing time.

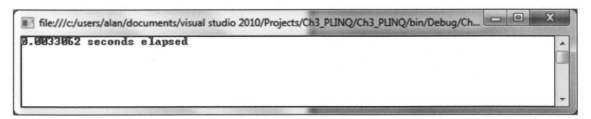

Figure 3–11. *The usage of AsParallel() significantly increased the query performance.*

■ **Tip** This isn't a comprehensive view of everything new .NET 4 brings to the table in terms of multithreading and parallel processing. For a good discussion of the many additional changes, consider *Introducing .NET 4 with Visual Studio 2010* by Alex Mackey (Apress, 2010).

CMS Parallelization Opportunities

Implementing parallel processing methods in the CMS is a tricky proposition, in no small part because it's unknown how large the resulting data sets will ultimately be. For example, if we blindly tack `AsParallel()` onto the query that retrieves a specific page from within the site tree, the resulting performance changes could vary wildly depending on the volume of data in the system, whether it's executing on a machine with multiple cores, and so on. Users of the CMS probably won't appreciate an artificially created overhead delay simply because a certain threshold of data doesn't exist.

For this reason, the CMS core itself doesn't implement any specific parallel processing methodology. An additional consideration is that the CMS is designed to allow embeddable controls to handle their own data management; it's a logic extension to implement parallel processing at the embeddable level, where more low-level information is available.

Creating a Data Mining Embeddable

Given that the CMS embeddable controls are simply web server controls that implement IEmbeddable, it's a simple enough matter to create one that demonstrates some parallel processing techniques by way of data mining.

■ **Note** *Data mining* refers to the act of processing data to look for patterns within the information. For example, one might want to process weather data to discover temperature trends over time or process purchase information to find which markets respond well to certain types of products or services.

Data mining is a rich and varied realm of mathematics and statistics; although we won't get too in depth with those concepts in this chapter, we can still look at some real-world situations that we may face as developers.

The first step on that path is the generation of a set of data that is significant enough to represent the types of information we'd encounter "in the wild." A small data set lacks the volume required to adequately demonstrate parallelization techniques and from a statistical perspective also prohibits the extraction of any meaningful pattern information.

There is an excellent site at http://generatedata.com, shown in Figure 3–12, that (for free) will assemble a variety of data sets that can be customized both in terms of content and output.

Figure 3–12. Using the generatedata.com site to create some sample data

I created an XML file of 5,000 records, which is the maximum the site permits. I then took the data within and repeated it to generate a slightly larger file. The resulting data structure consists of a name and the short form of a U.S. state; Listing 3–9 shows a few rows.

Listing 3–9. Some of the Sample Data Generated by the Site

```
<names>
    <name>
        <Name>Mira</Name>
        <State>WA</State>
    </name>
    <name>
        <Name>Ima</Name>
        <State>OR</State>
    </name>
```

```
<name>
    <Name>Keefe</Name>
    <State>OR</State>
</name>
<name>
    <Name>Wade</Name>
    <State>VA</State>
</name>
<name>
    <Name>Beatrice</Name>
    <State>NJ</State>
</name>

...etc.
```

`</names>`

The specific implementation of embeddable controls is covered in detail in Chapter 4 (along with coverage of MEF, on which the plug-in functionality is based). For now, we can focus on the Render() method of the embeddable; Listing 3–10 demonstrates loading the sample XML file using sequential LINQ processing.

■ **Tip** Normally we wouldn't put this type of processing directly into the Render() method; this is simply for the sake of a brief demonstration.

Listing 3–10. The Render() Method of a Data Mining Embeddable

```
protected override void Render(HtmlTextWriter writer)
{
    StringBuilder sb = new StringBuilder();

    System.Diagnostics.Stopwatch sw = System.Diagnostics.Stopwatch.StartNew();

    var people = from person in XElement.Load(@"C:\CMS\results.xml").Elements()
                 where person.Element("State").Value == "OR"
                 select person;

    sb.Append("Operation completed in ");
    sb.Append(sw.Elapsed.TotalSeconds.ToString());
    sb.Append(" seconds.<br/>");

    foreach (var p in people)
    {
        sb.Append(p);
        sb.Append("<br/>");
    }

    writer.Write(sb.ToString());
}
```

Using this embeddable on a page resulted in a total execution time of approximately 0.03 seconds to complete, as shown in Figure 3–13.

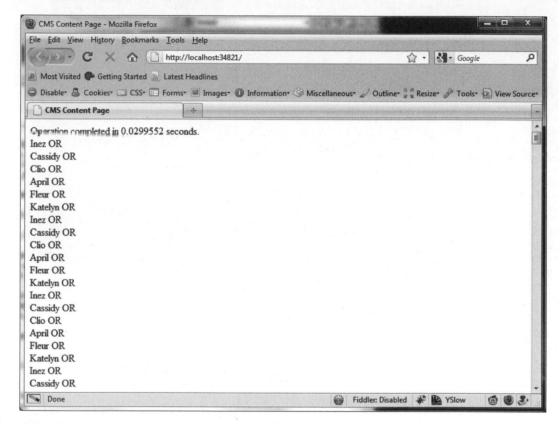

Figure 3–13. Executing the query via sequential LINQ

The application of PLINQ via the AsParallel() method, as shown in Listing 3–11, triggers automatic parallel query execution.

Listing 3–11. Using PLINQ's AsParallel() Method

```
var people = from person in XElement.Load(@"C:\CMS\results.xml").Elements().AsParallel()
             where person.Element("State").Value == "OR"
             select person;
```

Using this modified embeddable on a page resulted in an execution time of approximately 0.02 seconds, as shown in Figure 3–14.

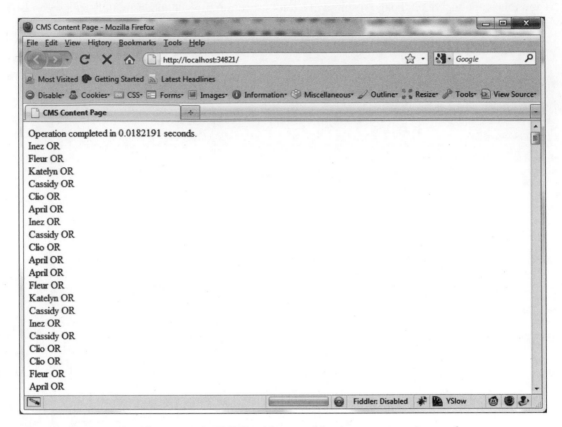

Figure 3–14. Executing the query via PLINQ with a resulting improvement in speed

Expanding the Data Mining Tasks

The benefits of parallel processing are typically most effectively realized as the size of the data structure or problem domain increases. Even on a single task (find all the users who live in Oregon), the application of PLINQ shaved one tenth of a second off the request processing time, which adds up quickly under load. We can further demonstrate the parallelization benefits by expanding the amount of work the embeddable is responsible for.

Listing 3–12 expands the tasks so that a list of distinct states is created, and then an operation is performed on each state.

Listing 3–12. Executing Multiple Queries in Parallel

```
protected override void Render(HtmlTextWriter wriler)
{
    StringBuilder sb = new StringBuilder();
```

```
System.Diagnostics.Stopwatch sw = System.Diagnostics.Stopwatch.StartNew();

// get a list of distinct states
var states = from person in XElement.Load(@"C:\CMS\results.xml").Elements().AsParallel()
             select person.Elements("State").Distinct();

writer.Write("Distinct states list created in {0} seconds<br/>",sw.Elapsed.TotalSeconds);

Parallel.ForEach(states, state =>
{
    var process =
      Task.Factory.StartNew(() => GetAllUsers(state.First<XElement>().ToString()));

    writer.Write("{0} processed in {1} seconds.<br/>",
                 state.First<XElement>().ToString(), process.Result);
});
}

protected string GetAllUsers(string state)
{
    System.Diagnostics.Stopwatch sw = System.Diagnostics.Stopwatch.StartNew();

    var result = from person in XElement.Load(@"C:\CMS\results.xml").Elements().AsParallel()
                 where person.Element("State").Value == state
                 select person;

    return sw.Elapsed.TotalSeconds.ToString();
}
```

Figure 3–15 shows the output of this embeddable.

The total execution time for the embeddable was approximately 1.98 seconds. What would the performance implication be if we were to execute the same processes in a sequential fashion? Listing 3–13 shows the same processes with the parallelization concepts removed.

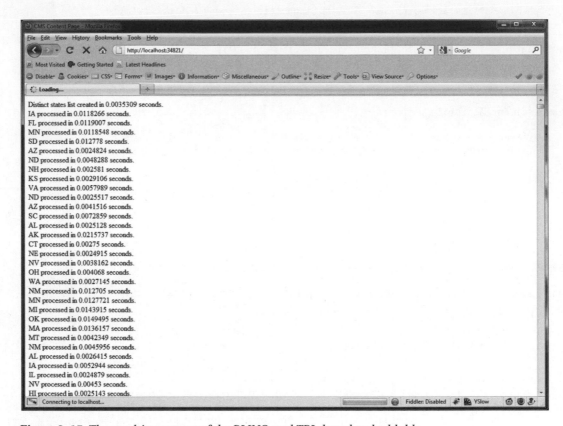

Figure 3–15. *The resulting output of the PLINQ and TPL-based embeddable*

Listing 3–13. *The Same Processes Handled Sequentially*

```
protected override void Render(HtmlTextWriter writer)
{
    StringBuilder sb = new StringBuilder();

    System.Diagnostics.Stopwatch sw = System.Diagnostics.Stopwatch.StartNew();

    // get a list of distinct states
    var states = from person in XElement.Load(@"C:\CMS\results.xml").Elements()
                 select person.Elements("State").Distinct();

    writer.Write("Distinct states list created in {0} seconds.<br/>",
                 sw.Elapsed.TotalSeconds);

    foreach (var state in states)
    {
        writer.Write("{0} processed in {1} seconds.<br/>", state.First<XElement>().ToString(),
```

```
            GetAllUsers(state.First<XElement>().ToString()));
    };

    writer.Write("Total execution time: {0} seconds.", swTotal.Elapsed.TotalSeconds);
}

protected string GetAllUsers(string state)
{
    System.Diagnostics.Stopwatch sw = System.Diagnostics.Stopwatch.StartNew();

    var result = from person in XElement.Load(@"C:\CMS\results.xml").Elements()
                 where person.Element("State").Value == state
                 select person;

    return sw.Elapsed.TotalSeconds.ToString();
}
```

The output as shown in Figure 3–16 tells the tale. The total execution time for the sequential version of the same tasks was approximately 4.08 seconds, a difference of 2.1 seconds.

■ **Tip** All in all, this represents something of a "perfect storm" with regard to performance. Not only is the problem somewhat data-intensive, but a costly operation (opening the source XML file) is performed on each element in the states set.

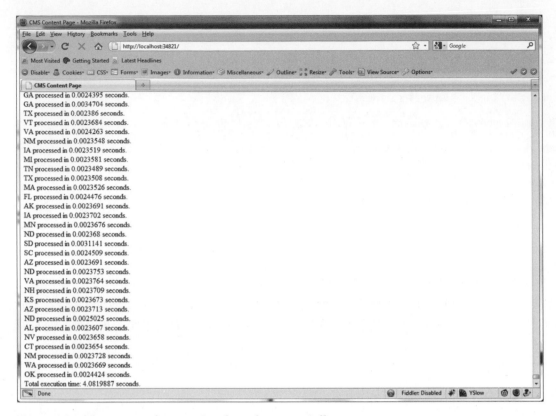

Figure 3–16. The output after running the code sequentially

Now that we've seen the benefits of parallelization, let's look at an opportunity for parallelization in the CMS.

Tagging

As more and more users tag and review content in the system, you're essentially creating a fantastic data mining opportunity whereby you can direct users to content within the scope of their interests that they may not have found otherwise. You can learn a lot about your audience in this manner, as well as gain insight into expanding that audience further.

As the dataset grows larger and larger, your potential for parallelization grows with it. Let's say that a particular user rates your article about the local auto dealership very highly; another user who rates a separate article on third-party automotive warranties may very likely be interested to learn about this other article. It is within your power to examine the choices these two users make and offer suggestions about relevant content accordingly.

Since this information is of the "fire and forget" variety (and can quite quickly increase in quantity), it's a pretty good candidate for parallelization opportunities. For example, if we're searching for related content based on review scores, we could divide workload across multiple threads quite easily; thread A could search for high review scores for similar content, thread B could search for midrange review scores, and so on. The information gathered can be easily assembled at the end of the process for display to the user; it is this property that makes it attractive for parallel processing.

We'll start off with designing some tables and systems for capturing user data. The intention is that we'll be creating controls that are embeddables; this gives us flexibility moving forward to change, add, or remove functionality. First we'll create a table for tags using the T-SQL code shown in Listing 3–14.

The table definition for tags is very straightforward. To define tag data, we need only the following two fields:

- The ID number of the tag

- The text of the tag

Listing 3–14. T-SQL cCode to Define a Table That Contains Tags

```
SET ANSI_NULLS ON
GO

SET QUOTED_IDENTIFIER ON
GO

CREATE TABLE [dbo].[Tags](
    [tagID] [int] IDENTITY(1,1) NOT NULL,
    [tagText] [nvarchar](250) COLLATE SQL_Latin1_General_CP1_CI_AS NOT NULL,
 CONSTRAINT [PK_Tags] PRIMARY KEY CLUSTERED ([tagID] ASC)
WITH (
    PAD_INDEX = OFF,
    IGNORE_DUP_KEY = OFF)
    ON [PRIMARY]
) ON [PRIMARY]
```

We've set the tagID column to be an auto-incrementing field that is also the primary key. Next, we need a table that will contain the tags that are applied to a particular piece of content. The table definition for this (see Listing 3–15) has the following requirements:

- The content ID number

- The ID number of the tag applied

- The ID of the user who applied the tag

Listing 3–15. T-SQL Code to Define the Tag Entries for a Particular Piece of Content

```
SET ANSI_NULLS ON
GO

SET QUOTED_IDENTIFIER ON
GO

CREATE TABLE [dbo].[ContentTags](
        [contentID] [int] NOT NULL,
        [tagID] [int] NOT NULL,
        [userID] [int] NOT NULL
) ON [PRIMARY]
```

Although this structure is fairly simple, it does open up a wide variety of uses. For example, when working with tags, it's useful to provide a list of currently applied tags for a piece of content when a user is looking to label that content; it's more convenient for a user to just click a list of tags to add or remove the tag from a list. A good example of this is the popular website Delicious, which allows users to create public bookmark lists and tag them for easy access (see Figure 3–17).

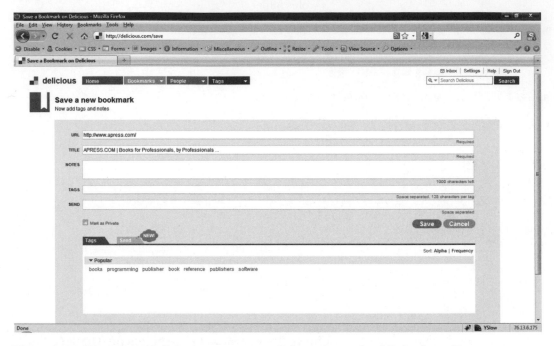

Figure 3–17. The website Delicious supports one-click tagging and public bookmarking.

The Tags tab at the bottom of the page lists commonly applied tags for the particular piece of content (in this case, a website or particular URL within a site); a single click on one of the tags automatically adds it to the TAGS textbox located immediately below NOTES. Clicking the tag a second time will automatically remove it from that textbox. This is a good option to provide users and is just one example of how to apply tags to a real-world site.

■ **Tip** If you've used Delicious in any capacity, you may have noticed that the tags tab allows you to sort the tags either by alphabetical order or by frequency of appearance. The data processing required for ordering tags by frequency of appearance is the sort of area I'd examine as a possible opportunity for parallelization.

Tagging on the Client

Normally I like to work entirely from the data backward, but some of our design considerations will be affected by how we are actually handling tags on the client side, so we'll spend a little time building the tagging embeddable and its necessary JavaScript code.

First let's add a new control to our embeddables folder called tags.ascx. The markup for the tags file is described in Listing 3–16. Note that this is not the final implementation; we're building a simple (and hard-coded) test for now. We will make this properly data-driven shortly.

Listing 3–16. The Markup and JavaScript for the Tags Control

```
<%@ Control Language="C#" AutoEventWireup="true" CodeFile="tags.ascx.cs"
Inherits="embeddables_tags" %>

<!-- can be moved to an external Javascript if you prefer -->
<script type="text/javascript">
    function ModifyTagList(tagname) {
        var tagboxContents = document.getElementById('txtTagBox').value;
        if (tagboxContents.indexOf(tagname) > -1) {
            tagboxContents = tagboxContents.replace(tagname + ' ', '');
            document.getElementById('txtTagBox').value = tagboxContents;
        }
        else {
            document.getElementById('txtTagBox').value += tagname + ' ';
        }
    }
</script>

<input id="txtTagBox" type="text" />

<p>
<a href="#" onclick="javascript:ModifyTagList('apress');return false;">apress</a>
<a href="#" onclick="javascript:ModifyTagList('book');return false;">book</a>
<a href="#" onclick="javascript:ModifyTagList('.net');return false;">.net</a>
<a href="#" onclick="javascript:ModifyTagList('c#');return false;">c#</a>
</p>
```

■ **Tip** Why does the JavaScript call in each hyperlink have return false; included? Without this, the hash (#) will be appended to the current URL when the user clicks it; http://mysite.com/homepage/ will turn into http://mysite.com/homepage/#. The previous method results in a cleaner implementation and experience for the user.

Let's take a look at what's happening here; if you're a JavaScript, guru you can safely skip this part, but everyone else would probably appreciate a breakdown of what's going on.

The ModifyTagList method accepts a single parameter: the name of the tag to add or remove from a particular location. The value of an element on the page (txtTagBox) is assigned to a variable called tagBoxContents. We examine this value and find whether a particular tag appears within it; if it does, we need to remove it (the user has clicked it a second time and therefore wants it removed from the list). If it does not, we need to add it to the `tagBoxContents` value. Finally, the value of `tagBoxContents` is assigned as the value of the `txtTagBox` element.

As you can see in Figure 3–18, the tagging embeddable is technically displayed third; this is because the template embeddable takes priority over user editable controls. It is secondary to the articles embeddable in the content hierarchy, though.

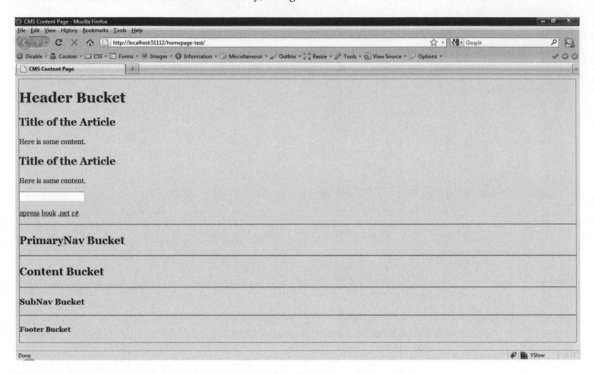

Figure 3–18. *The tagging controls are present in the content.*

Clicking one of these tags results in the tag being placed in the textbox; clicking it again results in its removal. The JavaScript code respects tags that are presently in the box, and because of the design we chose, we can enter a matching string of text, and it will be treated properly. For example, type **apress** in the box, and then click the corresponding tag link; the *apress* text should disappear immediately from the textbox (see Figure 3–19).

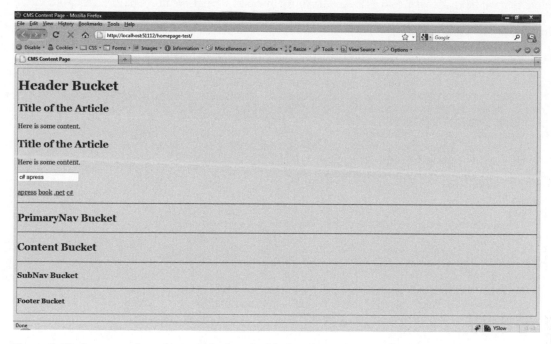

Figure 3–19. Some tags have been clicked and added to the textbox. Note the URL remained clean.

This lends itself to some obvious server-side decisions. We can easily split the textbox on the space character to get an array of tag elements; any tags that already exist in the system do not need to be added to the Tags table, and any that do not already exist will be added.

As a result of this, we need to process the information in a specific order, as follows:

- If a tag is new, add it to the system and get the newly assigned tag ID.

- If a tag is not new, retrieve its ID from the Tags table.

- Update the entries per user in the ContentTags table based on the array contents.

Before we start creating stored procedures to handle this, let's write a bit of the C# server-side code; we need to make some determinations about data processing before we set to the task of procedures.

Fleshing Out the Tagging Embeddable

The first thing we need to do is open up the tagging embeddable again and adjust things to favor a data-driven methodology, as shown in Listing 3–17. We'll do so by replacing the standard HTML input element with a .NET TextBox control; we'll also add a Panel, which will be used to contain a PlaceHolder. The PlaceHolder control will be the container for the actual tag links based on our database.

Note that we have also defined a few `CssClass` attributes; although we don't have a specific style for these elements yet, we will certainly want to put a little spit and polish on down the road, so placing hooks early is beneficial.

Listing 3–17. Modifying the tags.ascx Markup to Gacilitate Data-Driven Code

```
<%@ Control Language="C#" AutoEventWireup="true" CodeFile="tags.ascx.cs"
Inherits="embeddables_tags" %>
<!-- can be moved to an external Javascript if you prefer -->
<script type="text/javascript">
    function ModifyTagList(tagname) {
        var tagboxContents = document.getElementById('txtTagBox').value;
        if (tagboxContents.indexOf(tagname) > -1) {
            tagboxContents = tagboxContents.replace(tagname + ' ', '');
            document.getElementById('txtTagBox').value = tagboxContents;
        }
        else {
            document.getElementById('txtTagBox').value += tagname + ' ';
        }
    }
</script>

<asp:TextBox ID="txtTagBox" runat="server" CssClass="tagBox"></asp:TextBox>
<asp:Panel ID="pnlTagLinks" runat="server" CssClass="tagPanel">
    <asp:PlaceHolder ID="plcTagLinks" runat="server"></asp:PlaceHolder>
</asp:Panel>

<p>
<a href="#" onclick="javascript:ModifyTagList('apress');return false;">apress</a>
<a href="#" onclick="javascript:ModifyTagList('book');return false;">book</a>
<a href="#" onclick="javascript:ModifyTagList('.net');return false;">.net</a>
<a href="#" onclick="javascript:ModifyTagList('c#');return false;">c#</a>
</p>
```

Why did we leave the paragraph element and the demo links in the markup? Well, clicking the links no longer results in a tag being added to the TextBox. Let's look into this.

What's in a Name?

If you're familiar with pages constructed using .NET master pages or user controls, you've likely guessed the issue at hand. What you may not know is how easily .NET 4 allows you to correct the problem. The answer to the lack of updating tags is found in the HTML markup for the page that has been generated for the user. Let's view the source of this page and see where things went wrong (see Listing 3–18).

Listing 3–18. The ID Attribute Does Not Match What Our JavaScript Expects

```
<!DOCTYPE html>
<html xmlns="http://www.w3.org/1999/xhtml">
<head id="Head1"><title>CMS Content Page</title>
    <!-- stylesheets -->
    <link href="../css/main.css" rel="stylesheet" type="text/css" />
```

```html
<!-- client-side libraries -->
<script src="js/jquery-1.3.2.min.js" type="text/javascript"></script>
</head>
<body>
<form name="form1" method="post" action="?id=1" id="form1">
<div>
<input type="hidden" name="__VIEWSTATE" id="__VIEWSTATE"
value="/wEPDwUKMTEyMDI3NDAzMmRk6N+OdTiimk08O1j4Hrr5Cn1Gy9E=" />
</div>

<div>

        <input type="hidden" name="__EVENTVALIDATION" id="__EVENTVALIDATION"
value="/wEWAgKXgvvODwLs/J3YDmPBnk9FT+e0Zz6Lrs6vFr171iQd" />
</div>
    <div id="wrapper">


<header>
<h1>Header Bucket</h1>
<h2>Title of the Article</h2>
<p>Here is some content.</p>
<h2>Title of the Article</h2>
<p>Here is some content.</p>
<!-- can be moved to an external Javascript if you prefer -->
<script type="text/javascript">
    function ModifyTagList(tagname) {
        var tagboxContents = document.getElementById('txtTagBox').value;
        if (tagboxContents.indexOf(tagname) > -1) {
            tagboxContents = tagboxContents.replace(tagname + ' ', '');
            document.getElementById('txtTagBox').value = tagboxContents;
        }
        else {
            document.getElementById('txtTagBox').value += tagname + ' ';
        }
    }
</script>

<input name="header$ctl02$txtTagBox" type="text" id="header_ctl02_txtTagBox" class="tagBox" />
<div id="header_ctl02_pnlTagLinks" class="tagPanel">

</div>

<p>
<a href="#" onclick="javascript:ModifyTagList('apress');return false;">apress</a>
<a href="#" onclick="javascript:ModifyTagList('book');return false;">book</a>
<a href="#" onclick="javascript:ModifyTagList('.net');return false;">.net</a>
<a href="#" onclick="javascript:ModifyTagList('c#');return false;">c#</a>
</p>
</header>
<nav>
<h2>PrimaryNav Bucket</h2>
<!-- the remaining markup has been snipped for brevity -->
```

This is a long-standing issue in the .NET world and one that has prompted developers to come up with a variety of unique solutions, some more successful than others. When .NET renders the page and constructs the final output that will be delivered to the client, there are situations where the ID of a particular control is modified by the .NET Framework to ensure that the element has a unique ID within the page hierarchy.

Needless to say, this can wreak havoc on client-side code, which doesn't know about the control hierarchy modifications. The framework has had a `.ClientID` property for developer use for some time that would return the specific ID that has been generated, but this is really something of a hack; we're never presented with a choice in the matter of whether we want our controls to have renamed IDs. Sometimes it's a convenient lifesaver; other times it's a real pain in the butt.

To solve this in Visual Studio, if the Properties window is not present on the right side of the screen, press F4 to activate it. Switch to either Split mode or Design mode on the `tags.ascx` file, and click on the TextBox control. The Properties window to the right has a setting called ClientIDMode with a variety of settings. For now, select Static (see Figure 3–20).

Figure 3–20. In this case, ClientIDMode should be set to Static.

Now if we click the tag links again, everything functions as it did initially.

The ability to completely alter the way controls are named within a page is a huge time-saver and a real convenience when working with complex pages based on master pages or nested user controls (such as the CMS we're building now). If you're curious about what the other ClientIDMode settings do, they are detailed as follows:

- Inherit is the default setting; a control with this setting will assume the ClientIDMode settings of whatever parent control it has.

- Legacy uses the same naming conventions as older versions of the .NET Framework. If no ClientIDMode setting is defined anywhere in the control's hierarchy, this will be the default over Inherit.

- Predictable is primarily for use within data repeater-style controls. For example, if we defined a site tree, we may want the ID of the control to automatically bind to the primary key of the data source, which in this case would be the contentID field.

The Properties window is just a shortcut to defining the attribute in code. You'll notice that the tags.ascx file has been updated and the ClientIDMode property set on the TextBox control. If you prefer to do your editing by hand, you're of course welcome to do so (see Listing 3–19).

Listing 3–19. The ClientIDMode Property Defined in the Control Markup

```
<asp:TextBox ID="txtTagBox" runat="server" CssClass="tagBox"
ClientIDMode="Static"></asp:TextBox>
```

Now that we have resolved the client ID issues, it is safe to remove everything between the paragraph tags in the tags.ascx file, leaving us with only the JavaScript and .NET controls.

Handling Tag Input

The next step in the process is permitting the user to update the tag list and sending that data over to the server. One potential issue is that so far we have not set up any method for users to create accounts and establish user IDs, so technically we can't store the information based on the table schemas we defined earlier. For now, we'll assume that the user ID is -1, and we'll remove all entries with -1 a bit later.

We should start by adding a button to the control that will allow the user to update with the tags they've selected. You can use either a LinkButton or regular Button; my preference is to use a LinkButton (see Listing 3–20), but the decision is yours. Figure 3–21 shows the results of this change.

Listing 3–20. Using a LinkButton to Save the Tag Information

```
<%@ Control Language="C#" AutoEventWireup="true" CodeFile="tags.ascx.cs"
Inherits="embeddables_tags" %>
<!-- can be moved to an external Javascript if you prefer -->
<script type="text/javascript">
    function ModifyTagList(tagname) {
        var tagboxContents = document.getElementById('txtTagBox').value;
        if (tagboxContents.indexOf(tagname) > -1) {
            tagboxContents = tagboxContents.replace(tagname + ' ', '');
            document.getElementById('txtTagBox').value = tagboxContents;
        }
        else {
            document.getElementById('txtTagBox').value += tagname + ' ';
        }
    }
</script>
<asp:TextBox ID="txtTagBox" runat="server" CssClass="tagBox"
ClientIDMode="Static"></asp:TextBox>
<asp:LinkButton ID="lnkSaveTags" runat="server" CssClass="tagButton" ClientIDMode="Static"
    Text="Save my Tags"></asp:LinkButton>
<asp:Panel ID="pnlTagLinks" runat="server" CssClass="tagPanel">
    <asp:PlaceHolder ID="plcTagLinks" runat="server"></asp:PlaceHolder>
</asp:Panel>
```

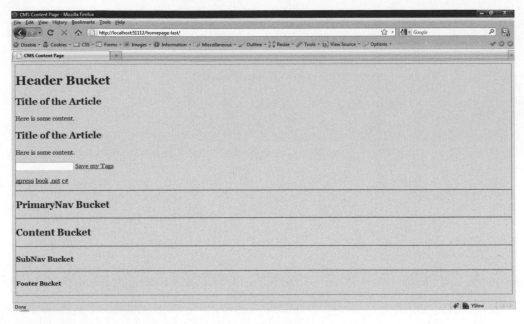

Figure 3–21. A LinkButton has been added to the embeddable.

Now we can define the behavior for what happens when a user clicks the Save button to preserve their tags. We know from our earlier data definition that we will be keying off the contentID value for most of the data related to user reviews; the question is how to access that contentID value given the fact that the address bar reads only /homepage-test/?

Luckily for us, the way the CMS performs URL rewriting effectively preserves this information, and it is accessible in the same way that it would be normally. The Request.QueryString collection is simply a list of key-value pairs that has been filled by the incoming request parameters; accessing this collection does not rely specifically on the address bar contents. An example is probably the easiest method of displaying this concept (see Listing 3–21 and Figure 3–22).

Listing 3–21. A Simple Test by Modifying tags.ascx.cs

```
using System;
using System.Collections.Generic;
using System.Linq;
using System.Web;
using System.Web.UI;
using System.Web.UI.WebControls;

public partial class embeddables_tags : System.Web.UI.UserControl
{
    protected void Page_Load(object sender, EventArgs e)
    {
        Response.Write("The contentID of this page is " + Request.QueryString["id"]);
    }
}
```

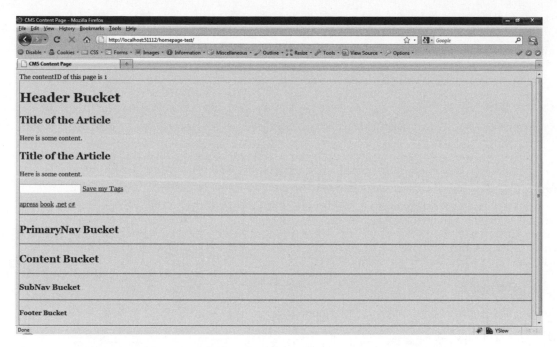

Figure 3–22. The contentID is accessible as though the URL had not been rewritten.

Since we don't have to jump through any hoops to access the information we need, we can turn our attention back to building our ideal API and then working backward (see Listing 3–22). A clean implementation is simply handing off the necessary information to the business tier when the LinkButton is clicked; the presentation tier doesn't need to handle any real responsibilities at this point (although we will likely want to display some output to the user to indicate the tags were successfully saved).

Listing 3–22. Building Our Ideal API from Usage and Working Backward

```csharp
using System;
using System.Collections.Generic;
using System.Linq;
using System.Web;
using System.Web.UI;
using System.Web.UI.WebControls;
using Business;

public partial class embeddables_tags : System.Web.UI.UserControl
{
    protected void lnkSaveTags_Click(object sender, EventArgs e)
    {
        int tempUserID = -1;
```

```
            bool success = MetaContent.SaveTags(Request.QueryString["id"], txtTagBox.Text,
tempUserID);
        }
}
```

■ **Note** This API implies that we will lump additional functionality within this overarching MetaContent class. This class will be used to hold tags, ratings and other forms of metadata (which is essentially data about data).

Tag Processing in the Business Tier

So far, we've created a few classes in our business tier that are essentially pass-throughs; the presentation tier uses them as communication channels to (and an abstraction of) the data tier. However, the requirements for tag processing are somewhat different. We need to parse the tag list so that we can determine the existence of tags in the system and how to proceed with the data at hand. Let's begin by creating an entity for the tags.

We'll use a class called Tag.cs in the CommonLibrary project's Entities folder. This will hold the property definition for a tag in the system (see Listing 3–23).

Listing 3–23. The Entity Definition for a CMS Content Tag

```
namespace CommonLibrary.Entities
{
    /// <summary>
    /// Defines the properties of a tag within the CMS
    /// </summary>
    public class Tag
    {
        public int? tagID { get; set; }
        public string tagText { get; set; }
    }
}
```

■ **Note** I used a nullable integer for the tagID property because newly generated tags (prior to being added to the database) will not yet have a tagID assigned to them.

Now that we have an entity defined, we can begin creating methods in the business tier to accommodate tags. In the Business project, we need a class called MetaContent; Listing 3–24 shows the code for this class.

Listing 3–24. The Skeleton of the MetaContent Class

```
using System;
using System.Collections.Generic;
```

```
using System.Linq;
using System.Text;

namespace Business
{
    public static class MetaContent
    {
        /// <summary>
        /// Manages the parsing and storage of tag data for a particular user and content
        /// </summary>
        /// <param name="contentID">the ID of a CMS page</param>
        /// <param name="tags">a space-delimited list of tags</param>
        /// <param name="userID">the ID of the current user</param>
        /// <returns>true if the save was successful</returns>
        public static bool SaveTags(string contentID, string tags, int userID)
        {
            return false;
        }
    }
}
```

We know that the incoming list of tags will be space-delimited, so we need a method that will split that list and assemble a generic List of tags for use in the data tier (see Listing 3–25).

Listing 3–25. A Method to Split a Tag List Based on Spaces

```
using System;
using System.Collections.Generic;
using System.Linq;
using System.Text;
using CommonLibrary.Entities;

namespace Business
{
    public static class MetaContent
    {
        /// <summary>
        /// Manages the parsing and storage of tag data for a particular user and content
        /// </summary>
        /// <param name="contentID">the ID of a CMS page</param>
        /// <param name="tags">a space-delimited list of tags</param>
        /// <param name="userID">the ID of the current user</param>
        /// <returns>true if the save was successful</returns>
        public static bool SaveTags(string contentID, string tags, int userID)
        {
            return false;
        }

        /// <summary>
        /// Splits a list of tags on the space character
        /// </summary>
        /// <param name="tags">a space-delimited list of tags</param>
        /// <returns>a generic list of Tags</returns>
```

```
        public static List<Tag> SplitTags(string tags)
        {
            var tagList = new List<Tag>();

            foreach (var t in tags.Split(' '))
            {
                tagList.Add(new Tag { tagID = null, tagText = t });
            }

            return tagList;
        }
    }
}
```

Although each tag in the list is initially configured such that the tagID property is null, as time progresses and the number of tags in the system grows, we'll likely encounter tags that have already been defined, and we should therefore use their tagIDs consistently. As such, let's add a method that we can use to send back a list of tags that have IDs assigned based on the contents of our database (see Listing 3–26).

Listing 3–26. Adding a Method for Filling in tagIDs Where Available

```
using System;
using System.Collections.Generic;
using System.Linq;
using System.Text;
using CommonLibrary.Entities;

namespace Business
{
    public static class MetaContent
    {
        /// <summary>
        /// Manages the parsing and storage of tag data for a particular user and content
        /// </summary>
        /// <param name="contentID">the ID of a CMS page</param>
        /// <param name="tags">a space-delimited list of tags</param>
        /// <param name="userID">the ID of the current user</param>
        /// <returns>true if the save was successful</returns>
        public static bool SaveTags(string contentID, string tags, int userID)
        {
            return false;
        }

        /// <summary>
        /// Splits a list of tags on the space character
        /// </summary>
        /// <param name="tags">a space-delimited list of tags</param>
        /// <returns>a generic list of Tags</returns>
        public static List<Tag> SplitTags(string tags)
        {
            var tagList = new List<Tag>();
```

```
            foreach (var t in tags.Split(' '))
            {
                tagList.Add(new Tag { tagID = null, tagText = t });
            }

            return tagList;
        }

        /// <summary>
        /// Checks the database to fill tagIDs where available
        /// </summary>
        /// <param name="tagList">a generic list of tags</param>
        /// <returns>the list of tags with any existing tagIDs filled in</returns>
        public static List<Tag> FillExistingTagIDs(List<Tag> tagList)
        {
            return Data.MetaContent.FillExistingTagIDs(tagList);
        }
    }
}
```

By default, T-SQL does not have any native method for handling arrays passed from server-side code. There are a variety of ways we can handle this situation; although functional, it would be an exercise in fairly poor performance if we ran a stored procedure for each tag provided. We could opt to assemble our SQL statements within a stored procedure dynamically. However, since the actual workload is very simple, we'll opt to not use a stored procedure, and rather we will create a single dynamic SQL statement in our Data project.

Create a new class file in the Data project called MetaContent.cs; we'll create a method called FillExistingTagIDs to fulfill the expectations of the Business project. Let's create this code first (see Listing 3–27), then we'll discuss the purpose of the more complex middle section.

Listing 3–27. The MetaContent Class in the Data Tier

```
using System;
using System.Data;
using System.Data.SqlClient;
using System.Collections.Generic;
using System.Linq;
using System.Text;
using CommonLibrary.Entities;

namespace Data
{
    public static class MetaContent
    {
        /// <summary>
        /// Checks the database to fill tagIDs where available
        /// </summary>
        /// <param name="tagList">a generic list of tags</param>
        /// <returns>the list of tags with any existing tagIDs filled in</returns>
        public static List<Tag> FillExistingTagIDs(List<Tag> tagList)
        {
            var existingTags = new List<Tag>();
```

```
        using (var conn = Factory.GetConnection())
        {
            var comm =
             new SqlCommand("SELECT tagID, tagText FROM Tags WHERE tagText IN (", conn);

            foreach (var t in tagList)
            {
                // removing potentially unsafe characters
                // from the incoming tag list before appending
                t.tagText = t.tagText.Replace("'", "''").Replace(";", "");

                comm.CommandText += "'" + t.tagText.ToLower() + "'";
            }
            comm.CommandText = comm.CommandText.Replace("''", "','");
            comm.CommandText += ")";

            try
            {
                conn.Open();
                var reader = comm.ExecuteReader();
                while (reader.Read())
                {
                    existingTags.Add(
                      new Tag { tagID = reader.GetInt32(0),
                                tagText = reader.GetString(1)
                      }
                    );
                }
            }
            finally
            {
                conn.Close();
            }
        }

        return existingTags;
    }
  }
}
```

■ **Note** It's a flat-out holy war among developers whether one should use solely stored procedures or dynamic SQL statements. I typically have a preference for stored procedures, if for no other reason than familiarity. A common argument is that stored procedures are better maintained by SQL Server in terms of performance plans, therefore the procedure execution should be faster. In the case of our tag code, it will be infrequently executed and likely very subject to change, so my concern is not particularly high for the performance of this limited process.

The purpose of the initial section of code is to loop through each tag, remove unsafe characters that might introduce SQL injection opportunities, and finally appending each tag name to a SQL statement (see Listing 3–28).

Listing 3–28. *Parsing Tags to Remove Unsafe Characters and Craft a SQL Statement*

```
var comm = new SqlCommand("SELECT tagID, tagText FROM Tags WHERE tagText IN (", conn);

foreach (var t in tagList)
{
    // removing potentially unsafe characters from the incoming tag list before appending
    t.tagText = t.tagText.Replace("'", "''").Replace(";", "");

    comm.CommandText += "'" + t.tagText.ToLower() + "'";
}
comm.CommandText = comm.CommandText.Replace("''", "','");
comm.CommandText += ")";
```

Essentially, the purpose of this method is to create a large, generalized SQL IN statement. The end result is that a statement such as SELECT tagID, tagText FROM Tags WHERE tagText IN ('foo', 'bar') will be passed to the database.

POST Problems

At this stage, before we have finished wiring these tiers together, the code can be compiled and run. If we were to do so, we could click any of the sample tag links to add them to the TextBox and then click the Save my Tags button. If we did so, we would see a result like the image in Figure 3–23; note that the issue occurs only when posting back to the server.

Figure 3–23. *There is an issue related to postbacks that we have not yet encountered.*

It's safe to assume that because we have taken on the responsibility for URL parsing and routing that we may have potentially confused .NET somewhere along the line. It's important to note that the URL changed after we clicked the LinkButton; the URL now includes ?id=1 at the end. Let's take a look at the source of the page (see Listing 3–29).

Listing 3–29. Note the Action Property of the Form Element

```
<!DOCTYPE html>
<html xmlns="http://www.w3.org/1999/xhtml">
<head id="Head1"><title>
        CMS Content Page
</title>
    <!-- stylesheets -->
    <link href="../css/main.css" rel="stylesheet" type="text/css" />

    <!-- client-side libraries -->
    <script src="js/jquery-1.3.2.min.js" type="text/javascript"></script>
</head>
<body>
    <form name="form1" method="post" action="?id=1" id="form1">
    <!-- the remaining markup has been snipped for brevity -->
```

The issue is that the action of the form is set to be ?id=1, which gets appended to the current URL. Prior to .NET 4, our solution would have to involve either using regular expressions to modify the action property of the form element or making additional checks and comparisons in the Global.asax file (which would therefore include additional code to resolve the values to friendly URLs).

.NET 4 introduces a much more convenient way of handling this situation, which should please developers who have encountered this issue in the past. We can now directly modify the action property of the form element without jumping through any hoops. Open the content.aspx.cs file, and modify the Form_Load method (see Listing 3–30).

Listing 3–30. We Can Directly Access the Action Property of the Form

```
protected void Page_Load(object sender, EventArgs e)
{
    int id = Convert.ToInt32(Request.QueryString["id"]);
    form1.Action = HttpContext.Current.Request.RawUrl.ToString().ToLower();
    LoadTemplate(id);
    LoadContent(id);
}
```

If we run the application again; clicking the LinkButton will no longer result in a Yellow Page of Death. Viewing the source confirms that our efforts were successful (see Listing 3–31).

Listing 3–31. The Action Property Has Been Modified Dynamically

```
<!DOCTYPE html>
<html xmlns="http://www.w3.org/1999/xhtml">
<head id="Head1"><title>
        CMS Content Page
</title>
    <!-- stylesheets -->
    <link href="../css/main.css" rel="stylesheet" type="text/css" />
```

```
<!-- client-side libraries -->
<script src="js/jquery-1.3.2.min.js" type="text/javascript"></script>
</head>
<body>
    <form name="form1" method="post" action="/homepage-test/" id="form1">
    <!-- the remaining markup has been snipped for brevity -->
```

Finalizing Tag Storage

With that issue resolved, we can now focus our attention on the final steps in storing our tags based on content. Let's open the MetaContent.cs class in the business tier and make the modifications shown in Listing 3–32.

Listing 3–32. Updating Tags When Available

```
using System;
using System.Collections.Generic;
using System.Linq;
using System.Text;
using CommonLibrary.Entities;

namespace Business
{
    public static class MetaContent
    {
        /// <summary>
        /// Manages the parsing and storage of tag data for a particular user and content
        /// </summary>
        /// <param name="contentID">the ID of a CMS page</param>
        /// <param name="tags">a space-delimited list of tags</param>
        /// <param name="userID">the ID of the current user</param>
        /// <returns>true if the save was successful</returns>
        public static bool SaveTags(string contentID, string tags, int userID)
        {
            try
            {
                // assemble a generic List of tag elements
                var tagList = SplitTags(tags);

                // determine which tags already exist in the system
                tagList = FillExistingTagIDs(tagList);
            }
            catch(Exception ex)
            {
                // we want to pass the exception up to the parent method
                throw ex;
            }
            return true;
        }

        /// <summary>
```

```
/// Splits a list of tags on the space character
/// </summary>
/// <param name="tags">a space-delimited list of tags</param>
/// <returns>a generic list of Tags</returns>
public static List<Tag> SplitTags(string tags)
{
    var tagList = new List<Tag>();

    foreach (var t in tags.Split(' '))
    {
        tagList.Add(new Tag { tagID = null, tagText = t });
    }

    return tagList;
}

/// <summary>
/// Checks the database to fill tagIDs where available
/// </summary>
/// <param name="tagList">a generic list of tags</param>
/// <returns>the list of tags with any existing tagIDs filled in</returns>
public static List<Tag> FillExistingTagIDs(List<Tag> tagList)
{
    var existingTags = Data.MetaContent.FillExistingTagIDs(tagList);

    foreach(var t in tagList)
    {
        foreach (var e in existingTags)
        {
            if (t.tagText == e.tagText)
            {
                t.tagID = e.tagID;
            }
        }
    }

    return tagList;
}
    }
}
```

The FillExistingTagIDs method has been significantly updated; first, it retrieves a list of tags in the system. Next, it loops through each tag passed into the method, and then a subloop iterates over each tag that already exists. If there is a matching tag between the two, the parent tag List is updated. The end result of this method is that we have a complete list of tags with IDs filled in where available.

Now we can add a few sample tags to the system and test the functionality of our business tier processing. The T-SQL statement shown in Listing 3–33 will add the values of the test links to the database.

Listing 3–33. *A Small T-SQL Statement to Create Some Sample Tags*

```
INSERT INTO Tags (tagText)
    SELECT 'apress'
UNION ALL
```

```
        SELECT 'c#'
UNION ALL
        SELECT '.net'
UNION ALL
        SELECT 'book'
```

■ **Tip** You could write this as a series of distinct INSERT INTO statements if you desire; I prefer the UNION ALL shorthand as a convenience. The end result is the same.

At this stage I'll set a breakpoint in the FillExistingTagIDs method on the final return statement. We'll use this breakpoint to examine the value of the tag List and see whether the IDs have been properly updated. Run the application; click one or two of the sample links, and then type a different tag. Click the Save my Tags link (see Figure 3–24).

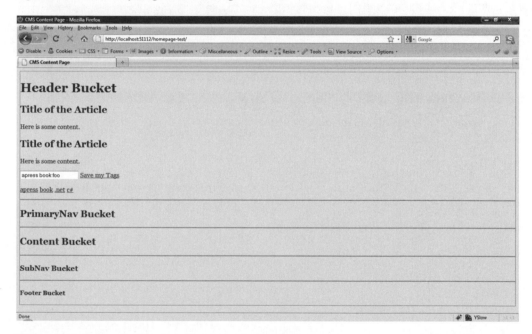

Figure 3–24. Two tags that should exist and a single new one

When the breakpoint is reached, we can hover over the tagList variable and examine the contents. When I ran my test, I used two prepopulated tags ("apress" and "book"), and I typed a third tag that does not exist in the system ("foo"). You should find that any prepopulated tags have had IDs assigned to them, and any tags that didn't previously exist still have a null tagID value. Figure 3–25 shows how the breakpoint looked on my machine.

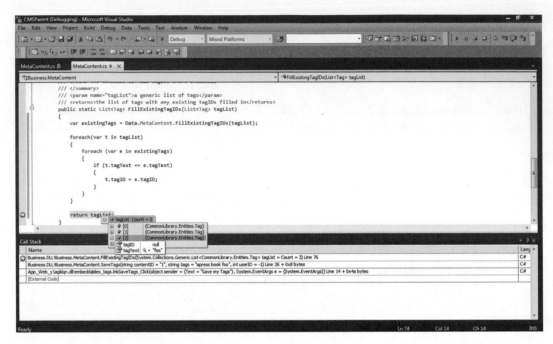

Figure 3–25. *The breakpoint we set allows us to examine the contents of the tagList variable.*

Inserting Tags

The final step in the processing and storage of tags is a method of inserting the new tags into the database. We can do so quite simply with a short stored procedure (see Listing 3–34).

Listing 3–34. *A Stored Procedure for Inserting a New Tag*

```
SET ANSI_NULLS ON
GO

SET QUOTED_IDENTIFIER ON
GO

CREATE PROCEDURE InsertNewTagEntity
        @tagText NVARCHAR(MAX)
AS
BEGIN
        SET NOCOUNT ON;

        INSERT INTO Tags VALUES (@tagText)
END
GO
```

It's trivial to modify the MetaContent class in the data tier to use this stored procedure (see Listing 3–35).

Listing 3–35. *The Data Tier Modified to Insert New Tags*

```csharp
using System;
using System.Data;
using System.Data.SqlClient;
using System.Collections.Generic;
using System.Linq;
using System.Text;
using CommonLibrary.Entities;

namespace Data
{
    public static class MetaContent
    {
        /// <summary>
        /// Checks the database to fill tagIDs where available
        /// </summary>
        /// <param name="tagList">a generic list of tags</param>
        /// <returns>the list of tags with any existing tagIDs filled in</returns>
        public static List<Tag> FillExistingTagIDs(List<Tag> tagList)
        {
            var existingTags = new List<Tag>();

            using (var conn = Factory.GetConnection())
            {
                var comm =
                 new SqlCommand("SELECT tagID, tagText FROM Tags WHERE tagText IN (", conn);

                foreach (var t in tagList)
                {
                    // removing potentially unsafe characters
                    // from the incoming tag list before appending
                    t.tagText = t.tagText.Replace("'", "''").Replace(";", "");

                    comm.CommandText += "'" + t.tagText.ToLower() + "'";
                }
                comm.CommandText = comm.CommandText.Replace("''", "','");
                comm.CommandText += ")";

                try
                {
                    conn.Open();
                    var reader = comm.ExecuteReader();
                    while (reader.Read())
                    {
                        existingTags.Add(
                          new Tag {
                            tagID = reader.GetInt32(0),
                            tagText = reader.GetString(1)
                          }
```

```
                    );
                }
            }
            finally
            {
                conn.Close();
            }
        }

        return existingTags;
    }

    /// <summary>
    /// Inserts a new tag entity into the database
    /// </summary>
    /// <param name="tagText">the name of the tag</param>
    public static void InsertNewTagEntity(string tagText)
    {
        using (var conn = Factory.GetConnection())
        {
            var comm = new SqlCommand("InsertNewTagEntity", conn);
             comm.Parameters.AddWithValue("@tagText", tagText);
             comm.CommandType = CommandType.StoredProcedure;
            try
            {
                conn.Open();
                comm.ExecuteNonQuery();
            }
            finally
            {
                conn.Close();
            }
        }
    }
}
}
```

Next, we need to modify the business tier so that the records will actually be inserted. We'll make our changes in the MetaContent class (see Listing 3–36).

Listing 3–36. The MetaContent Class in the Business Tier with the Final Changes for Saving New Tags

```
using System;
using System.Collections.Generic;
using System.Linq;
using System.Text;
using CommonLibrary.Entities;

namespace Business
{
    public static class MetaContent
    {
        /// <summary>
```

```
/// Manages the parsing and storage of tag data for a particular user and content
/// </summary>
/// <param name="contentID">the ID of a CMS page</param>
/// <param name="tags">a space-delimited list of tags</param>
/// <param name="userID">the ID of the current user</param>
/// <returns>true if the save was successful</returns>
public static bool SaveTags(string contentID, string tags, int userID)
{
    try
    {
        // assemble a generic List of tag elements
        var tagList = SplitTags(tags);

        // determine which tags already exist in the system
        tagList = FillExistingTagIDs(tagList);

        // insert new tags to the system
        InsertNewTagEntities(tagList);
    }
    catch(Exception ex)
    {
        // we want to pass the exception up to the parent method
        throw ex;
    }
    return true;
}

/// <summary>
/// Splits a list of tags on the space character
/// </summary>
/// <param name="tags">a space-delimited list of tags</param>
/// <returns>a generic list of Tags</returns>
public static List<Tag> SplitTags(string tags)
{
    var tagList = new List<Tag>();

    foreach (var t in tags.Split(' '))
    {
        tagList.Add(new Tag { tagID = null, tagText = t });
    }

    return tagList;
}

/// <summary>
/// Checks the database to fill tagIDs where available
/// </summary>
/// <param name="tagList">a generic list of tags</param>
/// <returns>the list of tags with any existing tagIDs filled in</returns>
public static List<Tag> FillExistingTagIDs(List<Tag> tagList)
{
    var existingTags = Data.MetaContent.FillExistingTagIDs(tagList);

    foreach(var t in tagList)
```

```
        {
            foreach (var e in existingTags)
            {
                if (t.tagText == e.tagText)
                {
                    t.tagID = e.tagID;
                }
            }
        }

        return tagList;
    }

    /// <summary>
    /// Inserts new tags into the database
    /// </summary>
    /// <param name="tagList">the generic list of tags</param>
    public static void InsertNewTagEntities(List<Tag> tagList)
    {
        foreach (var t in tagList)
        {
            if (t.tagID == null)
            {
                Data.MetaContent.InsertNewTagEntity(t.tagText);
            }
        }
    }
}
```

If we run the application, we can select one or two tags from the links provided and supply one additional new tag. We can then click Save my Tags, and the database should be updated with the new tag.

Content Tags

We've established a system where tags are added to the system as users input them; tags that don't already exist are added automatically when users enter tag names for content. What we need to do next is provide functionality where a particular piece of content gets tag ID data stored based on the user data provided.

We can start with a simple stored procedure that clears the content tag entries for a particular user and content ID (see Listing 3–37).

Listing 3–37. *A Small Stored Procedure to Clear the Content Tags for a User and Particular Content ID*

```
SET ANSI_NULLS ON
GO

SET QUOTED_IDENTIFIER ON
GO

CREATE PROCEDURE ClearContentTagsByUserAndContentID
        @contentID INT,
```

```
            @userID INT
AS
BEGIN
        SET NOCOUNT ON;

        DELETE FROM ContentTags WHERE contentID = @contentID
                AND userID = @userID
END
GO
```

Next, we need a procedure that will insert a new tag for a piece of content and a given user (see Listing 3–38).

Listing 3–38. A Stored Procedure for Inserting Tags for a Piece of Content and User

```
SET ANSI_NULLS ON
GO

SET QUOTED_IDENTIFIER ON
GO

CREATE PROCEDURE InsertContentTagsByUserAndContentID
        @contentID INT,
        @tagID INT,
        @userID INT
AS
BEGIN
        SET NOCOUNT ON;

        INSERT INTO ContentTags VALUES (@contentID, @tagID, @userID)
END
GO
```

We now need to modify the MetaContent class in the Ddata tier to use both of these procedures (see Listing 3–39).

Listing 3–39. Calling Our Stored Procedures in the Data Tier

```
using System;
using System.Data;
using System.Data.SqlClient;
using System.Collections.Generic;
using System.Linq;
using System.Text;
using CommonLibrary.Entities;

namespace Data
{
    public static class MetaContent
    {
        /// <summary>
        /// Checks the database to fill tagIDs where available
        /// </summary>
        /// <param name="tagList">a generic list of tags</param>
```

```csharp
        /// <returns>the list of tags with any existing tagIDs filled in</returns>
        public static List<Tag> FillExistingTagIDs(List<Tag> tagList)
        {
            var existingTags = new List<Tag>();

            using (var conn = Factory.GetConnection())
            {
                var comm =
                 new SqlCommand("SELECT tagID, tagText FROM Tags WHERE tagText IN (", conn);

                foreach (var t in tagList)
                {
                    // removing potentially unsafe characters
                    // from the incoming tag list before appending
                    t.tagText = t.tagText.Replace("'", "''").Replace(";", "");

                    comm.CommandText += "'" + t.tagText.ToLower() + "'";
                }
                comm.CommandText = comm.CommandText.Replace("''", "','");
                comm.CommandText += ")";

                try
                {
                    conn.Open();
                    var reader = comm.ExecuteReader();
                    while (reader.Read())
                    {
                        existingTags.Add(
                          new Tag {
                            tagID = reader.GetInt32(0),
                            tagText = reader.GetString(1)
                          }
                        );
                    }
                }
                finally
                {
                    conn.Close();
                }
            }

            return existingTags;
        }

        /// <summary>
        /// Inserts a new tag entity into the database
        /// </summary>
        /// <param name="tagText">the name of the tag</param>
        public static void InsertNewTagEntity(string tagText)
        {
            using (var conn = Factory.GetConnection())
            {
                var comm = new SqlCommand("InsertNewTagEntity", conn);
                comm.Parameters.AddWithValue("@tagText", tagText);
```

```csharp
            comm.CommandType = CommandType.StoredProcedure;
            try
            {
                conn.Open();
                comm.ExecuteNonQuery();
            }
            finally
            {
                conn.Close();
            }
        }
    }

    /// <summary>
    /// Clears the content tags for a piece of content and user
    /// </summary>
    /// <param name="contentID">the integer content ID</param>
    /// <param name="userID">the integer user ID</param>
    public static void ClearContentTagsByUserAndContentID(int contentID, int userID)
    {
        using (var conn = Factory.GetConnection())
        {
            var comm = new SqlCommand("ClearContentTagsByUserAndContentID", conn);
            comm.Parameters.AddWithValue("@contentID", contentID);
            comm.Parameters.AddWithValue("@userID", userID);
            comm.CommandType = CommandType.StoredProcedure;

            try
            {
                conn.Open();
                comm.ExecuteNonQuery();
            }
            finally
            {
                conn.Close();
            }
        }
    }

    /// <summary>
    /// Inserts a new tag for a user and content ID
    /// </summary>
    /// <param name="contentID">the integer content ID</param>
    /// <param name="tagID">the integer tag ID</param>
    /// <param name="userID">the integer user ID</param>
    public static void InsertContentTagsByUserAndContentID(int contentID,
                                                int tagID, int userID)
    {
        using (var conn = Factory.GetConnection())
        {
            var comm = new SqlCommand("InsertContentTagsByUserAndContentID", conn);
```

```
                comm.Parameters.AddWithValue("@contentID", contentID);
                comm.Parameters.AddWithValue("@tagID", tagID);
                comm.Parameters.AddWithValue("@userID", userID);
                comm.CommandType = CommandType.StoredProcedure;

                try
                {
                    conn.Open();
                    comm.ExecuteNonQuery();
                }
                finally
                {
                    conn.Close();
                }
            }
        }
    }
}
```

The final step in this process is to wire everything together in the business tier. The modifications have been made to the MetaContent class (see Listing 3–40).

Listing 3–40. The Business Tier Has Been Modified to Save Content Tags

```
using System;
using System.Collections.Generic;
using System.Linq;
using System.Text;
using CommonLibrary.Entities;

namespace Business
{
    public static class MetaContent
    {
        /// <summary>
        /// Manages the parsing and storage of tag data for a particular user and content
        /// </summary>
        /// <param name="contentID">the ID of a CMS page</param>
        /// <param name="tags">a space-delimited list of tags</param>
        /// <param name="userID">the ID of the current user</param>
        /// <returns>true if the save was successful</returns>
        public static bool SaveTags(string contentID, string tags, int userID)
        {
            try
            {
                // assemble a generic List of tag elements
                var tagList = SplitTags(tags);

                // determine which tags already exist in the system
                tagList = FillExistingTagIDs(tagList);

                // insert new tags to the system
                InsertNewTagEntities(tagList);
```

```csharp
            // insert tags for this content
            InsertNewContentTags(tagList, Convert.ToInt32(contentID), userID);
        }
        catch(Exception ex)
        {
            // we want to pass the exception up to the parent method
            throw ex;
        }
        return true;
    }

    /// <summary>
    /// Splits a list of tags on the space character
    /// </summary>
    /// <param name="tags">a space-delimited list of tags</param>
    /// <returns>a generic list of Tags</returns>
    public static List<Tag> SplitTags(string tags)
    {
        var tagList = new List<Tag>();

        foreach (var t in tags.Split(' '))
        {
            tagList.Add(new Tag { tagID = null, tagText = t });
        }

        return tagList;
    }

    /// <summary>
    /// Checks the database to fill tagIDs where available
    /// </summary>
    /// <param name="tagList">a generic list of tags</param>
    /// <returns>the list of tags with any existing tagIDs filled in</returns>
    public static List<Tag> FillExistingTagIDs(List<Tag> tagList)
    {
        var existingTags = Data.MetaContent.FillExistingTagIDs(tagList);

        foreach(var t in tagList)
        {
            foreach (var e in existingTags)
            {
                if (t.tagText == e.tagText)
                {
                    t.tagID = e.tagID;
                }
            }
        }

        return tagList;
    }

    /// <summary>
    /// Inserts new tags into the database
```

```
/// </summary>
/// <param name="tagList">the generic list of tags</param>
public static void InsertNewTagEntities(List<Tag> tagList)
{
    foreach (var t in tagList)
    {
        if (t.tagID == null)
        {
            Data.MetaContent.InsertNewTagEntity(t.tagText);
        }
    }
}

/// <summary>
/// Inserts new tags for a piece of content
/// </summary>
/// <param name="tagList">the generic list of tags</param>
/// <param name="userID">the integer user ID</param>
public static void InsertNewContentTags(List<Tag> tagList,
                                        int contentID, int userID)
{
    // call the fill method again to get all the tag IDs
    var existingTags = Data.MetaContent.FillExistingTagIDs(tagList);

    // clear out the existing tags for this content
    Data.MetaContent.ClearContentTagsByUserAndContentID(contentID, userID);

    foreach (var e in existingTags)
    {
      // the ID must be explicity converted from nullable
      Data.MetaContent.InsertContentTagsByUserAndContentID(
        Convert.ToInt32(e.tagID), contentID, userID
      );
    }
}
    }
}
```

Summary

.NET 4 has a lot to offer developers in terms of easing the difficulties present in parallel processing. We discussed the concepts behind parallelization as well as some of the potential (and common) pitfalls that are frequently encountered while developing parallel code. We explored the Task Parallel Library and PLINQ and then used them to create a CMS embeddable that operated on a sample data set of user information to compare and contrast performance implications. We also saw how to implement tagging in the CMS, which is another excellent source of data for data mining using parallization techniques. As we move forward, we'll explore embeddable controls in greater detail; MEF and its plug-in functionality form the backbone of development in the CMS.

■ ■ ■

Managed Extensibility Framework and the Dynamic Language Runtime

"He did not arrive at this conclusion by the decent process of quiet, logical deduction, nor yet by the blinding flash of glorious intuition, but by the shoddy, untidy process halfway between the two by which one usually gets to know things."

—Margery Allingham

There are many challenges in developing an enterprise-level system; those challenges are compounded when one begins down the tricky road of developing a plug-in architecture. Contracts and interfaces must be established, boilerplate code must be written, and exceptions must be handled and accounted for. It can be a truly daunting task as it ramps up in complexity. The whole effort can be distilled to a single core challenge: creating a system that is not overly complex but remains safely usable and provides the desired extensibility. This chapter examines the Dynamic Language Runtime and the Managed Extensibility Framework, both newly integrated into .NET 4; our coverage of these technologies will help us create such a system in less time and with less code.

Managed Extensibility Framework

Software reusability is something of a holy grail among developers, a lofty goal that has proven to be quite difficult to achieve in a practical sense. Much code has been written to solve unique problems in distinct situations. Rather than focus on the components themselves and where any given one could be repurposed, the Managed Extensibility Framework (MEF) defines a system that facilitates reuse in a generic fashion, leaving the specifics up to developers so that they may implement their components as the particular situation dictates. MEF was created to elegantly solve a lot of the problems and challenges with developing reusable software components, and it does so very effectively.

The Manual Way

It's completely possible in C# to create a flexible plug-in architecture without the aid of a framework such as MEF; at a basic level, one must perform at least the following tasks:

- Define the interface (contract) that plug-ins and calling code abide by

- Create components that implement this interface fully

- Create code in the host application that will load and execute plug-in components

Without question, the largest portion of work and design winds up in the final point; a system to execute plug-ins can quickly become very complex. Assemblies are loaded via .NET's reflection classes and executed by the host application based on both the implementation of the component itself and the abilities that the host application provides. A complete sample Forms application is detailed in Listing 4–1; the application looks in a specified directory for plug-ins that implement the IPlugin interface. This interface defines a method called Calculate that accepts two integers.

Listing 4–1. A Complete Implementation of a Basic Plug-in System

```
using System;
using System.Reflection;
using System.Windows.Forms;

namespace pluginTest
{
    public partial class Form1 : Form
    {
        public Form1()
        {
            InitializeComponent();
        }

        private void Form1_Load(object sender, EventArgs e)
        {
            Assembly objAssembly = Assembly.LoadFrom(Application.StartupPath + "/test.dll");
            IPlugin plugin = (IPlugin)ExamineAssembly(objAssembly, "IPlugin");

            double result = plugin.Calculate(1, 2);
        }

        /// <summary>
        /// Retrieves object metadata about a specified plugin
        /// </summary>
        /// <param name="objAssembly">the Assembly object to examine</param>
        /// <param name="interfaceName">the interface we expect to be defined</param>
        /// <returns>the plugin object</returns>
        public object ExamineAssembly(Assembly objAssembly, string interfaceName)
        {
            foreach(var objType in objAssembly.GetTypes())
            {
                if (!objType.IsPublic) continue;

                Assembly plugin;

                try
                {
```

```
            plugin = Assembly.LoadFrom(objAssembly.Location);
            return plugin.CreateInstance(objType.FullName);
        }
        catch(Exception ex)
        {
            // error handling here...
        }
    }
    return null;
    }
  }
}
```

Although functional, it's somewhat fragile and doesn't open up a lot of options for us. It will certainly allow plug-in capabilities, but it's neither portable nor flexible. If we were to create a new application that required plug-ins, we would have to move this code over and likely repurpose it.

The MEF Way

Although it's not really possible for us to escape the first two requirements of our list, MEF does a great job of opening up the third requirement and providing a way for us to include plug-ins in our system without a lot of tedious boilerplate code. Let's create a sample console application and take a look at how MEF handles a similar situation; we'll call our console application MEFPluginTest.

The System.ComponentModel.Composition.dll file is the brains of the whole MEF operation, so the first thing we should do is add a reference to it in our application, as shown in Figure 4–1.

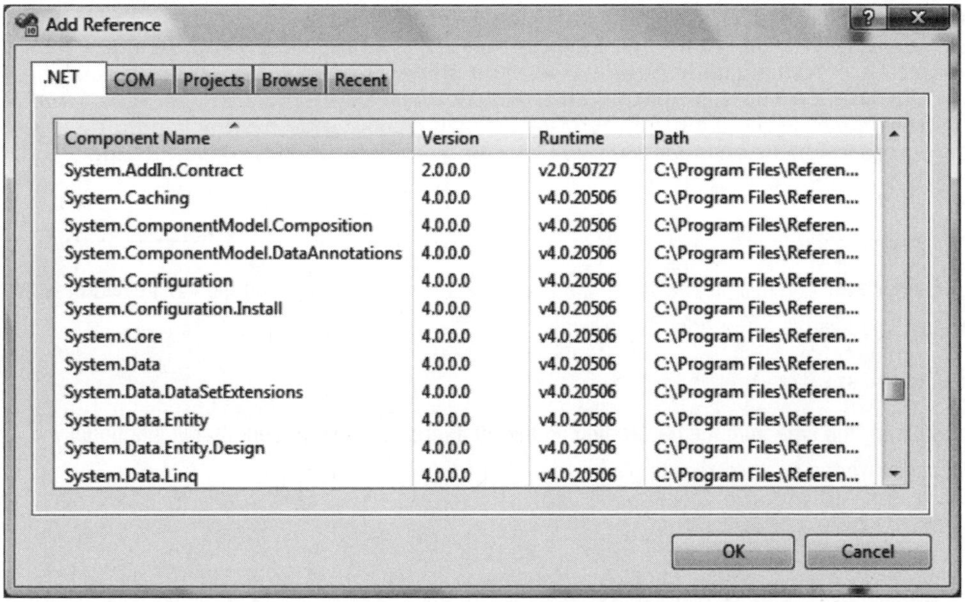

Figure 4–1. The System.ComponentModel.Composition library is included in .NET 4 by default.

Working from Usage to Implementation

Anecdotally, I find it is beneficial to design code working from the implementation backward. By creating our ideal usage first, rather than the plumbing to support it, we ensure that the code we use most often to accomplish a task is clean and manageable.

In plug-in terms, this approach serves an even greater purpose: designing reusable components is a difficult task, made more complex if the API used within those components is unwieldy or poorly designed. Therefore, for the purposes of this example we will create a new Class Library project called SharedLibrary, which will be used to house our contracts.

Exposing Libraries via MEF

One of the cornerstones of reusable, modular software is the use of interfaces. Coding to interfaces effectively decouples software components from one another, allowing the developer to switch methods and implementations on the fly. Listing 4–2 shows an example that compares instantiation types.

Listing 4–2. Coding to an Interface Allows for Better Flexibility As Requirements and Software Change

```
// concrete implementation; tightly coupled
Administrator admin = new Administrator();

// coding to an interface; loosely coupled
IUser admin = new Administrator();
```

In both cases, a new object called admin is created; the difference in the second case is that any object matching the interface requirements of the IUser type is considered acceptable. In effect, the interface defines a contract that implementing classes must abide by. From a coding standpoint, this means that you could define common properties and methods that a specific user in your system must have and then instantiate based on the IUser interface throughout your code. Adding additional user types would not require a significant modification of code on your part, shortening maintenance and coding times.

■ **Caution** This does have the potential to bite you in the rear if you are a big fan of using the var keyword, which indicates an implicitly typed variable. Consider the following:

```
var admin = new Administrator();
```

The var keyword will infer the type from the declaration on the right, creating a statement that is functionally identical to the first case from our previous example.

```
Administrator admin = new Administrator();
```

Therefore, you will have to explicitly use the interface declaration on the left side of the assignment for C# to be able to understand that you want to use it.

A Simple Plug-in Contract

Now that we have covered coding to an interface, we can create one that will serve to describe a simple plug-in. We will use this contract as a way to communicate to MEF and our application that there are libraries ready to be loaded that implement specific methods and properties.

First, create an interface in the SharedLibrary project called IPlugin. Listing 4–3 shows the code for this interface.

Listing 4–3. *The Interface for a Simple Plug-In*

```
namespace SharedLibrary
{
    public interface IPlugin
    {
        string MessageProperty { get; }
        string DiagnosticMessage();
        string DiagnosticParameters(int x, int y);
    }
}
```

Although simple, this plug-in will show us how to communicate between properties in MEF as well as methods (and methods with parameters supplied). Note that we do not need to add a reference to the System.ComponentModel.Composition library in this case; the interface does not need to specify the manner in which it will be applied.

Implementing the Plug-In

Our interface has been created; now we need a project that will contain the code for an implementation of that interface. Create a new Class Library called MEFTestLib, and add a new Class File called Test. You will also need a reference to the System.ComponentModel.Composition library for this project. Listing 4–4 shows the implementation of a sample MEF plug-in.

Listing 4–4. *Implementation of the Simple Plug-in in Test.cs*

```
using System;
using System.Collections.Generic;
using System.ComponentModel.Composition;
using System.Linq;
using System.Text;
using SharedLibrary;

namespace MEFTestLib
{
    [Export(typeof(IPlugin))]
    public class Test : IPlugin
    {
        public string MessageProperty
        {
            get { return "MEFTestLib.Test : Message property successfully updated."; }
        }

        public string DiagnosticMessage()
```

```
        {
            return "MEFTestLib.Test.DiagnosticMessage() : Successfully called the
DiagnosticMessage() method.";
        }

        public string DiagnosticParameters(int x, int y)
        {
            return "MEFTestLib.Test.DiagnosticParameters(int, int) : You passed " + x + " and
" + y + ".";
        }
    }
}
```

Most of this should be familiar ground; the Test class implements the IPlugin interface and returns some sample data. What's worth noting is the Export attribute located above the class declaration, as shown in Listing 4–5.

Listing 4–5. *Exposing Our Class to MEF*

```
[Export(typeof(IPlugin))]
```

■ **Tip** For this example, we're exporting the entire class. You're free to expose only certain properties or methods if desired; MEF is very flexible in that respect. In the CMS, it is assumed that the entire class has been exported.

This is the precise reason that we coded to an interface; the Export attribute indicates to MEF that we want to expose the Test class to host applications and that the expected type is IPlugin. Calling code will expect anything of type IPlugin to be exposed and available for use, meaning you could create quite a few libraries that implement IPlugin and have them all integrate seamlessly; this is the heart of how the CMS handles embeddables and extensibility.

■ **Caution** Implementing a single library in MEF is different from implementing multiple libraries. By that I mean if you have a common folder of libraries (which we will create shortly) and place multiple DLLs in it that export common methods and properties, your calling code must account for there being more than one available library. That requirement will become clearer in a moment.

Using the Plug-In

Now we can turn our attention back to the lonely MEFPluginTest console application we created a little while ago. Let's add a class to this project called PluginManager. The code in Listing 4–6 will do the actual legwork of communicating to and from our libraries.

■ **Tip** Notice in Listing 4–6 that I have defined the expected location for MEF plug-ins as `C:\MEFTestLibraries`; you're obviously free to choose any location you like. If you do choose another location and are following along with the source code downloaded from the Apress website, remember to update this location in that code as well.

Listing 4–6. *The PluginManager Class in the Console Application*

```
using System;
using System.ComponentModel.Composition;
using System.ComponentModel.Composition.Hosting;
using System.Collections.Generic;
using System.Reflection;
using System.Linq;
using System.Text;
using SharedLibrary;

namespace MEFPluginTest
{
    public class PluginManager
    {
        [Import(typeof(IPlugin))]
        public IPlugin TestPlugin { get; set; }

        public void ExecutePlugin()
        {
            try
            {
                var catalog = new AggregateCatalog();
                catalog.Catalogs.Add(new DirectoryCatalog(@"C:\MEFTestLibraries"));
                catalog.Catalogs.Add(new AssemblyCatalog(Assembly.GetExecutingAssembly()));

                var container = new CompositionContainer(catalog);
                container.ComposeParts(this);

                Console.WriteLine(TestPlugin.MessageProperty);
                Console.WriteLine(TestPlugin.DiagnosticMessage());
                // please excuse the "magic numbers"...
                Console.WriteLine(TestPlugin.DiagnosticParameters(1, 2));
            }
            catch (Exception ex)
            {
                Console.WriteLine(ex.Message);
                Console.WriteLine(ex.InnerException);
            }
            Console.ReadLine();
        }
    }
}
```

An AggregateCatalog is created that holds both a DirectoryCatalog and an AssemblyCatalog (more on those in a moment). With the locations defined, the available part is composed, and some of its methods are invoked with different parameters.

Notice that the hosting application has the most knowledge of both the plug-ins and the wiring required; this is how we want things to be. Our plug-ins should be dumb and blind, executing only when desired and having no real knowledge of where, when, or how they will be used. This is a core concept in the CMS.

Now we need to modify the Program.cs file to instantiate our PluginManager class and execute the plug-in, as in Listing 4–7.

Listing 4–7. *Calling the PluginManager Class*

```
using System;

namespace MEFPluginTest
{
    class Program
    {
        static void Main(string[] args)
        {
            var pm = new PluginManager();
            pm.ExecutePlugin();
            Console.ReadLine();
        }
    }
}
```

Go ahead and build the application (but do not run it yet). Once the application has compiled successfully, move the SamplePlugin.dll file from the /bin/Debug folder to C:\MEFTestLibraries (or whichever location you prefer if you've updated your code). Once that DLL has been moved to the correct location, run the application.

■ **Tip** One timesaving tip for developing MEF parts in this fashion is the use of the post-build events available in .NET projects. Select Properties ➤ Build Events for a Class Library, and then use the following command for the post-build event: copy $(TargetDir)$(TargetFileName) C:\MEFTestLibraries\$(TargetFileName). This will automatically move the DLL file to C:\MEFTestLibraries\ on a successful build.

Remember that .NET assemblies cannot be unloaded from a running AppDomain, so if your host application is running, you'll need to stop it before trying to overwrite the assembly, or you'll see a message indicating the post-build event failed.

If you are working within a share network environment, you may see a message like the one in Figure 4–2 when you try to run the host application.

Figure 4–2. Trying to load assemblies from an "unsafe" location generates an exception.

Under the default security settings, .NET is restricting access to assemblies located on network shares. Luckily, it's extremely easy to get around this problem with a quick fix: add a new App.config file to the MEFPluginTest console application, and modify it so that it contains the following.

Listing 4–8. Modifying App.config to Support Loading of Unsafe Assemblies

```
<?xml version="1.0" encoding="utf-8" ?>
<configuration>
    <runtime>
        <loadFromRemoteSources enabled="true"/>
    </runtime>
</configuration>
```

This instructs the runtime to permit the loading of assemblies in remote locations. Bear in mind that this could present a security risk and is really only necessary if you need to access assemblies located over a network or in some other untrusted location. Running this code with all assemblies on a local machine should not generate an error or require the App.config modification.

If you had previously received an error, this should remedy it, and you should see output as shown in Figure 4–3.

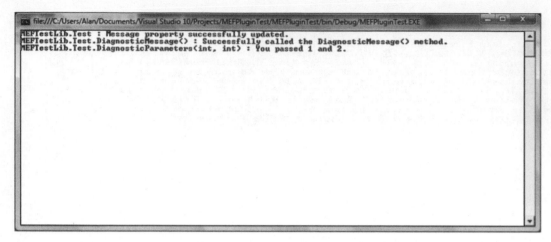

Figure 4–3. Our plug-in was successfully called from the host application via MEF.

Catalogs and Containers

So, we've created an interface that defines a plug-in, we've created a plug-in that implements that interface and exposes methods and properties to MEF via attribute metadata, and we've created a host application that will load assemblies that export the expected functionality we described. How does it all work?

One of the core constructs of MEF is the catalog, demonstrated in Listing 4–9. A catalog tells MEF that we expect imports and exports to exist in a particular location. There are three types of catalogs in MEF: the AggregateCatalog, the DirectoryCatalog, and the AssemblyCatalog.

Listing 4–9. Defining Catalogs to Inform MEF Where We Expect Exported Data

```
var catalog = new AggregateCatalog();
catalog.Catalogs.Add(new DirectoryCatalog(@"C:\MEFTestLibraries"));
catalog.Catalogs.Add(new AssemblyCatalog(Assembly.GetExecutingAssembly()));
```

The DirectoryCatalog indicates that we expect MEF plug-ins, or *parts* in MEF lingo, to exist in a particular directory; the AssemblyCatalog indicates that parts should live in a particular .NET assembly, and the AggregateCatalog is used for storing a combination of these locations.

With regard to the DirectoryCatalog, any .NET-accessible location will work fine, but I find it's beneficial while testing to have libraries stored in a common location; this is why we created the MEFTestLibraries folder at the root of the C: drive.

Once the location (or locations) for parts are established, MEF can examine those locations and retrieve the expected import types.

The real brain of the operation is the CompositionContainer, shown in Listing 4–10, which is responsible for wiring everything together. We add an instance of the current class so that all library dependences are connected properly, and finally we call ComposeParts, at which point we have access via MEF to our plug-in libraries.

Listing 4–10. The CompositionContainer Is Responsible for the Wiring and Composition of Objects

```
var container = new CompositionContainer(catalog);
container.ComposeParts(this)
```

Six lines of C# code is, I would argue, a very low barrier to entry in terms of developing a fairly advanced plug-in system. We were able to keep our interface as the primary bridge between components (in reality, the SharedLibrary would consist primarily of DTOs, if not entirely), and there are no concrete instances of plug-ins anywhere in the host application. In fact, the only reference we made was to the SharedLibrary; at compile time, the MEFPluginTest console application doesn't even know the SamplePlugin library exists at all. Is that really all we need to consider?

Supporting Multiple Parts

Earlier I mentioned that if we intend to have multiple MEF plug-ins available from a single location for import, we must accommodate that within our host application.

Create a new class library called SamplePlugin2, and add a new Class Library to it called Test. Next, add a reference to the SharedLibrary DLL so that we can use the IPlugin interface. Also, add a reference to System.ComponentModel.Composition so we can provide MEF metadata. Listing 4–11 details the code for Test in SamplePlugin2.

Listing 4–11. The SamplePlugin2 Library Is an Implementation of IPlugin with Different Output

```
using System;
using System.Collections.Generic;
using System.ComponentModel.Composition;
using System.Linq;
using System.Text;
using SharedLibrary;

namespace MEFTestLib
{
    [Export(typeof(IPlugin))]
    public class Test : IPlugin
    {
        public string MessageProperty
        {
            get { return "A totally different message property from a second plugin!"; }
        }

        public string DiagnosticMessage()
        {
            return "The DiagnosticMessage() method was called in the second plugin.";
        }

        public string DiagnosticParameters(int x, int y)
        {
            return "You passed " + x + " and " + y + ". The sum of these numbers is " + (x +
y) + ".";
        }
    }
}
```

Build (but do not run) the solution; once compiled, move SamplePlugin2.dll to the C:\MEFTestLibraries folder (or your desired location). You should now have two libraries in this folder, as shown in Figure 4–4.

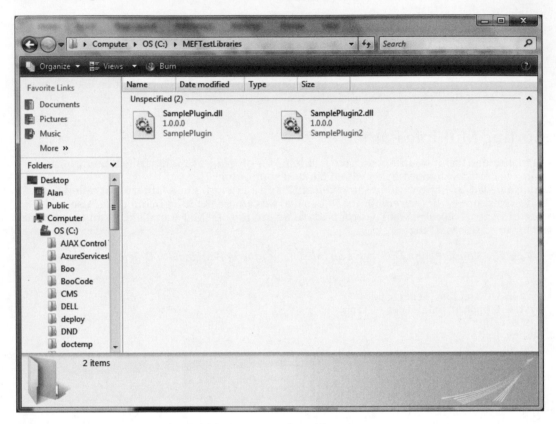

Figure 4–4. We now have multiple libraries in our shared location.

Now you can run the application; you should be presented with the rather unfriendly message displayed in Figure 4–5.

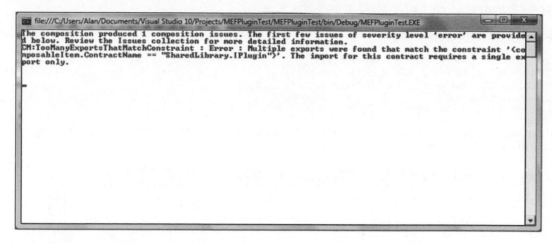

Figure 4–5. Multiple plug-ins exposing MEF exports causes an issue in our current design.

Listing 4–12. The Unfriendly, Although Informative, Error Message Provided by MEF

The composition produced 1 composition issues. The first few issues of severity level 'error' are provided below. Review the Issues collection for more detailed information.

CM:TooManyExportsThatMatchConstraint : Error : Multiple exports were found that match the constraint '(composableItem.ContractName == "SharedLibrary.IPlugin")'. The import for this contract requires a single export only.

What's the problem? The issue can be traced to how we actually imported the class in the host application. We assumed (without realizing it) that we would actually have one and only one instance of the plug-in class. Let's take a look at Listing 4–13 and see how to remedy the issue.

Listing 4–13. Improper Handling of Imports in Our Design

```
[Import(typeof(IPlugin))]
public IPlugin TestPlugin { get; set; }
```

The specific solution to this problem really depends on the implementation and usage of the plug-ins. Since we're simply displaying some test to the screen, we can create a generic list of IPlugin objects, as in Listing 4–14.

Listing 4–14. Handling Multiple Plug-in Imports

```
[Import(typeof(IPlugin))]
public List<IPlugin> TestPlugin { get; set; }
```

Next, we need to modify the actual calls to the plug-in to make use of a list; specifically, we need to enumerate the items in the list and iterate over them, calling the methods we want or accessing properties. Listing 4–15 shows how to iterate over the list of plug-ins.

Listing 4–15. *Iterating Over the List of IPlugin Objects*

```
foreach (var plugin in TestPlugin)
{
    Console.WriteLine(plugin.MessageProperty);
    Console.WriteLine(plugin.DiagnosticMessage());
    Console.WriteLine(plugin.DiagnosticParameters(1, 2));
    Console.WriteLine();
}
```

Running the application again should demonstrate that we have handled the situation, and the output is displayed as expected, as shown in Figure 4–6.

Figure 4–6. *The issue has been corrected, and multiple plug-ins are supported.*

I've included the complete listing of the host application in Listing 4–16, with the most recently updated lines in bold for convenience.

Listing 4–16. *The Complete Application Host Code*

```
using System;
using System.ComponentModel.Composition;
using System.Collections.Generic;
using System.Reflection;
using System.Linq;
using System.Text;
using SharedLibrary;

namespace MEFPluginTest
{
    public class PluginManager
    {
        [Import(typeof(IPlugin))]
        public List<IPlugin> TestPlugin { get; set; }
```

```
public void ExecutePlugin()
{
    try
    {
        var catalog = new AggregateCatalog();
        catalog.Catalogs.Add(new DirectoryCatalog(@"C:\MEFTestLibraries"));
        catalog.Catalogs.Add(new AssemblyCatalog(Assembly.GetExecutingAssembly()));

        var container = new CompositionContainer(catalog);
        container.ComposeParts(this);

        Console.WriteLine(TestPlugin.MessageProperty);
        Console.WriteLine(TestPlugin.DiagnosticMessage()),
        // please excuse the "magic numbers"...
        Console.WriteLine(TestPlugin.DiagnosticParameters(1, 2));
        foreach (var plugin in TestPlugin)
        {
            Console.WriteLine(plugin.MessageProperty);
            Console.WriteLine(plugin.DiagnosticMessage());
            Console.WriteLine(plugin.DiagnosticParameters(1, 2));
            Console.WriteLine();
        }
    }
    catch (Exception ex)
    {
        Console.WriteLine(ex.Message);
        Console.WriteLine(ex.InnerException);
    }
    Console.ReadLine();
}
}
}
```

Dynamic Language Runtime

Another method of providing extensibility in .NET 4 is via the Dynamic Language Runtime. The DLR sits right on top of the existing Common Language Runtime and seeks to provide features and functionality that developers used to dynamic languages (such as Ruby or Python) would be more comfortable with. It also aims to facilitate easier interaction between static .NET languages (such as C#) and dynamic .NET languages (such as IronPython). It's worth taking a moment to examine what a dynamic language is and is not and how it compares to a so-called static language.

■ **Note** We'll look at language interop later in the book; for now we're going to limit the discussion to C# and the use of specific language enhancements within it that change how C# developers can approach their code.

At a very basic level, a dynamic language is one in which the type checking is done at runtime instead of compile time. For example, in C#, the statement in Listing 4–17 is invalid and will prevent the code from compiling at all until the error is resolved.

Listing 4–17. The Type Is Known at Compile Time and Generates an Error

```
int myNumber = "Foobar!";
```

In a language such as Python (or its .NET implementation, IronPython), the type system is dynamic, meaning types are resolved at runtime; Listing 4–18 would be valid because the type is inferred from the value on the right side of the assignment operator.

Listing 4–18. This Is a Valid Python Statement; myNumber Is Assumed to be a String Based on Right Assignment

```
myNumber = "Foobar!"
```

■ **Note** It's a common mistake to believe that dynamic languages lack type systems.

The dynamic Keyword

The dynamic keyword that is new to C# 4 is another tool in the arsenal of a developer, and it's one to be used judiciously. Let's take a look at some of the concerns behind the dynamic keyword before we explore some interesting things we can accomplish with it.

The dynamic keyword supports the runtime evaluation of assignments in C#. It is distinct in function and purpose with regard to the var keyword, which is an implicit declaration; var is simply a shorthand where type information is still known at compile time. For example, the syntax in Listing 4–19 is invalid in C# and prevents the code from being compiled and executed; without a FooBar() method, the var keyword is unable to resolve properly, and a compile-time error is generated.

Listing 4–19. The Foo Class Lacks a FooBar() Method, and a Compile-Time Error Is Generated

```
public static class Foo
{
    static int Bar()
    {
        return 42;
    }
}

public void Test()
```

```
{
    var myNumber = Foo.FooBar(); // generates an error
}
```

Compare this with the dynamic keyword shown in Listing 4–20, which has an altogether different effect.

Listing 4–20. The Dynamic Keyword Will Resolve at Runtime

```
public static class Foo
{
    static int Bar()
    {
        return 42;
    }
}

public void Test()
{
    dynamic myNumber = Foo.FooBar(); // generates an error *AT RUNTIME ONLY*
}
```

This is what keeps C# developers up at night. It is entirely possible to use the dynamic keyword to act upon methods, properties, and so on, that may or may not exist. You will receive no compile-time errors and no red IntelliSense underlines to indicate that the FooBar() method is not a member of the Foo class; you receive nothing because *C# has not yet examined the Foo class to even know the method does not exist.* If you were to run the application, you would receive an exception when Test() was executed.

Benefits of the dynamic Keyword

The dynamic keyword *is* a static type; what makes it unique is that the act of type checking does not occur on this particular type, effectively making it dynamic and resolved at runtime. Objects declared with the type dynamic are actually statically typed objects that are ignored until runtime; it's kind of a clever hack to .NET's type system, in a way.

Let's look at a hypothetical use of the dynamic keyword. Earlier in the chapter we discussed the possibility of an interface called IUser that would support users in a system to be instanced without needing to couple to a particular type; the IUser interface provided a contract for us that more specific types could implement, and we could act on those types in an identical fashion because they all contained the same methods and properties (or at least the same basic set).

The dynamic keyword reduces the amount of code we need to create and maintain by establishing a sort of pattern-matching environment; consider the code in Listing 4–21.

Listing 4–21. A Theoretical Usage of the dynamic Keyword

```
public void ProcessUser(dynamic user)
{
    // we always want to greet the user
    DisplayMessage("Welcome, " + user.username);

    if (user is BasicUser)
    {
```

```
        // do nothing, basic user
    }

    if (user is Manager)
    {
        // display a key performance indicator dashboard for the specific manager
        DisplayKPIDashboard(user.userID);
    }

    if (user is Admin)
    {
        // display an admin console for adjusting site-wide settings
        DisplayAdminPanel(user.userID);
    }
}
```

Used properly, the dynamic keyword opens a wide variety of doors in terms of eliminating what could be perceived as boilerplate code. Instead of every specific type of user implementing the IUser interface, the dynamic keyword allows us to simply pass in any object that implements those fields naturally. It's roughly the same effect but with less code involved.

The dynamic keyword is not a replacement for interfaces but rather another option for how to approach the challenges of a specific system.

■ **Note** This type of object interaction and operation is affectionately referred to as *duck typing*. If it looks like a duck and quacks like a duck, it must be a duck. In dynamic programming terms, if two objects have identical properties and methods, then we can operate on them as if they were of identical types (even if they are not). The code in Listing 4–21 demonstrates this: BasicUser, Manager, and Admin are all different types, but we can act on them identically because they expose the same properties and methods. Each type "looks like" the others, so we can work with them interchangeably.

CMS Plug-Ins

Areas of a content management system lend themselves quite naturally to a plug-in-based architecture. In my experience, it's important to not go overboard with the approach; I've seen in many cases the end result is a system that is so concerned with being abstract that it becomes unwieldy and brittle (which is really the precise situation that a plug-in design is meant to avoid). To the CMS, although MEF is critical to its operation, the implementation is more like a gentle flavoring; it should enhance the end result, not overpower it.

■ **Note** The remainder of this chapter focuses on plug-ins via MEF; the usage of IronPython for additional plug-in behavior is discussed in more detail in Chapter 7, along with coverage of the basic language syntax.

IEmbeddable

If a single piece of code could be considered the keys to the castle in the CMS, the IEmbeddable interface is it. We discussed it briefly in Chapter 2, but we'll examine it again here in Listing 4–22.

Listing 4–22. The IEmbeddable Interface That Embeddables Rely On

```
using System;
using CommonLibrary.Permissions;

namespace CommonLibrary.Interfaces
{
    /// <summary>
    /// Interface that Embeddables are expected to implement.
    /// </summary>
    public interface IEmbeddable
    {
        Guid ContentID { get; set; }
        string EmbeddableName { get; }
        int EmbeddableID { get; }
        EmbeddablePermissions Permissions { get; }
    }
}
```

Throughout the CMS, the system relies on this interface as a way to communicate with the embeddable objects that make up a public-facing content page. The code in Listing 4–23, taken from the Business library of the CMS, is responsible for retrieving a catalog of assemblies that are exposed via MEF and implement IEmbeddable. These assemblies are added to a generic list called _embeddables by MEF automatically, and this list is returned by the method so that it can be used elsewhere in the system.

Listing 4–23. Loading MEF-Exposed Assemblies via IEmbeddable

```
[ImportMany(typeof(IEmbeddable))]
private List<IEmbeddable> _embeddables;

/// <summary>
/// Retrieves available plugins from the predefined location.
/// </summary>
/// <returns>A generic list of IEmbeddable objects.</returns>
public List<IEmbeddable> GetEmbeddablePlugins()
{
    var catalog = new AggregateCatalog();

    try { catalog.Catalogs.Add(new
DirectoryCatalog(ConfigurationManager.AppSettings["EmbeddablePluginFolder"])); }

    catch
    {
        // logging snipped
    }

    _container = new CompositionContainer(catalog);
```

```
    // grab all the available imports for this container
    try
    {
        _container.ComposeParts(this);
    }
    catch
    {
        // logging snipped
    }

    return _embeddables;
}
```

■ **Tip** Don't forget to ensure usage of the `ImportMany` attribute over `Import` if you expect to have multiple plug-ins, as is the case in the CMS; attempting to load multiple assemblies in this fashion with `Import` throws an exception.

Server Controls as Embeddables

The CMS uses .NET server controls to display public-facing content to users; as discussed, these controls implement IEmbeddable and are exposed via MEF. Examine Listing 4–24, which demonstrates a complete CMS embeddable sever control.

Listing 4–24. A Server Control Implementing IEmbeddable

```
using System.ComponentModel;
using System.ComponentModel.Composition;
using System.ComponentModel.Composition.Hosting;
using CommonLibrary.Interfaces;
using CommonLibrary.Permissions;

namespace Content
{
    [Export(typeof(IEmbeddable))]
    [ToolboxData("<{0}:Content runat=server></{0}:Content>")]
    public class Content : WebControl, IEmbeddable
    {
        public Guid ContentID { get; set; }

        public EmbeddablePermissions Permissions
        {
            get
            {
                return (EmbeddablePermissions.AllowedInContent |
                        EmbeddablePermissions.AllowedInFooter |
                        EmbeddablePermissions.AllowedInHeader |
                        EmbeddablePermissions.AllowedInPrimaryNav |
```

```
                    EmbeddablePermissions.AllowedInSubNav);
        }
    }

    public string EmbeddableName
    {
        get { return "Content"; }
    }

    public int EmbeddableID
    {
        get { return 1; }
    }

    protected override void Render(HtmlTextWriter writer)
    {
        StringBuilder sb = new StringBuilder();
        sb.AppendLine("<div id=\"content\">");
        sb.AppendLine("[Page content here]");
        sb.AppendLine("</div>");
        writer.Write(sb.ToString());
    }
}
}
```

■ **Tip** Why did we override `Render()` and not `RenderContents()`? Either is a valid option, but the `Render()` method won't wrap the output in any tags; typically, overriding `RenderContents()` triggers calls to `RenderBeginTag()` and `RenderEndTag()`, which in this case will cause the markup to be wrapped in `<span>` tags.

Note that the control must use the `Export` attribute to indicate to MEF that it uses `IEmbeddable`; it is this attribute that exposes the control to MEF. As discussed in Chapter 2, an embeddable in the CMS is expected to handle its own version control and data management via the ContentID GUID, which represents the specific version of the content to load.

There are a lot of benefits to opting for server controls as a way to provide this functionality. They're easily versioned, can be reused in the Visual Studio Toolbox, and are capable of being distributed for use in other applications. Also, developers of embeddables are responsible for the precise HTML output of the control. Figure 4–7 shows a page that uses the embeddable code in Listing 4–24.

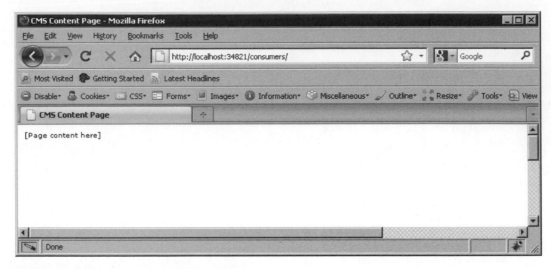

Figure 4–7. *Using the embeddable on a page*

Displaying Embeddables

The embeddables make their way to the page by being loaded into buckets, which themselves are loaded into a PlaceHolder control on the content.aspx page. Listing 4–25 shows the markup of this page.

Listing 4–25. *The Markup of content.aspx*

```
<%@ Page Language="C#" AutoEventWireup="true" CodeFile="content.aspx.cs" Inherits="content"
ClientIDMode="Static" %>

<!doctype html>
<html xmlns="http://www.w3.org/1999/xhtml">
<head id="Head1" runat="server">
    <title>CMS Content Page</title>

    <!-- client-side libraries -->
    <script src="/js/jquery-1.3.2.min.js" type="text/javascript"></script>
</head>
<body>
    <form id="form1" runat="server">
    <div id="nav" runat="server" visible="false">
        <p><a href="/admin/home.aspx">&laquo; Back to admin site</a></p>
    </div>
    <div id="page">
        <asp:PlaceHolder ID="cmsControls" runat="server"></asp:PlaceHolder>
    </div>
    </form>
</body>
</html>
```

■ **Tip** The `<div>` with an ID of nav is used to display a link back to the admin side of the CMS for users who have logged in and are previewing pages.

The `content.aspx` page passes off the responsibility for managing embeddable controls to the business tier, as shown in Listing 4–26. The `PageAssembler` class handles the actual creation of a page, including which buckets exist and which embeddables live within them.

Listing 4–26. Calling the Business Tier's PageAssembler Class to Get a Final Page

```
if (Request.QueryString["id"] != null)
{
    // it's important to set the form action - PostBacks fail if the URL differs from it
    Guid id = new Guid(Request.QueryString["id"]);
    form1.Action = HttpContext.Current.Request.RawUrl.ToString().ToLower();

    // The PageAssembler is where all the action and excitement lives
    PageAssembler pa = new PageAssembler(this);
    this.Page = pa.GetAssembledPage(id);
}
else
{
    return;
}
```

■ **Note** You may have noticed that the `content.aspx` page is expecting a GUID; although the system relies on GUIDs to handle the retrieval of data and the creation of content versions, users will arrive via friendly URLs. We will discuss how to create a custom URL-mapping system in Chapter 9. For now, just note that although users will navigate the system using friendly, memorable URLs (such as `/about-us/`), the system will use GUIDs behind the scenes.

PageAssembler

Listing 4–27 shows the MEF-relevant portions of the `PageAssembler` class in the business tier. It enforces the business rules, such as the singleton nature of buckets on a CMS page and the actual addition of embeddable controls to a bucket.

Listing 4–27. The PageAssembler Class, Responsible for Creating CMS Pages

```
using CommonLibrary.Entities;
using CommonLibrary.Interfaces;
using Business;

namespace Business
```

```
{
    public class PageAssembler
    {
        private List<Control> _embeddables;
        private Page _page;
        private PlaceHolder _cmsControls;

        /// <summary>
        /// Loads the content for a page.
        /// </summary>
        /// <param name="id">the ID of the page</param>
        private void LoadContent(Guid id)
        {
            Business.Content business = new Business.Content();
            List<ContentRow> content = business.LoadContent(id);
            foreach (var c in content)
            {
                LoadBuckets(c.bucketControl, c.embeddableID);
            }
        }

        /// <summary>
        /// Loads the top-level buckets for a page
        /// </summary>
        /// <param name="bucketName">the name of the bucket control</param>
        /// <param name="embeddableID">the ID of the embeddable we need to load</param>
        private void LoadBuckets(string bucketName, int embeddableID)
        {
            var bucket = _page.LoadControl("~/core/buckets/" + bucketName);
            bucket.ID = bucketName.Replace(".ascx", "");

            if (_cmsControls.FindControl(bucket.ID) == null)
            {
                _cmsControls.Controls.Add(bucket);
            }

            if (embeddableID > 0)
            {
                LoadEmbeddables(bucketName, embeddableID);
            }
        }

        /// <summary>
        /// Loads the current embeddable(s) for a bucket.
        /// </summary>
        /// <param name="bucketName">the name of the bucket control</param>
        /// <param name="embeddableID">the ID of the embeddable we need to load</param>
        private void LoadEmbeddables(string bucketName, int embeddableID)
        {
            var parentBucket = _cmsControls.FindControl(bucketName.Replace(".ascx", ""));
            var embeddables = parentBucket.FindControl("embeddables");
            foreach (var e in _embeddables)
            {
                if (((IEmbeddable)e).EmbeddableID == embeddableID)
```

```
            {
                embeddables.Controls.Add(e);
            }
        }
    }

    /// <summary>
    /// Executes the embeddables for a particular page
    /// </summary>
    private void ExecuteEmbeddables()
    {
        var business = new Business.Plugins();
        _embeddables = business.ExecuteEmbeddablePlugins(_page);
    }
}
}
```

From a development perspective, a page in the CMS is simply a collection of one or more user controls that contain one or more server controls within; Figure 4–8 illustrates this concept. The watch values for this breakpoint show that the LoadBuckets() method will add the content.ascx bucket to the page (if it doesn't already exist, then add an instance of an embeddable to it, in this case an embeddable with an ID of 4). This process repeats until a page is constructed.

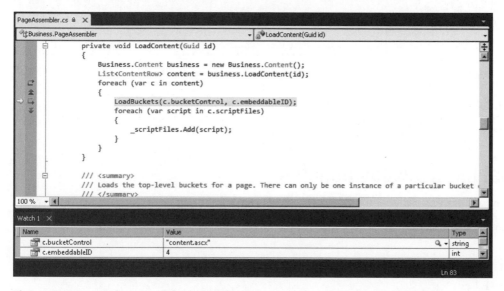

Figure 4–8. *A sample page with a single bucket containing a single embeddable*

Figure 4–9 shows the data structure behind the scenes as multiple embeddables are loaded by MEF. The CMS passes the relevant information in (the GUID for the content being retrieved) and receives only the most relevant information in return (the ID of the embeddable, the name of it, and the permissions for where it is allowed to live on a page).

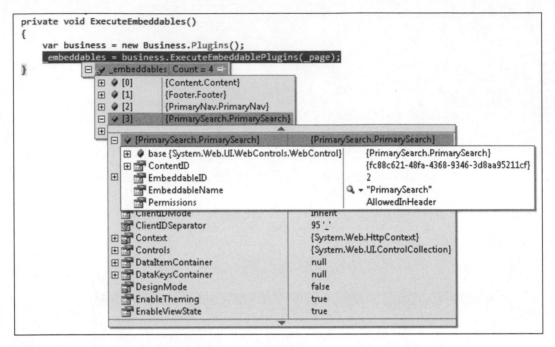

Figure 4–9. *A sample page with multiple embeddables*

It's a straightforward architecture that emphasizes simplicity and clarity, as well as flexibility. Everything is transparent operationally, and the CMS strives to reduce the chattiness between components as much as possible, relying on a single GUID wherever possible.

Additional Methodology Benefits

It should be obvious at this point that the CMS has a significant amount of behavior provided solely by the strengths of MEF. Besides being a lightweight and easy method of creating complex system behaviors, MEF provides several other benefits, particularly in terms of how we can handle problem situations.

Missing DLLs

The nature of embeddables in the CMS is that they are fully 100 percent optional, from both a discovery and a usage perspective. That means that even if the database contains an entry for a page indicating that a particular embeddable should be added to the page, the complete lack of that library won't cause a problem during the loading and execution of a page. Plug-ins can be added and removed without triggering application pool recycles or disrupting the loading of pages on the client side.

For example, if we were to delete the embeddable server control we created earlier and load that page again, we would be presented with the markup shown in Listing 4–28. The <div> with an ID of page has been highlighted to indicate where the markup would normally have been added.

Listing 4–28. A Page Will Still Load When an Embeddable Is Missing

```html
<!doctype html>
<html xmlns="http://www.w3.org/1999/xhtml">
<head id="Head1" runat="server">
    <title>CMS Content Page</title>

    <!-- client-side libraries -->
    <script src="/js/jquery-1.3.2.min.js" type="text/javascript"></script>
</head>
<body>
    <form id="form1" runat="server">
    <div id="nav" runat="server" visible="false">
        <p><a href="/admin/home.aspx">&laquo; Back to admin site</a></p>
    </div>
    <div id="page">

    </div>
    </form>
</body>
</html>
```

For example, if we were to delete the embeddable server control we created earlier and load that page again, we would be presented with the markup shown in Listing 4–28. The <div> with an ID of page has been highlighted to indicate where the markup would normally have been added.

Exceptions in Embeddables

MEF is also very forgiving regarding exceptions being thrown in plug-in libraries. Although we want to encourage proper exception handling behavior in developers building CMS controls, it's also desirable that a misbehaving control not bring down a particular page. In general, it would be better to simply display no content rather than an unhandled exception.

If we take the code from Listing 4–24 and modify it to include code that should throw an exception as in Listing 4–29, the page will still load without any notable problems for the client. The markup generated would be identical to Listing 4–28, where the <div> with an ID of page simply didn't have the embeddable's output in it.

Listing 4–29. This Should Trigger an Exception When We Attempt to Divide by Zero

```csharp
protected override void Render(HtmlTextWriter writer)
{
    int zero = 0;
    int test = 0 / zero;

    StringBuilder sb = new StringBuilder();
    sb.AppendLine("<div id=\"content\">");
    sb.AppendLine("[Page content here]");
    sb.AppendLine("</div>");
```

```
        writer.Write(sb.ToString());
}
```

■ **Note** This was a conscious decision made during the development of the system. It was deemed preferable to simply ignore failed embeddables and leave a blank spot on the page rather than disrupt processing any further.

A More Complex Emeddable

Although the tree-based structure of CMS content is discussed in more detail in Chapter 6, it's sufficient at this point to note that pages are stored in a hierarchy; a CMS page may have a single, direct parent or no parent at all. This information is often very useful to display to a user, so one of the embeddables available with the sample code for this book is a Breadcrumb embeddable.

Breadcrumbs

Breadcrumbs are the sets of links, typically located at the top of web pages, that denote the path back to the home page from your current location. Creating a breadcrumb embeddable will allow us to peek back upward into the CMS and create a real-world control.

Listing 4–30 shows the skeleton of a breadcrumb embeddable. At this point, it can be loaded onto a CMS page, although nothing will be displayed; based on its permissions, it is only valid in the Content bucket.

Listing 4–30. The Skeleton of a CMS Breadcrumb Embeddable

```
using System;
using System.ComponentModel;
using System.ComponentModel.Composition;
using System.Text;
using System.Web.UI;
using System.Web.UI.WebControls;
using CommonLibrary.Interfaces;
using CommonLibrary.Permissions;

namespace Breadcrumbs
{
    [Export(typeof (IEmbeddable))]
    [DefaultProperty("Text")]
    [ToolboxData("<{0}:Breadcrumbs runat=server></{0}:Breadcrumbs>")]
    public class Breadcrumbs : WebControl, IEmbeddable
    {
        #region IEmbeddable Members

        public Guid ContentID { get; set; }

        public EmbeddablePermissions Permissions
        {
            get { return (EmbeddablePermissions.AllowedInContent); }
```

```
        }

        public string EmbeddableName
        {
            get { return "Breadcrumb Navigation"; }
        }

        public int EmbeddableID
        {
            get { return 7; }
        }

        #endregion

        protected override void Render(HtmlTextWriter writer)
        {
            writer.Write();
        }
    }
}
```

■ **Tip** The ID of the embeddable in the downloadable code is 7; if you're creating this embeddable from scratch, you may have a different number depending on what you've already created.

Navigating the CMS Tree

The CMS provides a number of features for exposing both a raw tree structure that contains page information, as well as mapping tools that convert this data into forms that .NET controls (such as the site tree) can use. Listing 4–31 shows the usage of these methods, where a tree is assembled and the basic structure of the breadcrumb HTML is created.

Listing 4–31. Getting Access to the Site Tree and Beginning to Construct Links

```
private string GetLinks()
{
    var mapper = new Mapper();
    Tree tree = mapper.GetTree();
    Node parent = tree.FindPage(ContentID);

    var sb = new StringBuilder();
    sb.Append("<ul class=\"crumbs\">");

    string output = String.Empty;
    GetPreviousParent(ref output, tree, parent, true)

    sb.Append(output);
    sb.Append("</ul>");
    return sb.ToString();
```

```
}
```

The GetPreviousParent method, shown in Listing 4–32, is called recursively to work backward from the current page to the parent, so long as the page has a GUID specified for its parent. The output string is passed by reference to maintain a pointer throughout the iterations, and each new page is inserted to the beginning of that string.

Listing 4–32. *Assembling Markup to be Delivered to the Client*

```csharp
private void GetPreviousParent(ref string output, Tree tree, Node node, bool isCurrentPage)
{
   var content = new StringBuilder();

   if (isCurrentPage)
   {
      content.Append("<li class=\"active\">");
      content.Append(node.Title);
      content.Append("</li>");
   }
   else
   {
      content.Append("<li><a href=\"");
      content.Append(node.FriendlyUrl);
      content.Append("\">");
      content.Append(node.Title);
      content.Append("</a></li>");
   }

   var innerLinks = new StringBuilder(output);
   innerLinks.Insert(0, content.ToString());
   output = innerLinks.ToString();

   if (node.ParentID.HasValue)
   {
      Node parent = tree.FindPage(node.ParentID.Value);
      GetPreviousParent(ref output, tree, parent, false);
   }
}
```

Note the conditional check for isCurrentPage, which is marked true only on the first iteration; the desired effect is that the current page is displayed as text rather than a link that can be clicked.

Once the Render method has been updated to call the GetLinks method, as shown in Listing 4–33, the embeddable will be fully functional.

Listing 4–33.

```csharp
protected override void Render(HtmlTextWriter writer)
{
   writer.Write(GetLinks());
}
```

Figure 4–10 shows the output of the Breadcrumb embeddable on a sample site with a small amount of CSS applied to spruce it up.

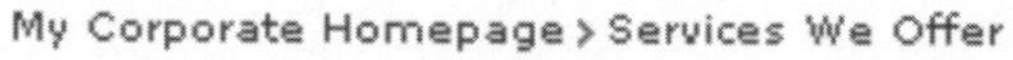

My Corporate Homepage > Services We Offer

Figure 4–10. *The functional breadcrumb navigation*

As you can see, the skeleton for an embeddable is lightweight and designed to stay out of the way; neither the CMS nor the embeddables need know much about one another, but more advanced features can be accessed via the CMS libraries directly if desired.

Summary

We began with a discussion of the Managed Extensibility Framework and the problems it was designed to solve. We examined how to create a simple plug-in for a console application and how to accommodate having multiple plug-ins in the same physical location. We expanded the discussion to the Dynamic Language Runtime and the new dynamic keyword in .NET 4. Next, we moved on to the actual creation of server controls that the CMS can use for the assembly of public-facing pages, and we discussed the PageAssembler class that manages that assembly. This code is the real core of the CMS; everything beyond this is layered onto this base functionality. We ended by creating a fully functional embeddable that displays breadcrumb navigation to the end user as they move through a site. As we advance into Chapter 5, we'll begin working with jQuery and look at ways to easily enhance the user experience of the CMS.

CHAPTER 5

■ ■ ■

jQuery and Ajax in the Presentation Tier

"Measuring programming progress by lines of code is like measuring aircraft building progress by weight."

—Bill Gates

The landscape of the Internet has changed dramatically over the past few years. Users expect more functionality out of web applications, to the point that the line between web and desktop is somewhat blurred. The issue is complicated by the nature of web browsers themselves; different manufacturers have implemented different parts of individual standards, added their own custom features that other browsers don't support, and so on. A web developer is left to try to create identical functionality and appearance across any number of distinct browsers that may or may not support any number of features. It appears quite daunting indeed. Luckily, there exists a quality JavaScript framework called jQuery that aims to bridge developer and user desire with browser results. We'll begin with a discussion of the problem domain, explore jQuery, and look at some clever ways to add Ajax functionality to the CMS. We'll improve on the style and design of the public-facing site as well.

■ **Note** jQuery has a vibrant community built up around it, constantly evolving the framework with plug-ins, innovative applications, and so on. This chapter is not meant to be an exhaustive look at everything the jQuery library can do (which anyone will tell is "quite a bit") but rather focuses on getting you up to speed on some core practices and applications of the library in the context of the CMS. For a very in-depth look at the nuances of jQuery, I recommend *Embracing jQuery: User Experience Design* by Brennan Stehling and Cindi Thomas (Apress, 2010).

An Introduction to jQuery

jQuery is an extremely popular JavaScript framework created by John Resig. The goal of jQuery is to provide a way for developers to leverage JavaScript across a variety of browsers without having to concern themselves with the low-level plumbing involved in writing JavaScript that operates identically across those browsers. The real power of the framework is in its syntax and brevity coupled with its highly extensible nature.

The $() Factory

Arguably the most common action in jQuery is the selection of particular elements on the page that need to be modified in some fashion; this is accomplished via the $() factory. The $() factory is the window to jQuery's selection capabilities, capable of accepting CSS classes, element IDs, types of elements, XPath queries, and more, making it an extremely flexible and versatile method of affecting changes upon a page's markup. This is a key tenet of jQuery: simplicity makes code easier to understand and maintain.

For example, Listing 5–1 shows a snippet of JavaScript that uses jQuery to add some class information to elements on a page. In almost all cases, jQuery code that involves event handling or working with page elements is placed within the $(document).ready() function. This ensures that the entire document has been loaded but fires before the page contents themselves are displayed. If the document were not ready, actions could be triggered for elements that didn't presently exist, which would could cause unpredictable behavior (or simply stop script execution altogether).

Listing 5–1. jQuery Code to Modify a Few Stylistic Elements and Display a Traditional Alert Box

```
<script type="text/javascript">
    $(document).ready(function () {
        $('h1').addClass('underlined');
        $('h4').addClass('italicized');
        alert('Hello via jQuery!');
    });
</script>
```

■ **Tip** In CSS, classes are prefixed with a period, while IDs are prefixed with a pound sign. For instance, `<div class="foo"></div>` would be accessed with `.foo { attribute: value; }`, while `<div id="bar"></div>` would be accessed with `#foo { attribute: value; }`. What's the difference? IDs should be unique on a page, while classes can appear multiple times; we should have only one `<div>` with an ID of "bar," but we could have many `<div>`s with classes of "foo."

The jQuery Object

The $() factory is just a shorthand wrapper for the jQuery object. The previous code could be written like this:

```
<script type="text/javascript">
    jQuery(document).ready(function () {
        jQuery('h1').addClass('underlined');
        jQuery('h4').addClass('italicized');
        alert('Hello via jQuery!');
    });
```

```
</script>
```

Why is this important? You may encounter a collision if third-party libraries or frameworks also use the $() factory for their own code. If you do have a problem, you'll need to use the fully qualified jQuery call.

Listing 5–2 defines the CSS classes that the jQuery snippet in Listing 5–1 is expecting. If used on a sample page, the <h1> elements will be underlined, and the <h4> elements will be italicized.

Listing 5–2. Two CSS Classes That jQuery Will Apply to the Page

```
<style type="text/css">
    .underlined { text-decoration: underline; }
    .italicized { font-style: italic; }
</style>
```

You can see in Figure 5–1 that jQuery has successfully modified the Document Object Model (DOM) and displayed our alert box to the client.

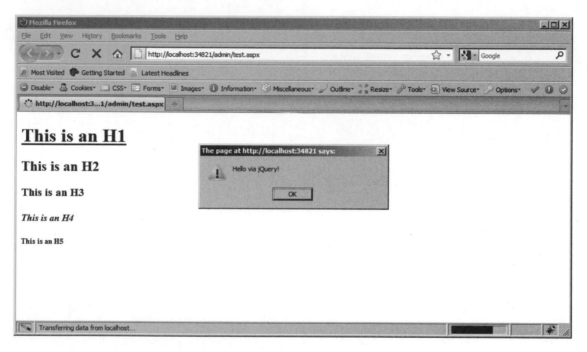

Figure 5–1. jQuery has modified the DOM and displayed our alert box.

137

Implicit Iteration

What may not be obvious at first glance is what is missing from the jQuery code we have written thus far; it's not that we haven't performed a necessary step. It would be more accurate to say jQuery made things so simple that we didn't *have* to perform certain steps. If we modify the code to select <h2> elements instead of <h1>, as shown in Listing 5–3, things may become a bit clearer. Figure 5–2 shows the results.

Listing 5–3. Modifying <h2> Instead of <h1>

```
<script type="text/javascript">
    $(document).ready(function () {
        $('h4').addClass('italicized');
        alert('Hello via jQuery!');
    });
</script>
```

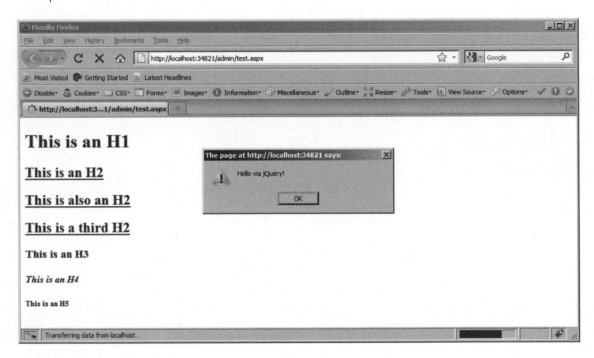

Figure 5–2. Implicit iteration in action

jQuery methods typically use what is called *implicit iteration*. This means that they are designed by default to operate on sets of elements instead of individual ones; you are not required to loop through the results and apply a change to each one. Implicit iteration assumes that the change should be applied to all matching elements within the DOM and does so accordingly. When we specified the <h2> element, jQuery automatically applied the underlined style to each <h2> element. Knowing that jQuery is somewhat all-encompassing with its selectors means that careful (read: clean) construction of HTML and CSS is very important to ensuring your pages behave the way you intend. As we move forward, we'll see how to become more specific with our selectors to pinpoint specific items or groups of items as opposed to broad, sweeping grabs of DOM elements. With that in mind, jQuery's use of implicit iteration results in code that is generally simpler, shorter, and easier to maintain.

Ajax via jQuery

One of the more popular choices for developing powerful and interactive websites is Ajax, which comes from "asynchronous JavaScript and XML." Jesse James Garrett wrote a well-known article called "AJAX: A New Approach to Web Applications" that popularized the concepts and informed many developers of an effective way to leverage various browser and server technologies to create web pages that are capable of operating and updating in an asynchronous fashion. The individual technologies that make up a typical Ajax design were not new, but the manner in which they were combined brought a new level of capability (as well as complexity) to the web arena.

■ **Note** Technically, the term Ajax is a misnomer these days; you could accomplish the same effects without JavaScript or XML. JavaScript remains the most popular choice among developers for creating client-side code, and XML is still widely used for the transmission of data between server and client. You could opt for a combination of VBScript and JavaScript Object Notation (JSON) if desired. It's important to note that the term wraps desired application functionality and does not specifically refer to the technologies used anymore.

The key to Ajax functionality in the modern browser environment is the XMLHttpRequest object. This object allows the client to speak to the server in an asynchronous fashion; this permits browsers to update the contents of a page (or a portion of a page) without refreshing the parent page. This experience is typically "smoother," resulting in smaller requests between client and server as opposed to whole-page refreshes. However, as with many other aspects of web development, for quite some time the various browser manufacturers did not have a consistent method of asynchronous functionality. The XMLHttpRequest object is accessed differently between Mozilla and Microsoft browsers, for example.

Using the XMLHttpRequest object in a manual fashion (without the benefits and conveniences of a well-tested framework) is not difficult, but requires a developer to accommodate the ways various browsers implement this functionality. Listing 5–4 shows a brief skeleton of asynchronous JavaScript that fetches an XML file from a server using the GET verb.

Listing 5–4. Using the Low-Level XMLHttpRequest Object to Request an XML File

```
<script type="text/javascript">
   var xhr = null;

   if (window.XMLHttpRequest)
   {
      xhr = new XMLHttpRequest();
   }

   else if (window.ActiveXObject)
```

```
    {
        xhr = new ActiveXObject("Microsoft.XMLHTTP");
    }

    if (xhr != null)
    {
        xhr.Open("GET", "Http://domain.com/some_file.xml", true);
    }
</script>
```

Note the conditional check if (window.XMLHttpRequest). This portion of the conditional is attempting to use the browser's native XMLHttpRequest object, while the else if (window.ActiveXObject) check seeks to open the Internet Explorer implementation (which is obviously an ActiveX object). This is a broad and generic check; there are specific ActiveX versions particular to different Internet Explorer versions, making robust XMLHttpRequest object code a somewhat more complex endeavor. This code also excludes necessary error handing and status checks, such as the response code (200, 404, 500, and so on) when fetching the XML file. The requirements for stable and reliable handwritten Ajax code can be quite substantial.

jQuery simplifies both the task of asynchronous communication as well as the handling of how to properly implement such communication between different browser families. Listing 5–5 shows the general pattern for Ajax operations in jQuery. A call to the $.ajax() method requires, as a minimum, a valid url parameter and a function to execute after successful communication between client and server.

Listing 5–5. Asynchronous Communication via jQuery

```
<script type="text/javascript">
    $.ajax({
        url: "http://domain.com/some_file.xml",
        success: function(html) {
            // handle the response here…
        }
    });
</script>
```

The $.ajax() method hides the low-level implementation details of the XMLHttpRequest object from you, as well as provides parameters for providing data, setting the type of HTTP verb to use, and handling both success and failure statuses. jQuery politely abstracts away the plumbing and allows you to focus on the project at hand, which can be quite a timesaving boon as cross-browser development can be quite complex.

■ **Tip** Remember that the $() factory method is a convenience wrapper around the jQuery() object. The $.ajax() call could also be read as jQuery.ajax().

Caching and Ajax

Frequently the purpose of asynchronous page communication is to update a portion or portions of a web page without requiring the heavier operation of requesting, generating, and retrieving a complete page update. This function is in contrast to caching techniques, which have become a critical component of scalable website design.

■ **Note** We will discuss distributed caching and scalability options in Chapter 6.

Browsers and servers can be very cache-happy with content that is viewed as static or unchanging. As a result, it's not uncommon to find that the results of an Ajax request to the server returns cached content, negating the effort of updating a portion of a page with fresh material.

We can avoid this particular issue in several ways. The first relies on the interpretation of HTTP verbs. It is possible to use the POST verb instead of the GET verb to make a content request to the server. By design, POSTs are not *supposed* to be cached (although they *can* be); the reason for this is a POST request is expected to have side effects of some kind on the server. For example, when you fill out a form on a web page, the contents are typically sent to the server via a POST message and trigger additional behaviors or operations on the server. The GET verb is intended to be side effect free and therefore subject to caching when possible.

You can specify the type of request made via jQuery by supplying type and data parameters when applicable. By default, jQuery will use the GET verb when using the $.ajax() method. Listing 5–6 shows how to configure the method to use the POST verb instead. Note the inclusion of the data parameter, which accepts input in the form of key=value, delimited with an ampersand (&). This data will be automatically inserted into the body of the POST message.

Listing 5–6. Asynchronous POST by Supplying a Verb Type and Data Parameters

```
<script type="text/javascript">
    $.ajax({
        type: "POST",
        url: "http://domain.com/some_page.aspx",
        data: "foo=1&bar=2&foobar=3",
        success: function(html) {
            // handle the response here...
        }
    });
</script>
```

Avoiding Caching on GET Requests

Although using the POST verb will technically work, a more straightforward and appropriate method is to provide randomized parameters to the end of a particular request URL to trigger the server to return the most up-to-date version of the resource in question. jQuery will handle this behavior automatically if we provide a cache parameter to indicate how we want the request to be created, as shown in Listing 5–7.

Listing 5–7. Asynchronous GET with the Cache Parameter Set to False

```
<script type="text/javascript">
    $.ajax({
        type: "GET",
```

```
        url: "http://domain.com/some_page.aspx",
        cache: false,
        success: function(html) {
            // handle the response here…
        }
    });
</script>
```

With the cache parameter set to false, the URL that jQuery will create has a random number appended to it as a value for an underscore parameter; using the dummy URL we supplied in the example, it would become something like http://domain.com/some_page.aspx?_=1259397606799. The server would interpret this as a unique request for the resource and ensure that a noncached copy is delivered to the client.

Lightweight Content Delivery with Ajax and HTTP Handlers

As mentioned previously, the creation of complete pages is a heavy operation for the server to complete. HTTP Handlers are a convenient way for developers to return content to the client that does not require the overhead of a complete page. For example, you may want a Handler that loads images from a remote source and renders them to the client; Listing 5–8 shows a typical request to such a handler.

Listing 5–8. Usage of Our Theoretical Image Handler

```
<img src="remoteImage.ashx?imgID=12345" alt="remote image" />
```

They are lighter-weight than typical pages and have the file extension .ashx. They are also the building block for the more complex .aspx page. Handlers can be quite effectively used via Ajax to provide noncached content in a situation where the rest of the page is cached at one or more levels.

Let's say for a moment that you were seeking a way to provide a small amount of noncached content to the client on a website that uses .NET's OutputCaching; for the purposes of our example, it will just be the current date and time of the page request. Because the original developers opted to have their controls and templates inherit from various levels of custom base classes, the ability to invoke PartialPageCaching is not available, and making the appropriate modifications across several projects is time or cost-prohibitive. A fairly quick solution to the problem is to create an HTTP Handler to deliver the content and use jQuery to call the Handler in an asynchronous (and noncached) fashion.

The actual execution of this is straightforward. Visual Studio refers to HTTP Handlers as *Generic Handlers*. Create a new project and add a generic handler to it called TimeHandler.ashx, as shown in Figure 5–3.

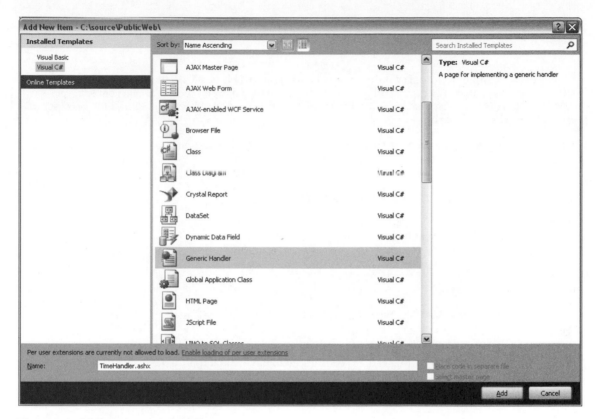

Figure 5–3. Adding a generic handler

By default, the Handler will have some superfluous code and assemblies we won't need. Pared down, the `.ashx` file should now look like Listing 5–9.

Listing 5–9. *The Simplified Handler Code*

```
using System;
using System.Web;

public class TimeHandler : IHttpHandler
{
    public void ProcessRequest(HttpContext context)
    {
        context.Response.ContentType = "text/plain";
        context.Response.Write("Hello World");
    }

    public bool IsReusable
    {
        get
```

```
    {
        return false;
    }
  }
}
```

Now it's a simple matter of creating a method to append a bit of HTML that contains the current timestamp to the outgoing Response object. Note that we have changed the Response.ContentType parameter to text/html in Listing 5–10; this MIME type is important for ensuring that the browser renders our output properly.

Listing 5–10. Returning the Current Time Appended to the Outgoing Response

```csharp
private HttpContext _context;

public void ProcessRequest(HttpContext context)
{
    _context = context;
    _context.Response.ContentType = "text/html";
    DisplayTime();
}

public void DisplayTime()
{
    _context.Response.Write("<p>The current time is <em>" + DateTime.Now + "</em>.</p>");
}
```

Finally, the last step is to create a page (which I have called HandlerTest.aspx) that will host our Handler for us. The page in Listing 5–11 is configured to have an OutputCache expiration of 40 minutes.

Listing 5–11. A Page with OutputCaching

```
<%@ Page Language="C#" AutoEventWireup="true" CodeBehind="HandlerTest.aspx.cs"
Inherits=" HandlerTest" %>
<%@ OutputCache Duration="2400" VaryByParam="*" %>

<!DOCTYPE html PUBLIC "-//W3C//DTD XHTML 1.0 Transitional//EN"
"Http://www.w3.org/TR/xhtml1/DTD/xhtml1-transitional.dtd">
<html xmlns="Http://www.w3.org/1999/xhtml">
<head runat="server">
    <title>jQuery Generic Handler Caching Test</title>
    <script src="jquery-1.3.2.min.js" type="text/javascript"></script>
</head>
<body>
    <form id="form1" runat="server">
    <div id="cached">
        <p>The cached time is <em><%=DateTime.Now %></em>.</p>
    </div>

    <div id="noncached">
        <!-- noncached output will go here -->
    </div>
```

```
<script type="text/javascript">
    $.ajax({
        type: "GET",
        url: "TimeHandler.ashx",
        cache: false,
        success: function(html) {
            $("#noncached").append(html);
        }
    });
</script>

    </form>
</body>
</html>
```

When run, the jQuery $.ajax() method will automatically fetch the TimeHandler.ashx's output in a noncached call using the GET verb. The jQuery method $.append() will add whatever markup is returned to the <div> element with an ID of "noncached," It will then (assuming a successful 200 status code from the server) append the contents of that request to the <div> element with an ID attribute of noncached.

■ **Tip** Remember that jQuery uses implicit iteration. By adhering to the XHTML specification and maintaining unique IDs for elements on the page, this call will update only one element in the DOM. For the sake of organization, I recommend using elements with unique IDs as repositories for noncached content retrieved via jQuery's Ajax calls; specific content will go in specific locations, and by using IDs and adhering to the XHTML specification, you will ensure the final page looks as intended.

Figure 5–4 shows the result of running this page. You can see that the time has changed after the page has been refreshed in the noncached section, although the rest of the page remains cached as intended.

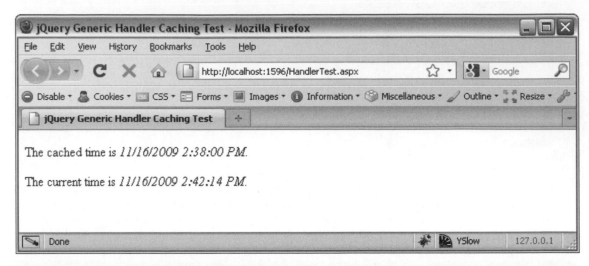

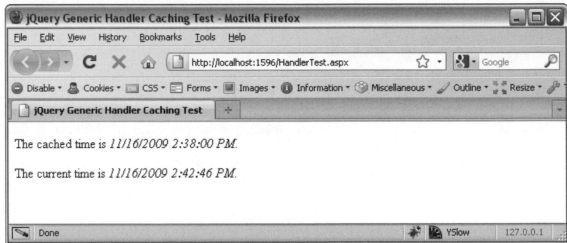

***Figure 5–4.** Refreshing the page shows the noncached output in addition to the cached output*

The "trick," if you will, is that the actual markup returned to the client is always the same. Listing 5–12 details the markup that the client receives when browsing this particular page.

***Listing 5–12.** The Markup That the Client Receives on Each Request*

```
<!DOCTYPE html PUBLIC "-//W3C//DTD XHTML 1.0 Transitional//EN"
"Http://www.w3.org/TR/xhtml1/DTD/xhtml1-transitional.dtd">
<html xmlns="Http://www.w3.org/1999/xhtml">
<head><title>
    jQuery Generic Handler Caching Test
```

```
</title>
    <script src="js/jquery-1.3.2.min.js" type="text/javascript"></script>
</head>
<body>
    <form name="form1" method="post" action="HandlerTest.aspx" id="form1">
<div>
<input type="hidden" name="__VIEWSTATE" id="__VIEWSTATE"
value="/wEPDwUJOTU4MjMyMzI1ZGQCfpeY54+jXCEVr6SAUzKWolFFXA==" />
</div>

        <div id="cached">
            <p>The cached time is <em>11/16/2009 2:38:00 PM</em>.</p>
        </div>

        <div id="noncached">
            <!-- noncached output will go here -->
        </div>

        <script type="text/javascript">
            $.ajax({
                type: "GET",
                url: "TimeHandler.ashx",
                cache: false,
                success: function(html) {
                    $("#noncached").append(html);
                }
            });
        </script>

    </form>
</body>
</html>
```

This markup is indeed cached by .NET's OutputCaching and dutifully returned on each page request in identical fashion until the cache expires. However, the jQuery call is asynchronous, and the cache parameter is set to false, so *the JavaScript that the client executes generates a unique request from within a cached page*. When the DOM is modified, the user sees the updated content within the DOM. This is an important point to emphasize: the page is in fact cached 100 percent, but the call made within that cached page is unique on each request.

This kind of lightweight content delivery can be a critical factor in ensuring that your site maintains stability and responsiveness under the pressure of heavy user load. HTTP Handlers provide an excellent method of quick content assembly, and jQuery provides you with effective options for making quick, asynchronous calls to skirt around caching issues easily and without a lot of unnecessary plumbing on your part. Judicious application is required, however, because using too many noncached components can defeat your scalability efforts by shifting the workload back to the server in the form of guaranteed-unique requests.

Handling Asynchronous Errors

In an ideal world, code would just work properly the first time (and every subsequent time). In reality, we know that's not the case, and effective error handling is key to establishing stable production environments. jQuery makes it trivial to handle exceptions or problems that occur on the server side while processing asynchronous requests and allows you to respond to those error conditions however you see fit. Similar to the success parameter, jQuery allows you to define an error parameter and specify whatever actions you want to take on the client side. To demonstrate this functionality, let's induce an exception in our Handler; in particular, we'll cause a "divide by zero" exception, shown in Listing 5–13, and we'll make sure that it is not properly handled by a try / catch block.

■ **Note** This is the same approach we used to trigger exceptions in embeddable controls in Chapter 3.

Listing 5–13. Causing an Unhandled Exception in Our Handler

```
public void DisplayTime()
{
    var zero = 0; // C# won't allow direct n / 0 operations
    _context.Response.Write("<p>The current time is <em>" + DateTime.Now + "</em>.</p>");
    _context.Response.Write("<p>1 over 0 equals " + (1 / zero) + "</p>");
}
```

Running the code within Visual Studio will trigger an unhandled exception on the division by zero operation as expected, but the page will continue to render properly, just without the desired output from the handler. If we examine the request in Firebug, we can see that the exception caused a 500 Internal Server Error for the Handler request; none of our desired output was rendered into the noncached element, but no error information was rendered either. It's visible only when examining the request pipeline, as shown in Figure 5–5.

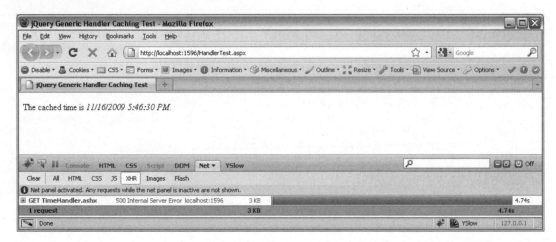

Figure 5–5. The exception triggers a 500 status to be returned from the server, and no output is added to the DOM.

Now that there is a reproducible error to work with, the jQuery asynchronous call can be modified with an error parameter that handles these types of responses from the server. In this case, we'll modify the DOM with a message indicating there was a problem server-side; Listing 5–14 shows the modified jQuery code.

Listing 5–14. Adding an Error Parameter to Handle Server-Side Faults

```
<script type="text/javascript">
    $.ajax({
        type: "GET",
        url: "TimeHandler.ashx",
        cache: false,
        success: function(html) {
            $("#noncached").append(html);
        },
        error: function(html) {
            $("#noncached").append("<p>There was an error on the server. Please try
again.</p>");
    });
</script>

    </form>
</body>
</html>
```

■ **Caution** Although jQuery does a good job of error handling, if the fault lies with the server, the error should be handled at the server. Consider this type of error handling a last line of defense, or, more accurately, as one more weapon in the war against unhandled exceptions. Need proof? A successful call to this handler returns approximately 40 to 50 bytes back to the client, whereas the unhandled server exception returns more than *3,000* bytes back; examining the response in Firebug will show you that it actually returns the entire .NET "yellow screen of death" page to the client. That's 75 times more noncached data coming back to the client (per request) in this instance, which adds up very quickly, not to mention the extra performance penalty incurred by the unhandled exception.

We can see in Figure 5–6 that jQuery has handled the error condition for us and displayed the appropriate message to the client. Although in some cases you might just want to ignore the error and display nothing, jQuery does provide you the necessary hooks to handle the errors as you deem fit for your application.

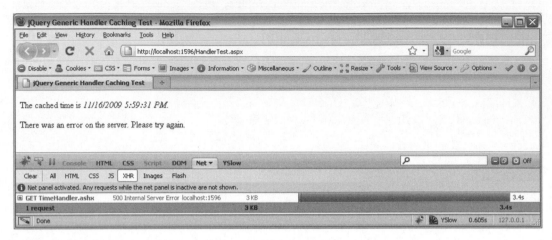

Figure 5–6. The error was detected and handled by jQuery.

Handling DOM Modifications

There is an additional case we should examine with regard to dynamically modifying our page: the nature of such updates has a specific effect when the content we are inserting is itself designed to modify a page. For example, JavaScript supports page modification in a variety of ways; a common method is the document.write() function, which allows direct insertion into the DOM. Google Analytics is one such external script that makes use of this method of modification. Were you to load the Google Analytics script via an asynchronous handler, the results would likely be surprising because the page would immediately go completely blank.

The easiest way to examine the problem and solve it is with an example. Consider the page in Listing 5–15, which I have called dom.aspx. The page uses jQuery to load the output of a ContentHandler.ashx file and add it to an element with an ID of noncached.

Listing 5–15. A Sample Page for Modification via jQuery

```
<%@ Page Language="C#" AutoEventWireup="true" CodeBehind="dom.aspx.cs"
Inherits="jQueryPlayground.dom" %>

<!DOCTYPE html PUBLIC "-//W3C//DTD XHTML 1.0 Transitional//EN"
"http://www.w3.org/TR/xhtml1/DTD/xhtml1-transitional.dtd">
<html xmlns="http://www.w3.org/1999/xhtml">
<head runat="server">
    <title>DOM Modification Test</title>
    <script src="js/jquery-1.3.2.min.js" type="text/javascript"></script>
</head>
<body>
    <form id="form1" runat="server">
    <div>
        <h1>
            DOM Modification Test</h1>
```

```
    <p>
        This will be overwritten by the Javascript.</p>
    <p id="noncached">
        <!-- non-cached content here -->
    </p>
    </div>
    </form>
    <script type="text/javascript">
        $.ajax({
            type: "GET",
            url: "ContentHandler.ashx",
            cache: false,
            success: function (html) {
                $("#noncached").append(html);
            }
        });
    </script>
</body>
</html>
```

Although we have not yet created the ContentHandler.ashx handler, the page looks like Figure 5–7 when viewed in a browser.

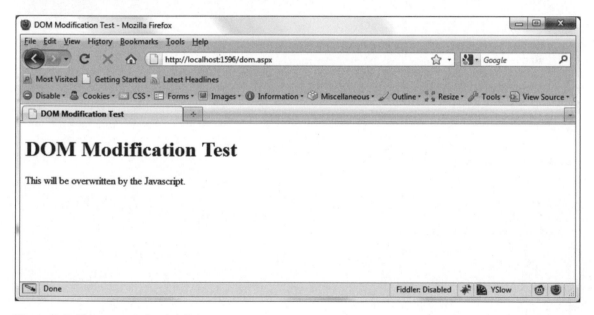

Figure 5–7. *The output of a simple page*

Listing 5–16 demonstrates a simple handler to fulfill the page requirements. Note that the output of the handler is a single line of JavaScript that uses the document.write() method to add content to a page.

Listing 5–16. *A Simple Handler That Returns JavaScript*

```
using System;
using System.Web;

namespace jQueryPlayground
{
    public class ContentHandler : IHttpHandler
    {
        public void ProcessRequest(HttpContext context)
        {
            context.Response.ContentType = "text/html";
            context.Response.Write("<script type=\"text/javascript\">document.write('This
should be the only content of the page.');</script>");
        }

        public bool IsReusable
        {
            get
            {
                return false;
            }
        }
    }
}
```

Figure 5–8 demonstrates the results of running the dom.aspx page with this code in the handler. Although we were expecting the element with ID noncached to have the text in the handler appended to it, the entire page has been replaced instead. What happened?

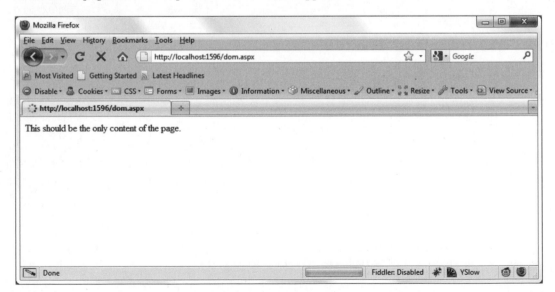

Figure 5–8. *The JavaScript has significantly modified our page.*

Proper usage of document.write() is predicated on the intention of the page itself being loaded fully before it is called. If you call it after a document has fully loaded, a new document is created instead. This is the cause of our troubles: the dom.aspx page loads in entirety, and the asynchronous call appends content from the generic handler after this point. When the browser executes the JavaScript returned by the handler, the document.write() function creates a new document, and the old markup is lost, creating the output shown in Figure 5–8.

Luckily, we are perfectly within our right and ability to override the document.write() function in our own code and handle the behavior as needed by our application. It is important to override the function before it is called and used, however; Listing 5–17 shows how to override this function with jQuery.

Listing 5–17. *Overriding the document.write() Method*

```
<script type="text/javascript">

    $.ajax({
        type: "GET",
        url: "ContentHandler.ashx",
        cache: false,
        success: function (html) {
            $("#noncached").append(html);
        }
    });
</script>
```

Viewing the dom.aspx page in the browser again confirms that we have caught and handled the document.write() method. The output of the handler has been successfully appended to the desired page, as shown in Figure 5–9.

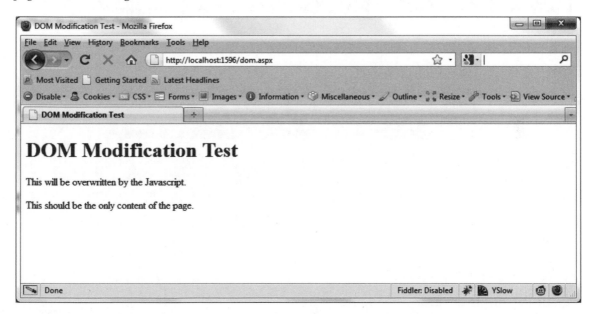

Figure 5–9. *Overriding document.write() to append the output to the desired element*

■ **Caution** Although functional in this case, this is not necessarily an ideal solution for all situations. In the same fashion as handling URL mapping, you are taking on a significant responsibility by overriding the browser's rendering methods; this can cause some unexpected behavior when dealing with third-party JavaScript and should be approached carefully.

Improving the CMS Admin with jQuery

jQuery has a well-deserved reputation for being powerful as well as flexible. We've already seen how easy it is to work with in terms of both DOM modification and Ajax; now we can apply some of these techniques to the admin site and move toward a more attractive, user-friendly interface.

Let's begin by examining Figure 5–10, Figure 5–11, and Figure 5–12; these images show the user interface as it appears on the admin side of the CMS. Figure 5–10 shows the embeddable editor, where system users will likely spend the majority of their time. The first panel is automatically open by default and displays the basic attributes that all content in the system will have.

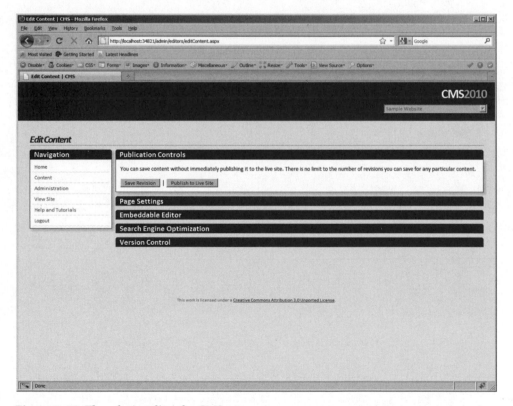

Figure 5–10. The admin editor for CMS pages

Figure 5–11 shows the home page after the user has clicked some of the panels to expand them. We will apply jQuery's animation capabilities to smoothly expand and collapse the panels; this small touch looks more polished than having them abruptly appear.

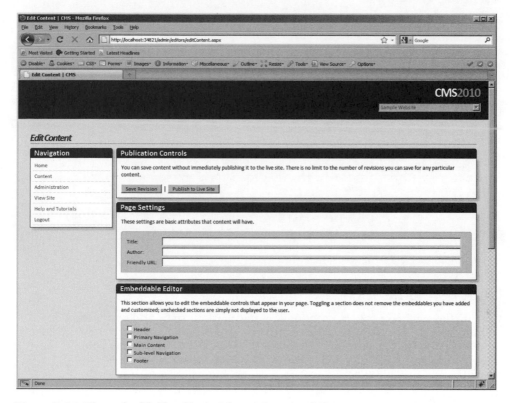

Figure 5–11. *The embeddable editor with panels expanded*

Finally, Figure 5–12 shows the home page if the user has disabled JavaScript. There are a few important points in this image: note that the panels are all expanded by default (a specific instance of graceful degradation). Also, a small paragraph has appeared in the footer to notify the user that JavaScript is disabled and it should be reenabled to allow the CMS to provide the full user experience as intended.

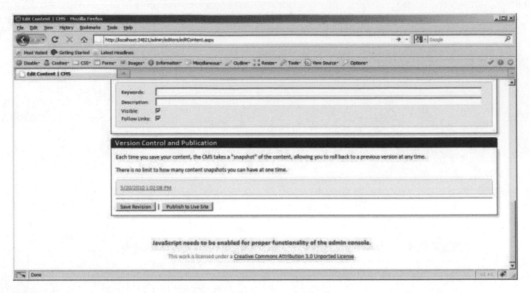

Figure 5–12. The admin home page with JavasSript disabled

Creating Collapsible Panels

We can begin work on the admin console by creating reusable markup, style, and scripts for the collapsible panels on the right side of the page. The idea behind these panels is to use simple, clear markup (and as little of it as possible). Listing 5–18 shows the markup for a collapsible panel.

Listing 5–18. The Markup for a Collapsible Panel

```
<div class="collapseWrapper">
   <h3>
      Title Goes Here
   </h3>
   <div class="collapse">
     <p>
        Content goes here; you can add quite a bit to these particular elements.
     </p>
   </div>
</div>
```

■ **Tip** You don't *have* to specify a class for the inner `<div>`. You could use CSS to target the applicable styles to the first `<div>` after an `<h3>` within an element of class `collapseWrapper` using the `next()` method. I chose this way for clarity, but either way will work just fine. The biggest determining factor is whether you want to apply the `collapse` styles to other elements that may not be in this specific hierarchy.

Why did we use a class instead of an ID? Throughout the CMS we're striving to adhere to web standards where possible, and the XHTML specification dictates that an element on any given page, if provided an ID, must have a unique one. It is a violation of the specification to have two elements with the same ID; it is not a violation to have multiple elements with the same classes applied.

Now that we have the basic structure of the panels, we need to style them to match the design we looked at earlier; Listing 5–19 contains the CSS that gives a collapsible panel its appearance. The style is fairly straightforward; the <h3> element has bold, white text and a black background. The rest of the box is styled to be in stark contrast to the header, and some visual enhancements have been applied to the borders and underneath the boxes themselves, as shown in Figure 5–13.

Listing 5–19. The CSS for the Collapsible Panel

```
.collapseWrapper *
{
    font-family: Calibri;
}
.collapseWrapper h3
{
    -moz-border-radius-topleft: 5px;
    -moz-border-radius-topright: 5px;
    background-color: #000;
    color: #FFF;
    font-size: 1.2em;
    margin: 0;
    padding: 0 4px 0 10px;
}
.collapse
{
    -moz-box-shadow: 5px 5px 5px #CCC;
    border: 1px solid #000000;
    margin: 0;
    padding: 0 11px 11px;
}
```

■ **Tip** If you already have some experience with CSS, you may be wondering what the -moz-border-radius and -moz-box-shadow properties are. They are a Mozilla-specific implementation of CSS3's new rounded corner and drop-shadow features, eliminating the need for prefabricated images or other hacks. Internet Explorer users won't benefit from this set of properties and will instead see the normal, 90-degree corners without any shadowing. This is an example of *graceful degradation*, because the absence of these features is a purely aesthetic concern and doesn't change the functionality of the page at all.

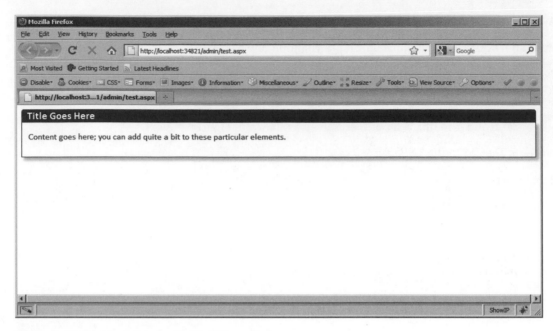

Figure 5–13. *The sample panel with CSS applied*

Expanding with jQuery

If you recall from earlier in the chapter, we discussed how jQuery automatically defaults to an implicit iteration type of behavior when selecting elements in the DOM. We can use that to our advantage in creating the expanding and collapsing behavior of our panels; Listing 5–20 is all that is necessary for the behavior of the panels throughout the admin side of the CMS.

Listing 5–20. *The jQuery Code to Handle the Panel Behaviors*

```
<script type="text/javascript">
    $("h3").click(function () {
        $(this).next(".collapse").slideToggle(100);
    });
    $(".collapseWrapper").children(".collapse").hide();
    $(".collapseWrapper:eq(0)").children(".collapse").show();
</script>
```

Let's look at this in detail. The first task of this script is to attach code to the click event of every `<h3>` element on the page. This may not be the behavior you want; it may be too broad. If you intend to use `<h3>` elements on the admin page for purposes other than headers in the panels, you will want to be more specific and opt for `$(".collapseWrapper h3")` because this current implementation will affect every `<h3>` in the DOM, whereas the latter would not.

The code attached to the click function identifies the next element (using the appropriately named `next()` method) after the `<h3>` that has a `class` attribute of `collapse` and toggles the visibility of that element using a sliding animation (via the `slideToggle()` method) that takes an integer value of 100 milliseconds to complete.

Note the effects of implicit iteration; we didn't need to loop over the elements in the DOM or take any additional steps in code to attach the desired behavior to every element we wanted to select. Let's say we add a second panel to the page, as Figure 5–14 shows; although the markup has changed, we haven't had to adjust the jQuery code to accommodate it; jQuery handled it for us automatically.

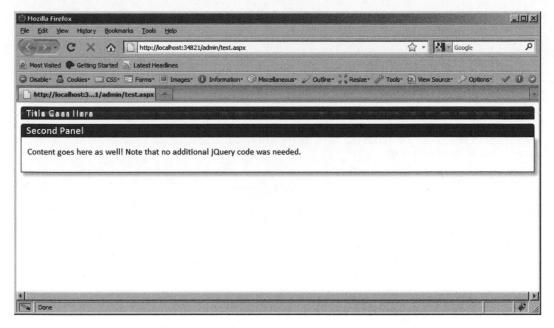

Figure 5–14. Implicit iteration saved us the extra coding to attach to every <h3>.

The next two lines of the script automatically hide and show particular elements in the panel; the first hides all subelements of any element that has the class attribute collapseWrapper. This is the code responsible for the behavior we saw in Figure 5–10 where the user browses to the home page and each panel is closed. The second line completes the desired behavior and opens the subelement with class attribute collapse under the first element in the page with a class attribute collapseWrapper. The end result of these two lines is that when the user browses to the page, the first panel is expanded, and the remainder are closed.

It is this design pattern that ensures the page exhibits graceful degradation; if the user does have JavaScript disabled, all the panels will still be visible because we have used jQuery to hide them. Without JavaScript enabled, that action cannot complete and the panels remain visible, guaranteeing that the user can still operate the full functionality of the page.

Displaying the JavaScript Disabled Message

We can apply this same pattern to display the error message in the footer of the page if the user has JavaScript disabled. First we need an element in the page that we can select with jQuery to modify its behavior, shown in Listing 5–21.

Listing 5–21. A Simple Paragraph Element to Hold Our Message

```
<p id="nonScript">
    JavaScript needs to be enabled for proper functionality of the admin console.
</p>
```

Styling this element as in Listing 5–22 adds a touch of visual flair and ensures the element will stand out; the properties defined make the message bright red, bold, and slightly larger than the baseline text size in the client browser.

Listing 5–22. Styling the Error Message So That It Stands Out

```
#nonScript
{
    font-family: Calibri;
    font-size: 1.2em;
    font-weight: bold;
    color: #f00;
}
```

Now all that is needed is a bit of jQuery, demonstrated in Listing 5–23, to hide that particular element when the page is loaded.

Listing 5–23. The jQuery Code to Handle the Panel Behaviors

```
<script type="text/javascript">
    $("h4").click(function () {
        $(this).next(".collapse").slideToggle(100);
    });
    $(".collapseWrapper").children(".collapse").hide();
    $(".collapseWrapper:eq(0)").children(".collapse").show();

    $("#nonScript").hide();

</script>
```

Figure 5–15 displays the output of this material. With JavaScript disabled, the panels are all visible, as is the red error message. Although certain features may rely on JavaScript to be functional, we aren't leaving the user high and dry without any indication of what's gone wrong if they happen to arrive without JavaScript enabled.

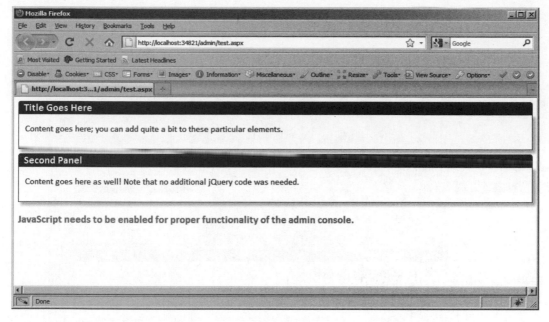

Figure 5–15. With JavaScript disabled, the message appears, and the panel is automatically expanded.

Poka-Yoke Devices

One of the traits of the better web applications in the wild is the use of *poka-yoke devices*. Not limited to web applications, poka-yoke devices are everywhere. They stop us from opening a microwave that's currently warming up our food, turning on a car that's already in gear, or putting the SIM card in our cell phones upside down. They're so ubiquitous that we often don't even notice they're there, but we certainly would if they were absent. In short, poka-yoke devices are mistake-proofing mechanisms that help keep users on track and reduce the frustration of using an application.

■ **Tip** Robert Hoekman does an excellent job discussing the many ways to help harden web applications against user errors in his book *Designing the Obvious: A Common Sense Approach to Web Application Design* (New Riders Press, 2006).

The CMS uses jQuery to add poka-yoke devices in a few critical locations; the most notable of these is on the admin editor for page content. If a user makes a change to anything on the page and attempts to navigate away (by clicking the back button, a link to a new page, and so on), the browser is instructed to alert the user that the page has been modified and give them an opportunity to save their changes or discard them. Figure 5–16 shows this device in action; it's such a simple action but could make the difference between a happy user and an ex-user.

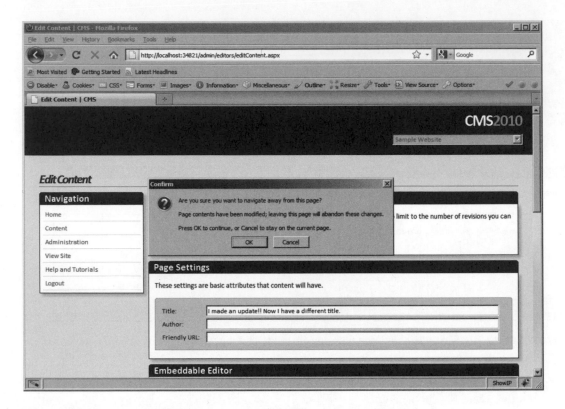

Figure 5–16. *The browser alerts the user that they will lose changes if they don't save.*

The first step to creating such a device is establishing a flag that will be used to denote whether a page has been modified (or is "dirty") and hasn't yet been saved. Listing 5–24 shows how to do this.

Listing 5–24. Beginning the Poka-Yoke Device

```
var isDirty = false;

$(document).ready(function () {
});
```

Next, we need to decide what exactly constitutes a "change" that should set the isDirty flag to true. The obvious first choice is the modification of text fields on the page. To handle this, we need to intercept the keydown() event of the text fields and set the flag at that point. Listing 5–25 shows how to attach code to the keydown() event.

Listing 5–25. Attaching Code to the keydown() Event of the Text Fields on the Page

```
var isDirty = false;

$(document).ready(function () {


});
```

Finally, we attach some code to the unbeforeunload() event of the browser, as shown in Listing 5–26; this event will fire when the user attempts to leave the current page. The browser will unload the current page before loading the new one. It is this transitional event that gives us an opportunity to prompt the user for confirmation that this is how they want to proceed.

Listing 5–26. Attaching Code to the unbeforeunload() Event

```
var isDirty = false;

$(document).ready(function () {



});
```

Logically, some element on the page must be responsible for saving a revision of the page or publishing it to the live site. Therefore, we must have a way to flip the isDirty flag to false so that the user will not be prompted unnecessarily. Listing 5–27 shows how the CMS exempts the Save Revision and Publish to Live Site buttons by marking the isDirty flag false.

Listing 5–27. The Submit Buttons Should Mark the Page as Saved

```
var isDirty = false;

$(document).ready(function () {

        $('h2').addClass('underlined');
    $(function () {
      document.write = function (input) {
         $("#noncached").append(input);
      }
    });
    $('input[type=text]').keydown(function () {
      isDirty = true;
    });
    $('input[type=text]').keydown(function () {
      isDirty = true;
    });
     window.onbeforeunload = (function () {
        if (isDirty) {
            return ('Page contents have been modified; leaving this page will abandon these
changes.');
        }
```

```
  });
$('input[type=text]').keydown(function () {
   isDirty = true;
});

$('input[type=submit]').click(function () {
   isDirty = false;
});

  window.onbeforeunload = (function () {
      if (isDirty) {
          return ('Page contents have been modified; leaving this page will abandon these
changes.');
      }
  });

});
```

The simple act of prompting the user before leaving from a page that hasn't been saved is invaluable; as developers it cost us precisely 14 lines of JavaScript/jQuery code (excluding whitespace). That's positively trivial compared to helping ensure users aren't making needless mistakes and losing content that may have taken considerable time to customize.

Summary

We took a high-level tour of jQuery, the problems it solves, and the benefits it brings to developers looking to expedite and simplify the creation of their client-side code. Next we covered Ajax as a technology in general and how jQuery handles asynchronous requests between client and server. Then we built an HTTP Handler to deliver content in a lightweight, low-overhead fashion and used jQuery to call that Handler from a cached page and update it with noncached content. Next we used jQuery's animation capabilities to enhance the appearance of the administrative portion of the site and learned how to apply graceful degradation techniques to smooth the experience for users who may have JavaScript disabled. Finally, we discussed poka-yoke devices and how to help mistake-proof the user experience on the administrative side of the CMS. As we advance onto distributed caching solutions, we'll look to bullet-proof the system itself, reducing server load and enhancing the stability of the CMS as a whole.

## CHAPTER 6

Distributed Caching via Memcached

"If you want to set off and go develop some grand new thing, you don't need millions of dollars of capitalization. You need enough pizza and Diet Coke to stick in your refrigerator, a cheap PC to work on, and the dedication to go through with it."

—John Carmack

When working with large-scale applications that serve millions of requests a day (or more), even a well-written data-intensive application can begin to show cracks. These issues may appear in the form of slow responses, timeouts, or a complete loss of service until the incoming traffic is reduced. Besides disk I/O, one of the most costly tasks in your performance budget is the communication to and from your database. Although today's relational database management systems (RDBMSs) are excellent at storing execution plans and retrieving data quickly, sometimes the sheer volume of requests and minor delays in handling them are overwhelming to one component or another along the processing pipeline. The obvious solution is to cache frequently used or infrequently changing data to avoid the trip to the database. It's not a silver bullet, however. For applications that are deployed on multiple servers (for example, in a load-balanced environment), the in-session cache quickly becomes insufficient for reasons we will look at shortly. In this chapter, we'll discuss the solution to that problem: the distributed cache. We'll cover what it is, what it is not, and best practices for using it. We'll also create a tree structure for our CMS and explore how a distributed cache is an ideal location for storing such objects; we'll also learn why configuring Memcached properly is critical for effective cache usage.

What Is a Distributed Cache, and Why Is it Important?

The easiest way to define a distributed cache is by comparison to the typical in-session cache. Let's assume we have a hypothetical application on a single-server environment; our lone machine hosts the application and probably the database as well. In this situation, it's perfectly acceptable (and absolutely faster) to use the in-session cache provided by .NET. Assuming good data layer design, your cache hit ratio should quickly get very high, and the database traffic will reduce accordingly.

■ **Tip** *Cache hit ratio* refers to the percentage of requests to the cache that result in successful returns of data. For any specific data point, you need to first check the cache for the presence of a specific key-value pair. If this value exists, you can retrieve it and move on; otherwise, you have to make a request for that data point from your data source (RDBMS, XML feed, flat file, and so on) and then insert the value into the cache for retrieval next time. Obviously, you want the cache hit ratio to be as high as possible; spending processing time on excessive cache misses is worse than having no cache at all sometimes.

The limitations of this design become apparent only when moving to more complex application hosting architectures. Consider an environment where your application is hosted on five web servers that are positioned behind a load balancer. The load balancer handles incoming HTTP requests and directs traffic to servers that are capable of handling additional traffic, spreading the workload across each of the five machines (ergo, "load balancing").

The .NET cache that you're familiar with is tied to the particular instance of the application instance on a specific box; what that means is if your user hits box A and stores the value for the key "foo" in the cache, their next request may result in them communicating with box B. The .NET cache is not distributed, so box B has no knowledge of the key-value pair "foo" that exists on box A. The consequence of this is that the ratio of cache hits to misses is painfully low, particularly as the number of servers increases. You may be able to get away with this in an environment with few boxes and light traffic, but when things ramp up, it's going to represent a potentially serious bottleneck.

Memcached

Enter Memcached to save the day. Memcached is a free, open source, distributed cache application that was written by Danga Interactive, the company behind the massively popular LiveJournal. Let's consider the nature of LiveJournal for a moment. If you're not familiar with this site, it is sufficient to say that LiveJournal is a very popular blogging web site where users can also befriend one another and establish communities. With an entity like an online blog, it quickly becomes apparent that a lot of the data is infrequently changing; blog posts tend to be static entities (this is not a hard and fast rule, but a typical generalization of behavior). It doesn't make a lot of sense to constantly request infrequently changing data from the database when a cache is typically much faster at handling precanned individual data points.

Memcached was developed to allow LiveJournal to distribute its cache across any number of servers and alleviate these costly database trips. Since then, it has become wildly popular, having been adopted by Facebook, Twitter, Digg, and YouTube, just to name a few. Part of the strength of Memcached is that many experienced developers and engineers in a variety of companies have contributed to the code, adding features and increasing stability and performance. The net effect is that we have at our disposal a battle-worn piece of software that has been proven time and time again in real-world, production environments at the enterprise level...plus, it's totally free.

■ **Tip** How important is Memcached (and the broader category of distributed caches) to the scalability potential of high-volume web presences? When Facebook introduced the option to create a specific friendly URL for individual profile pages, 200,000 people used this feature in the first 3 minutes. Each username has to be checked for availability, so Facebook created a specific Memcached tier with 1TB of memory allocated to handle this. Within the hour, 1 million people had used the service, which functioned solely because of the quick nature of the Memcached tier and not having to make costly database trips. You can read more about this at Facebook's engineering blog at http://www.facebook.com/note.php?note_id=39391378919.

Memcached can be hosted on either Windows or Unix environments. Once an instance of Memcached is running, it listens on a particular port (11211 by default) for requests and has a limited API for CRUD (create, read, update, and delete) operations, plus some diagnostic commands. You typically do not speak to Memcached directly; more commonly, you will use a client to do so. Clients offer a variety of benefits, including handling data compression/decompression and the low-level TCP/IP or UDP communication requirements so you aren't forced to implement them yourself (although you're certainly free to do so). Furthermore, Memcached is supposed to be fault-tolerant; if you have 10 servers handling Memcached requests, you should be able to remove any of them from the pool at any time without issue. Client libraries help to manage the server pool and identify healthy, responsive boxes.

Can You Iterate Over Memcached Items?

As a result of its internal structure, one thing that Memcached does *not* support by default is iteration and listing of all its contents. For example, you can't structure a for loop to output every item in the cache; it's not a limitation but rather a side effect of the overall system design. This makes proper and efficient key name management critical to the success of your caching efforts.

If desired, you could create a list in memory of registered keys, but managing and polling the Memcached instance to ensure the accuracy of the list as keys expire will likely be more infrastructure than it's worth given the low overhead of key creation.

Acquiring a Memcached Client Library

A variety of Memcached clients are available that support a large number of languages and platforms. For the purposes of this chapter, we will use the .NET Memcached client library available from http://sourceforge.net/projects/memcacheddotnet/. This project contains DLLs that you can import into your .NET applications that will connect to a Memcached server.

When you download and extract this project, you will find a variety of source control folders present. The libraries themselves are present in the \memcacheddotnet\trunk\clientlib\src folder. You'll want to open the .NET 2.0 version of the solution and build it; this will create the actual DLLs for use in your application as shown in Figure 6–1. The \clientlib\lib folder and subfolders contain additional libraries such as log4net that are dependencies of the client library.

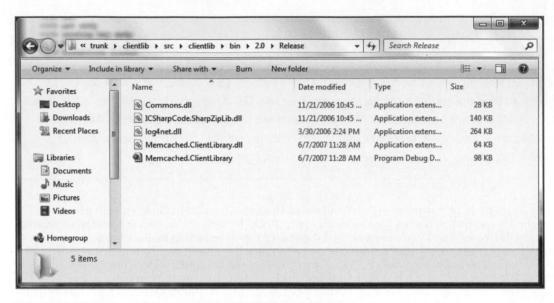

Figure 6–1. The output of a successful build of the client library

Now that you have the client libraries available to speak to a Memcached server, we need to actually set up an instance of a Win32 port. A free port of Memcached is available at http://jehiah.cz/projects/memcached-win32/. Feel free to download and explore the source code if you like; for the purposes of this chapter, we need to concern ourselves only with the binaries.

Getting Started with Memcached

Once you've acquired the Win32 version of the Memcached server, open a new command prompt window and make your way to the directory where you've placed it. Type memcached -vv, and press Enter. This will spin up a new Memcached instance in verbose mode (omitting the -vv parameter will start the instance with no output sent to the console window). You can also start Memcached as a Windows service, but we're not going to cover that at this point; for now, we want to have access to the play-by-play actions that occur, and we won't have that if we spin up a Windows service.

When Memcached starts, you'll see the default slab allocations including the accepted maximum object size (in bytes) for the slab and a total of how many objects of that maximum size will fit. A *slab* is an abstraction of memory that accommodates objects within a certain size range. The nice thing here is that you don't have to do any particular coding to align objects with slabs; Memcached will handle that for you automatically. Figure 6–2 displays the default slab allocations. We will discuss configuration considerations regarding slab sizes later in this chapter.

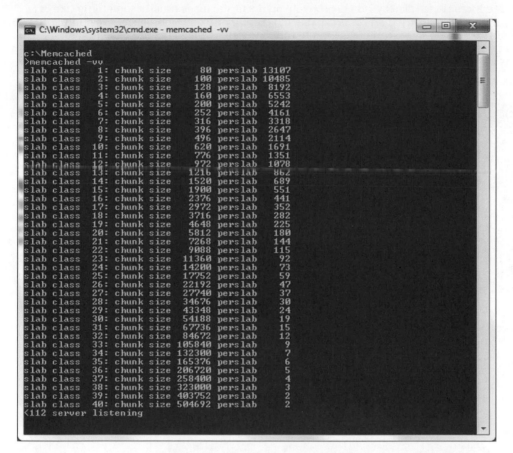

Figure 6–2. Running a Memcached instance in verbose mode to see activity as it happens

■ **Note** Memcached, in its initial form, relied on the glibc `malloc` call. This resulted in address space fragmentation and various performance problems after any individual instance had been active for several days straight. Eventually, the Memcached instance would simply crash. The newer versions of Memcached use a custom slab allocation system where items are automatically placed into particular buckets based on their size; for example, by default there are only 2 spaces for large items in the 500,000+ slab, but more than 13,000 spaces in the size 80 slab. The reason? It's more likely that you will store many small items as opposed to many large items. You can (and likely will) resize and redefine these slab classes when you spin up an instance. For now, the defaults work fine, although by the end of the chapter we will have identified conditions in which the defaults are unsuitable, as well as how to change them.

The last line Memcached displays via the console output at startup is usually something like <112 server listening. At this point, the server is capable of accepting incoming requests. We don't *have* to use handwritten code to do so; we can use Telnet to communicate with the instance if desired. Open a new command window and type telnet localhost 11211. The Memcached instance will report that a new client has made a connection to the server, as demonstrated in Figure 6–3.

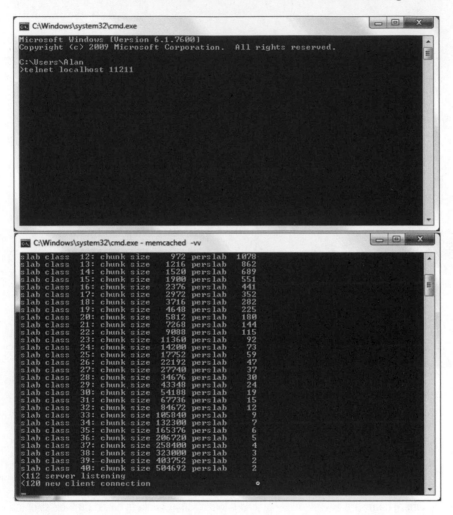

Figure 6–3. Connecting via Telnet on the default port, 11211. The Memcached instance displays a new connection.

Working with Memcached via a direct connection such as Telnet requires a fairly in-depth knowledge of the Memcached protocol, in no small part because the messages returned when you get the syntax wrong can be less than helpful in sorting out the problem. With that said, being able to connect via Telnet can be very useful in diagnosing application issues, examining the health of the cache, and so on, once you've got it running in a production environment. At the time of this writing, the current protocol lives at http://github.com/memcached/memcached/blob/master/doc/protocol.txt; it's definitely worth bookmarking and having readily accessible at all times.

■ **Note** Before we get into the code, let me take a moment to mention this critical point: caching is *hard*. It's simple enough to dump objects into the cache and retrieve them, but knowing what to cache and when to cache it (and maybe more importantly when to expire it) is the key to an effective caching layer. It seems easiest to simply cache everything and cache it often, but your application's requirements may not be in line with this approach. Also, caching can occasionally hide bugs (of many types) if applied too early in the development process; this is part of why we are discussing it later in the game.

One of the strengths of the .NET 4 Framework is the ability to swap providers for your cache (including the OutputCache). As such, if we want to engineer flexibility in our caching options, we should opt to hide the specific implementation details away in our libraries and work through abstractions and wrappers. The next few examples will use the client libraries we built directly to see how they work; then we'll wrap them in other code to hide what's actually being done.

Using the Client Libraries Directly

Create a new console application called MemcachedTest. Add a reference to the MemcachedClient library, and then add the code in Listing 6–1 to the Program.cs file.

Listing 6–1. Using the Win32 Memcached Client to Store and Retrieve Three Objects

```
using System;
using System.Text;
using Memcached.ClientLibrary;

namespace MemcachedTest
{
    class Program
    {
        static void Main(string[] args)
        {
            MemcachedClient cache = new MemcachedClient();

            string[] serverPool = { "127.0.0.1:11211" };
            SockIOPool pool = SockIOPool.GetInstance();
            pool.SetServers(serverPool);
            pool.Initialize();

            cache.Add("Test", "Value");
            cache.Add("Foo", "Bar");
            cache.Add("Number", 5);

            Console.WriteLine(
```

```
            "{0}, {1}, {2}", cache.Get("Foo"), cache.Get("Test"), cache.Get("Number")
        );
        Console.ReadLine();
    }
  }
}
```

The code is actually pretty straightforward; first, we configure a pool of servers as an array and add our particular instance to it by calling SetServers(). Next, we add objects to the cache in the traditional key-value pair format with the Add() method. Finally, we retrieve items with the Get() method and output the values to the console window, as shown in Figure 6–4.

■ **Caution** When storing and retrieving objects via the Memcached client, you are dealing with the .NET type object. As such, it is up to you to enforce good coding practices; if you store a string object in the cache and try to retrieve it into an integer variable, you will not receive an error within the IDE or when compiling. The exception will be thrown at runtime when the value is read from the Memcached instance. In a moment, we'll create a generic class that will help clarify the intention of code that handles object transmission.

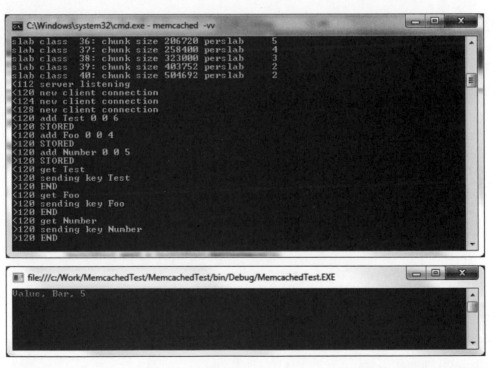

Figure 6–4. Memcached performs very fast lookups, particularly when the objects involved are small.

Writing a Memcached Library

Now that we know we have connectivity to our instance, we can extract the code for communicating with Memcached out and hide it in a separate library. Create a new class library called MemcachedLib, add a reference to the client library, and add a file called Client.cs to the project (you can also delete the default class file while you're at it). We'll also create a private MemcachedClient to hold the client library instance and check for its existence when we initialize our code (see Listing 6–2).

Listing 6–2. A Static Class to Hold Connections to a Memcached Instance

```
using System;
using System.Collections.Generic;
using System.Text;
using Memcached.ClientLibrary;

namespace MemcachedLib
{
    public static class Client
    {
        private static string[] _serverPool = { "127.0.0.1:11211" };
        private static MemcachedClient _memcached;
        private static SockIOPool _pool;

        public static MemcachedClient InitClient()
        {
            if (_memcached == null) _memcached = new MemcachedClient();
            if (_pool == null)
            {
                _pool = SockIOPool.GetInstance();
                _pool.SetServers(_serverPool);
                _pool.Initialize();
            }
            return _memcached;
        }
    }
}
```

Earlier we briefly mentioned that the items stored in and retrieved from the cache are of type object and therefore subject to both (un)boxing and type conversion errors. We can address some of these concerns by creating a class that accepts generic types. Add a new class file to the library called CacheItem.cs. This class will serve as the basic entity that handles cache operations (see Listing 6–3).

Listing 6–3. A Generic Class to Facilitate Strongly Typed Object Transmission to a Memcached Instance

```
using System;
using System.Collections.Generic;
using System.Text;

namespace MemcachedLib
{
    public class CacheItem<T>
    {
        public string Key { get; set; }
```

```
        public T Value { get; set; }

        public void Save()
        {
            Memcached.ClientLibrary.MemcachedClient m = Client.InitClient();
            m.Add(Key, Value);
        }

        public T Get()
        {
            Memcached.ClientLibrary.MemcachedClient m = Client.InitClient();
            this.Value = (T)m.Get(Key);
            return this.Value;
        }
    }
}
```

The CacheItem objects are responsible for self-storage and retrieval; in this case, it's a matter of personal preference for me. You could simply opt for the class to have a string Key property and a Value property of generic type T and leave it at that, making another class responsible for storage and retrieval. As we'll see in the next example, making the object responsible for these tasks lends itself to a very natural syntax.

■ **Note** At this point, we are still tied to the specific implementation of the Memcached client library based on the code in the Save() and Get() methods. We will extract that functionality at a later point to fully decouple the CacheItem class from the Memcached client.

Let's return to the console application again and modify it to use this new generic class. Add a reference to the MemcachedLib project, and make the bold modifications to the Program.cs file (see Listing 6–4). Figure 6–5 displays the output.

Listing 6–4. Using the New Generic Class to Communicate with the Memcached Instance

```
using System;
using System.Text;
using MemcachedLib;
using System.Diagnostics;

namespace MemcachedTest
{
    class Program
    {
        static void Main(string[] args)
        {
            AddTest();
            GetTest();

            Console.ReadLine();
```

```
        }

        private static void AddTest()
        {
            CacheItem<string> test =
              new CacheItem<string> { Key = "Test", Value = "Value" };
            test.Save();

            CacheItem<string> foo = new CacheItem<string> { Key = "Foo", Value = "Bar" };
            foo.Save();

            CacheItem<int> number = new CacheItem<int> { Key = "Number", Value = 5 };
            number.Save();
        }

        private static void GetTest()
        {
            CacheItem<string> test = new CacheItem<string> { Key = "Test" };
            CacheItem<string> foo = new CacheItem<string> { Key = "Foo" };
            CacheItem<int> number = new CacheItem<int> { Key = "Number" };

            Console.WriteLine("{0}, {1}, {2}", test.Get(), foo.Get(), number.Get());
        }
    }
}
```

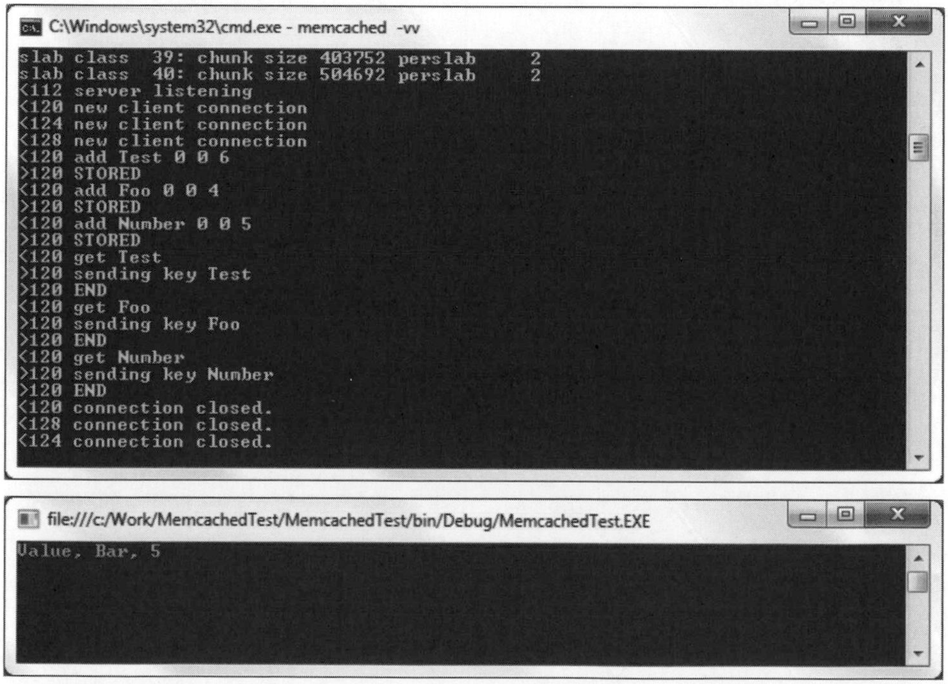

Figure 6–5. The new generic class gives better control over how we deal with objects in Memcached.

Testing the Library

You may have noticed that we added a reference to System.Diagnostics to the Program.cs file but haven't used anything in that namespace yet. We're going to modify the Program class to iterate over our cache operations 1,000 times and test how long it takes to complete the operations. We want to identify any potential performance bottlenecks as well as determine how efficiently the .NET Framework is managing the memory related to our objects (see Listing 6–5).

Listing 6–5. Running the Initial Methods 1,000 Times with a Stopwatch Attached to Determine Approximate Execution Time

```
namespace MemcachedTest
{
    class Program
    {
        static void Main(string[] args)
        {
            for (int i = 0; i < 1000; i++)
            {
                Stopwatch sw = new Stopwatch();
                sw.Start();
                AddTest();
                Console.WriteLine("Operation took {0}ms.", sw.ElapsedMilliseconds);
                sw.Stop();
                sw.Reset();

                sw.Start();
                GetTest();
                Console.WriteLine("Operation took {0}ms.", sw.ElapsedMilliseconds);
                sw.Stop();
                sw.Reset();
            }

            Console.ReadLine();
        }
    }
}
```

Figure 6–6 demonstrates the sort of result we want to see. Even after 1,000 iterations, the operations are still taking betwen 3 and 5 milliseconds to complete. The memory usage of the application was also consistent across the runs, taking up a rough maximum of 25KB to 26KB throughout, as shown in Figure 6–7.

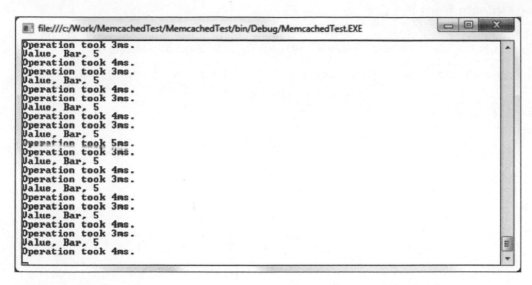

Figure 6–6. *Execution times are very consistent, even after 1,000 consecutive runs.*

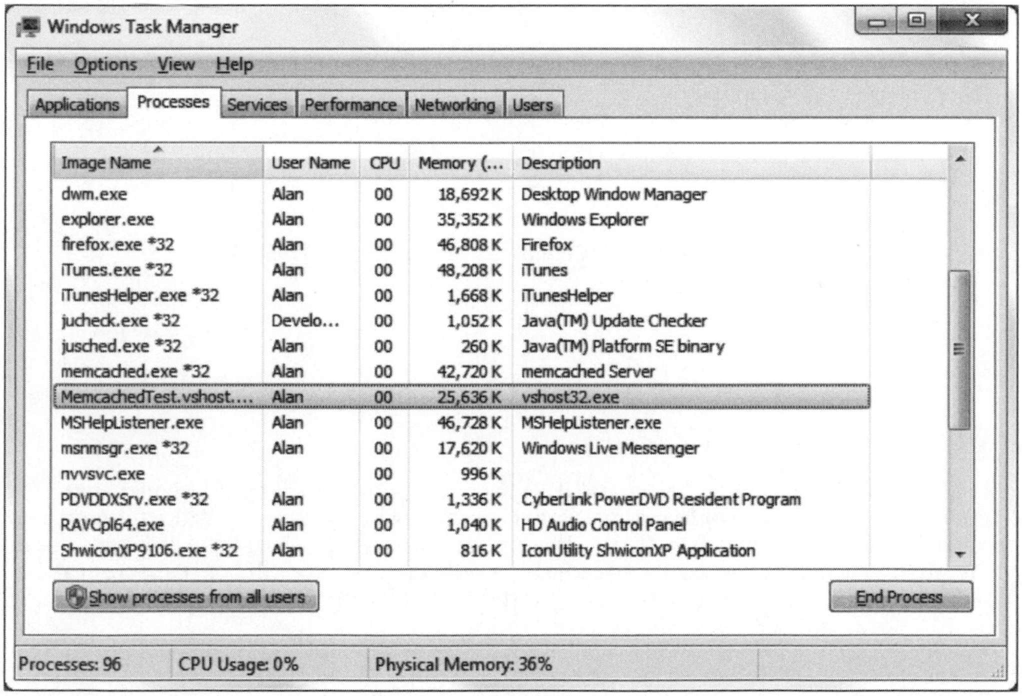

Figure 6–7. *Memory usage remained consistent across the 1,000 runs.*

Deleting Objects from the Cache

The final primary operation is deletion, which is extremely straightforward. The Delete() method, added to the CacheItem class, will handle removing objects from the cache (see Listing 6–6).

Listing 6–6. A Generic Class to Facilitate Strongly Typed Object Transmission to a Memcached Instance

```
using System;
using System.Collections.Generic;
using System.Text;

namespace MemcachedLib
{
    public class CacheItem<T>
    {
        public string Key { get; set; }
        public T Value { get; set; }

        public void Save()
        {
            Memcached.ClientLibrary.MemcachedClient m = Client.InitClient();
            m.Add(Key, Value);
        }

        public T Get()
        {
            Memcached.ClientLibrary.MemcachedClient m = Client.InitClient();
            this.Value = (T)m.Get(Key);
            return this.Value;
        }

        public void Delete()
        {
            Memcached.ClientLibrary.MemcachedClient m = Client.InitClient();
            m.Delete(this.Key);
        }
    }
}
```

Complex Object Types

So far the objects we've stored have been simple .NET types such as int and string. Although the Memcached client library is capable of handling most of the plumbing and infrastructure for us, there are still some considerations we need to factor in with regard to class design. To demonstrate this, create a new class file called CustomObject.cs in the MemcachedTest project. This class will hold a theoretical business entity that exposes CustomerID, CustomerName, and Salary properties (see Listing 6–7).

Listing 6–7. A Simple Custom Object Representing a Business Tier Entity

```
using System;

namespace MemcachedTest
{
    public class CustomObject
    {
        public int CustomerID { get; set; }
        public string CustomerName { get; set; }
        public decimal Salary { get; set; }
    }
}
```

Now we can modify the Program.cs file to store and retrieve objects of this CustomObject type to Memcached (see Listing 6–8).

Listing 6–8. Modifying the Main Program to Store a CustomObject in the Cache

```
namespace MemcachedTest
{
    class Program
    {
        static void Main(string[] args)
        {
            AddTest();
            GetTest();

            Console.ReadLine();
        }

        private static void AddTest()
        {
            CacheItem<CustomObject> customObj =
              new CacheItem<CustomObject> {
                Key = "Customer",
                Value = new CustomObject {
                  CustomerID = 1, CustomerName = "John Smith", Salary = 100000
                }
              };
            customObj.Save();
        }

        private static void GetTest()
        {
            CacheItem<CustomObject> customObj =
              new CacheItem<CustomObject> { Key = "Customer" };
            customObj.Get();
        }
    }
}
```

Running this code will trigger an exception as shown here. What's the problem with this code?

Type 'MemcachedTest.CustomObject' in Assembly 'MemcachedTest, Version=1.0.0.0,
Culture=neutral, PublicKeyToken=null' is not marked as serializable.

The issue is that the CustomObject class has not been marked with the Serializable attribute; alternatively, you could implement ISerializable if desired and handle serialization manually. The built-in binary serialization in .NET is sufficient for resolving this problem, as demonstrated in Listing 6–9; Figure 6–8 shows the output.

Listing 6–9. The Class Has Been Marked with the Serializable Attribute

```
using System;

namespace MemcachedTest
{
    [Serializable]
    public class CustomObject
    {
        public int CustomerID { get; set; }
        public string CustomerName { get; set; }
        public decimal Salary { get; set; }
    }
}
```

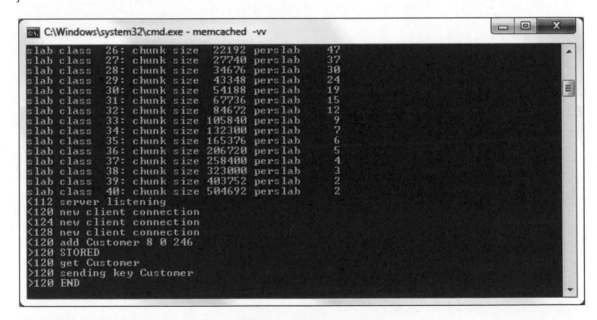

Figure 6–8. The CustomObject has been serialized and stored correctly.

Protocol Considerations

Earlier I mentioned that knowledge of the Memcached protocol is useful in designing an effective cache layer. In this case, although our code is functional, we've introduced a potentially subtle bug that wouldn't be totally obvious without viewing the verbose output of the Memcached instance.

Our CacheItem class uses the Add() method of the MemcachedClient library, which appears to work properly. The issue is exposed only when we run the Add() method on the same object repeatedly before the object has expired; see Figure 6–9 to see the problem in action. Note that the output displays "NOT STORED," indicating no change has been made to the cache.

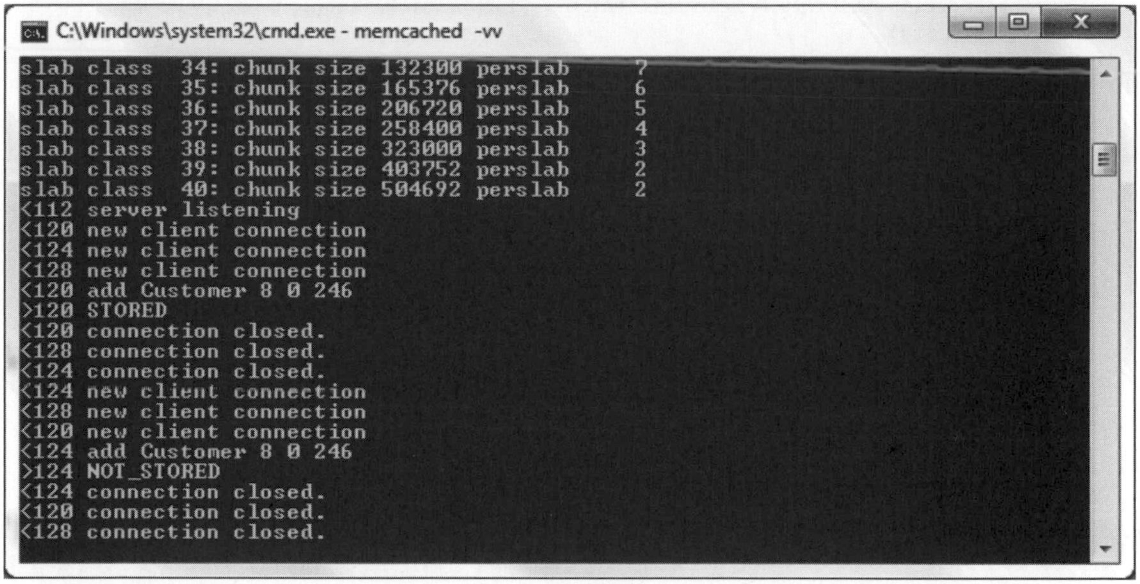

***Figure 6–9.** The add method doesn't overwrite existing objects in the cache.*

The MemcachedClient library defines a method called Set() that will automatically override the value of an item regardless of whether it has expired; Add() is a conditional method that modifies the contents of the cache only if the object in question either does not exist or has reached its expiration point. Note that this behavior is not dictated by the library itself but by the Memcached protocol; SET overwrites automatically while ADD is conditional.

We can resolve this issue in a variety of ways including method overloads or alternative methods (creating separate Add() and Set() methods in the CacheItem class). Since we're using .NET 4, we can take advantage of a new feature: optional parameters. This type of parameter allows us to specify some value (if desired) or operate on a default value if none is provided, as shown in Listing 6–10. This is a very convenient way to add conditional logic without excessive repetition (affectionately known as "don't repeat yourself"). The code from Listing 6–10 gives results as shown in Figure 6–10.

Listing 6–10. Optional Parameters Provide a Cleaner Approach Than Overloads in This Case

```
public class CacheItem<T>
{
    public string Key { get; set; }
    public T Value { get; set; }

    public void Save(bool overwrite = false)
    {
        Memcached.ClientLibrary.MemcachedClient m = Client.InitClient();
        if (overwrite)
        {
            m.Set(Key, Value);
        }
        else
        {
            m.Add(Key, Value);
        }
    }

    public T Get()
    {
        Memcached.ClientLibrary.MemcachedClient m = Client.InitClient();
        this.Value = (T)m.Get(Key);
        return this.Value;
    }
}
```

Using ILDASM to Learn About .NET Features

With regard to new features in the C# language (such as optional parameters) as well as existing ones, any time you want more information about how something works under the hood it is definitely worth opening up Intermediate Language Disassembler (ILDASM) and poking around the IL code that is generated by the compilation process. Remember that although C#, VB .NET, and all the other .NET languages may not take advantage of every single feature of the .NET runtime, the IL code absolutely can; a working knowledge of IL is certainly advantageous if you want to take full command of the framework.

You can view the IL for this class library by starting a new Visual Studio command prompt, navigating to the folder where your .DLL exists and typing ildasm "MemcachedLib.dll". If you open the Save() method, you'll see the method signature is .method public hidebysig instance void Save([opt] bool overwrite) cil managed, and the default value is set on line 3 via .param [1] = bool(false).

```
C:\Windows\system32\cmd.exe - memcached -vv

slab class   31: chunk size   67736 perslab   15
slab class   32: chunk size   84672 perslab   12
slab class   33: chunk size  105840 perslab    9
slab class   34: chunk size  132300 perslab    7
slab class   35: chunk size  165376 perslab    6
slab class   36: chunk size  206720 perslab    5
slab class   37: chunk size  258400 perslab    4
slab class   38: chunk size  323000 perslab    3
slab class   39: chunk size  403752 perslab    2
slab class   40: chunk size  504692 perslab    2
<112 server listening
<120 new client connection
<124 new client connection
<128 new client connection
<120 set Customer 8 0 246
>120 STORED
<120 connection closed.
<128 connection closed.
<124 connection closed.
<124 new client connection
<128 new client connection
<120 new client connection
<124 set Customer 8 0 246
>124 STORED
```

Figure 6–10. The set method automatically replaces the object in the cache.

Memcached Internals and Monitoring

Although in an ideal world nothing would ever break, sometimes things do go off the rails, and being able to identify the cause (or at least narrow it down) is valuable when the clock is ticking. The Memcached protocol defines a method (conveniently called STATS) for retrieving statistics about the state of the instance; this feature is exposed in the MemcachedClient library via the Stats() method.

We will make this modification to the Client class in the MemcachedLib project (Listing 6–11). The results are shown in Figure 6–11.

Listing 6–11. Retrieving Statistics from Registered Cache Instances

```
using System;
using System.Collections;
using System.Collections.Generic;
using System.Text;
using Memcached.ClientLibrary;

namespace MemcachedLib
{
    public static class Client
    {
        private static string[] _serverPool = { "127.0.0.1:11211" };
        private static MemcachedClient _memcached;
        private static SockIOPool _pool;

        public static MemcachedClient InitClient()
```

```csharp
    {
        if (_memcached == null) _memcached = new MemcachedClient();
        if (_pool == null)
        {
            _pool = SockIOPool.GetInstance();
            _pool.SetServers(_serverPool);
            _pool.Initialize();
        }
        return _memcached;
    }

    public static string Stats()
    {
        InitClient();
        StringBuilder results = new StringBuilder();

        Hashtable table = _memcached.Stats();

        foreach (DictionaryEntry serverInstance in table)
        {
            Hashtable properties = (Hashtable)serverInstance.Value;

            foreach (DictionaryEntry property in properties)
            {
                results.Append(
                    String.Format("{0,-25} : {1}\n", property.Key, property.Value)
                );
            }
        }

        return results.ToString();
    }
}
}
```

■ **Tip** `String.Format()` allows you to specify a variety of formatting options, such as the one used in Listing 6–10 to pad space between the first and second properties being appended to the `results` variable. It is similar in function to the `object.ToString()` overloads (such as the ability to specify currency output) but with a richer set of capabilities. An in-depth discussion of the `String.Format()` method is available in the MSDN library at http://msdn.microsoft.com/en-us/library/b1csw23d%28VS.100%29.aspx.

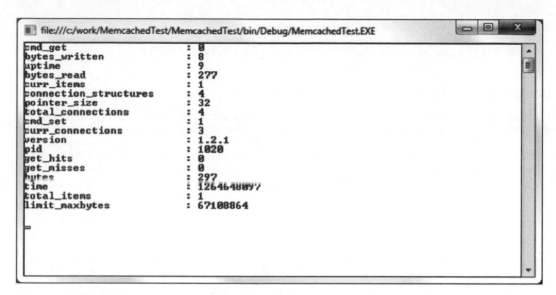

Figure 6–11. We can now retrieve nicely formatted statistic information about an instance.

The most critical statistics provided in this output are get_hits and get_misses. These two values make up the cache hit ratio, which is a critical diagnostic metric in determining the health of the cache. Ideally the misses will be very low, although in production it will likely never be zero. The reason for this is that the typical pattern of cache item storage is first checking for the presence of an item in the cache. If it exists, return it; otherwise, take the necessary steps to generate the data and then store it in the cache. If you're in a situation where the get_misses field is high (or worse, higher than the get_hits value), then it's time to step back and examine the business logic that relates to the items in the cache because there is likely a serious flaw.

■ **Tip** The Win32 version of Memcached is unfortunately not in lockstep with the Unix-based Memcached releases. The newer versions on the Unix side include richer statistics, including a property called evictions that will allow you to see the relative churn of the cache. Items are evicted by Memcached when slab space is low, so knowing how frequently this is happening can be a key step in slab optimization. In production environments, my personal experience (and what I hear from others) is that the Win32 port is fine for development and testing, but one or more dedicated Unix boxes hosting the most up-to-date version of Memcached are the norm.

Building a Cache-Friendly Site Tree

In Chapter 2 we established data structures and code for handling individual pieces of content such that a user arriving at a page would have a combination of buckets and embeddable controls delivered to them to form a complete page. What we failed to address at the time was the creation of a tree structure suitable for describing the hierarchy of a CMS site in a navigable fashion. Now that we have a robust caching infrastructure, the creation of a tree structure will fill this gap as well as demonstrate some Memcached considerations that have been hinted at but not yet enumerated.

Visualizing the Tree

In the context of the CMS, the tree can be visualized as an *unbalanced* collection of *nodes*, which are object representations of the pages in the site. Each node can have zero to *n child nodes*, and each child node can have zero to *n* child nodes of its own, and so on. Nodes at the same level are referred to as *siblings*. The CMS tree is considered unbalanced because there is no requirement that a node have a specific number of children or siblings; there are other types of tree structures (such as binary trees) that impose such restrictions but are unsuited to the nature of a web site hierarchy.

Figure 6–12 demonstrates a representation of a typical unbalanced tree.

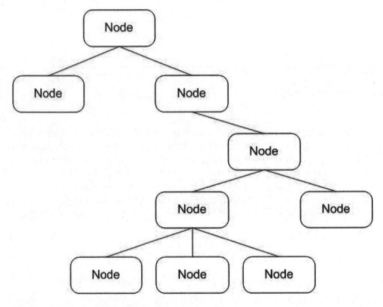

Figure 6–12. An unbalanced tree structure

It seems an obvious first step to begin the construction of this tree by creating the Node object and populating it with relevant fields.

Defining a Node

The code in Listing 6–12 demonstrates the implementation of the Node object in the CMS. There are some basic properties such as the ID of the content and the author, some search engine optimization features such as keywords and a description (covered more in-depth in Chapter 9), and some tree-specific settings such as a List of Node objects and a Guid indicating the immediate parent Node. It's not necessary to have a parent as the first Node in the tree, called the *root*, which by definition will not have a parent.

Listing 6–12. Defining a Structure for a Node, Which Represents a CMS Page

```
using System;
using System.Collections.Generic;
using System.Linq;
using System.Text;

namespace Business.SiteTree
{
    [Serializable]
    public class Node
    {
        // Basic settings (ID, who wrote it, etc.)
        public Guid ContentID { get; set; }
        public string Title { get; set; }
        public string Author { get; set; }
        public string FriendlyUrl { get; set; }

        // SEO-specific settings
        public string Keywords { get; set; }
        public string Description { get; set; }
        public bool Visible { get; set; }
        public bool FollowLinks { get; set; }

        // Tree-specific settings
        public List<Node> Pages { get; set; }
        public Guid? ParentID { get; set; }

        public Node()
        {
            Pages = new List<Node>();
        }
    }
}
```

■ **Note** The Node class has been marked with the Serializable attribute, which as we've discussed is required for the object to be stored in Memcached.

Defining the Tree

Given that a Node object has a list of child Nodes, it seems that we have a sufficient structure and a Tree object is superfluous. The CMS (as implemented in a real-world production environment) had an additional stipulated requirement: although each site should have a home page that contains the majority of subpages, it's occasionally necessary to have one-off pages (called *single pages*) that don't live within the normal tree structure. These pages are typically promotional events or short-lived content that don't need to fall within the categories defined in the normal hierarchy.

Since we must have the capacity to have pages outside the normal hierarchy, we'll need to create a Tree object that can hold our Nodes in a flexible way. Listing 6–13 demonstrates the basic Tree object.

Note that the Tree contains a List<Nodes> object. With this present, we can insert any number of Nodes at the top-level, and each one can have zero to *n* children. This meets the business requirements of the system while offering us an object that can wrap Nodes and provide useful functionality without cluttering the Node objects themselves.

Listing 6–13. *Defining the Structure for a Tree*

```
using System;
using System.Collections.Generic;
using System.Linq;
using System.IO;
using System.Runtime.Serialization;
using System.Runtime.Serialization.Formatters.Binary;
using System.Text;

namespace Business.SiteTree
{
    [Serializable]
    public class Tree
    {
        #region Public Methods
        public List<Node> Pages { get; set; }

        /// <summary>
        /// Initializes the list of page nodes
        /// </summary>
        public Tree()
        {
            Pages = new List<Node>();
        }
        #endregion
    }
}
```

■ **Note** The Tree class has also been marked with the Serializable attribute to facilitate storage in Memcached.

Finding Nodes

Now that the Tree supports a list of Node objects, we need a way to find a specific Node at some unknown level within the Tree. As has been the case throughout the system, we'll begin with the intended usage and work backward so that our API is clean and usable. Listing 6–14 demonstrates a simple way to retrieve a specific Node from the Tree.

Listing 6–14. *Finding a Node Within the Tree*

```
// Create an instance of a tree; assume for now that it has been filled with Nodes
Tree site = new Tree();

// Create a GUID that represents content
```

```
Guid contentID = new Guid("9aafa5d0-c20f-41de-9c04-b8284c8cc4cb");

// Get a complete Node object using only the GUID
Node page = site.FindPage(contentID);
```

Ideally, all we will need to know about a page is the GUID that uniquely identifies it in the CMS. Based on that information, we shouldn't need to concern ourselves with how to search through the tree or how many levels deep we need to go to find the Node in question. This API means we can fire and forget and let the Tree back end figure out the logistics for us.

Listing 6–15 shows an implementation that permits this type of functionality. Note that we have split the methods into two regions: Public Methods and Private Methods. The public-facing methods should be as simple as possible, calling one or more private methods to accomplish the required functionality

■ **Note** The total implementation for the Tree class is moderately long at approximately 270 lines of code, including the XML comments for each method. As such, we'll walk through only the most relevant methods in this chapter; for topics such as reordering Nodes or arbitrary relocation, the downloadable code for this book will serve as demonstration.

Listing 6–15. Implementation for Finding a Node Within the Tree

```
namespace Business.SiteTree
{
    [Serializable]
    public class Tree
    {
        #region Public Methods
        public List<Node> Pages { get; set; }

        /// <summary>
        /// Initializes the list of page nodes
        /// </summary>
        public Tree()
        {
            Pages = new List<Node>();
        }

        /// <summary>
        /// Finds a page node for a given content ID
        /// </summary>
        /// <param name="contentID">the unique identifier for the content</param>
        /// <returns>The page node for the content ID provided</returns>
        public Node FindPage(Guid contentID)
        {
            Node page = new Node();
            Search(this.Pages, contentID, ref page);
```

```
            return page;
        }
         #endregion

    #region Private Methods
    /// <summary>
    /// Recursively searches the tree structure for a page node
    /// </summary>
    /// <param name="tree">The list of page nodes</param>
    /// <param name="contentID">The page node content ID to search for</param>
    /// <param name="page">
    /// A reference to a page node that is filled by the method
    /// </param>
    private void Search(List<Node> tree, Guid contentID, ref Node page)
    {
        foreach (var p in tree)
        {
            if (p.ContentID == contentID)
            {
                page = p;
            }
            else
            {
                Search(p.Pages, contentID, ref page);
            }
        }
    }
}
```

The Search() method operates in a recursive fashion; if a specific Node is not properly matched at the current level, the method will be called again, and the current Node's children will be provided as the first parameter. This permits a top-down search of the structure until (and if) a match is found.

Inserting Nodes

Now that the Tree provides a way to find Nodes located at any depth, we need a way to insert them. If a Node has a parent, we'll need to use the FindPages() method to first locate the parent, and then we'll insert the Node as one of its children. If no parent is supplied, we can assume that the Node lives as a top-level single page.

Listing 6–16 demonstrates our intended manner of Node insertion, assuming that there is a Node already defined called ParentNode. Leaving the second parameter as null indicates a top-level page.

Listing 6–16. Inserting a Node as a Child to Another Node

```
tree.InsertPage(NewNode, ParentNode);
```

Listing 6–17 contains the implementation for inserting a Node based on whether a parent is provided. If a parent ID is provided, the FindPage() method is used to retrieve that Node from the Tree, and then the Node to be inserted is added as one of its children.

Listing 6–17. Inserting a Node into the Tree namespace Business.SiteTree

```
{
    [Serializable]
    public class Tree
    {
        #region Public Methods
        /// <summary>
        /// Inserts a page node below a particular parent
        /// </summary>
        /// <param name="page">The page node to insert</param>
        /// <param name="parentID">
        /// The nullable parent ID; pages without a parent ID are top-level pages
        /// </param>
        public void InsertPage(Node page, Guid? parentID)
        {
            if (parentID.HasValue)
            {
                Node parent = FindPage(parentID.Value);
                page.ParentID = parentID.Value;
                parent.Pages.Add(page);
            }
            else
            {
                this.Pages.Add(page);
            }
        }
        #endregion
    }
}
```

Serializing/Deserializing the Tree for Memcached Storage

Serializing an object in binary form is extremely easy in the .NET Framework, taking only a few lines to implement. The code in Listing 6–18 is all that is necessary to handle this functionality.

Listing 6–18. Inserting a Node into the Tree

```
namespace Business.SiteTree
{
    [Serializable]
    public class Tree
```

```
    {
        #region Public Methods
        /// <summary>
        /// Serializes a tree using binary serialization
        /// </summary>
        /// <returns>A MemoryStream containing the serialized information</returns>
        public MemoryStream SerializeTree()
        {
            MemoryStream ms = new MemoryStream();
            IFormatter formatter = new BinaryFormatter();
            formatter.Serialize(ms, this);
            return ms;
        }

        /// <summary>
        /// Deserializes a binary serialized tree
        /// </summary>
        /// <param name="serializedNode">The MemoryStream object containing the tree</param>
        /// <returns>A deserialized Tree object</returns>
        public Tree DeserializeTree(MemoryStream serializedTree)
        {
            IFormatter formatter = new BinaryFormatter();
            serializedTree.Seek(0, SeekOrigin.Begin);
            return (Tree)formatter.Deserialize(serializedTree);
        }
        #endregion
    }
}
```

The tree is very responsive even as the number of objects grows considerably. Figure 6–13 shows the output of three different tests; in the first, a Tree object was created, and 200 Nodes were inserted at random depths. The second test used 2000 Nodes, and the third used 20,000. Even at a size of 20,000 Nodes, the Tree could be serialized in approximately .80 seconds.

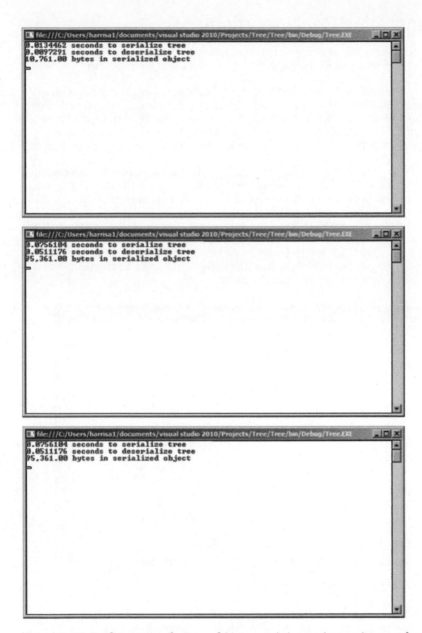

Figure 6–13. Performance of a Tree object containing an increasing number of Nodes

Memcached Configuration Considerations

At this point, we have developed a Memcached wrapper that facilitates the quick storage and retrieval of items from the cache, and we've also developed a custom tree structure that supports binary serialization.

Earlier in the chapter, we examined the Memcached concept of slabs as a form of custom memory allocation. Objects being inserted into the cache (or updated within it) are automatically placed in the slab container best suited to the size of the object in question; if a slab can't contain an object because of a lack of available space, then an existing object will be evicted. Under heavy load, this creates a potential performance bottleneck as potentially large objects will constantly be entering and leaving the cache.

Refer to Figure 6–2, which describes each of the slabs as configured automatically by Memcached. Figure 6–14 shows the size of a serialized Tree that contains 2,000 Nodes. Based on the slab allocations and their chunk sizes as shown in Figure 6–2, we won't be able to fit many Tree objects of this size in the cache before we begin to run out of space and evict items.

In the case of Figure 6–14, the object is 95,361 bytes. Memcached will then look at the slabs to find the most appropriate size; according to Figure 6–2, that would be slab 33 as the chunk size is 105,840 bytes. A chunk can be thought of as a container for an object; our 95k object fits in a chunk suited for objects between 84,673 bytes and 105,840 bytes. Slab 33 can currently hold 9 of these chunks. Once 9 chunks have been filled, objects will begin to expire from the cache.

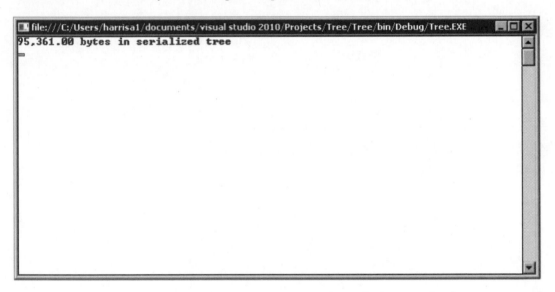

Figure 6–14. A sample Tree with 2,000 Nodes is approximately 95KB when serialized.

This is the reason we created the Tree object at this point in the book. It is a real-world object with a demonstrable size consideration that highlights the need for Memcached configuration to avoid what can quickly become a very serious performance bottleneck. Memcached supports a variety of configuration options that can aid in performance tuning, although some understanding of the Memcached slab allocation structure is necessary. For example, the slab size is dictated by a multiplier against the base size; the default of 1.25 produces the slab sizes shown in Figure 6–2. Figure 6–15 shows what happens if we set the -f parameter (which stands for "factor") to 6.0 instead of the default 1.25.

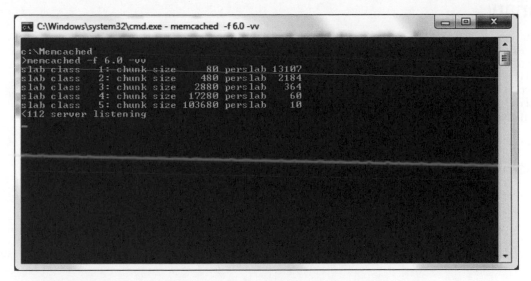

Figure 6–15. Memcached configured with a 6.0 slab growth factor

With the default Memcached configuration, we could hold 9 objects in the appropriate slab; by reconfiguring to a different growth factor, we have 60 available chunks (an increase of approximately 6.7 times) in the appropriate slab and should experience less cache churn as a result.

This is just an example of how to adjust Memcached for the type of object being stored; the growth factor in your slabs will be dictated by the size of the Tree objects you're storing, as well as the size of any other objects you plan to store. For instance, if you don't plan to host more than one site within a CMS instance, you can probably get away with the default slab configuration. If you plan to host 20 or 30 sites, you will likely need to segment slabs accordingly.

Memcached excels with small objects but can quite capably handle larger ones like our Tree. Understanding how the cache allocates space and determines where objects live is critical to identifying performance issues and (where possible) eliminating them before they cause you a headache.■

■ **Tip** I can't emphasize enough the importance of planning for caching *early* and implementing it *late*, coupled with careful evaluation of metrics gathered on objects that are destined for life in the cache. Identify the performance bottlenecks, and resolve what can be resolved in code or configuration; then look to caching to aid where appropriate. A distributed cache is of no use to you as a developer when it is constantly expiring items because they don't meet default size conventions, and a performance problem hidden by the cache remains a problem to be addressed (sooner or later).

Summary

In this chapter, we learned about Memcached and the problems that it solves when scaling outward in a high-traffic environment. We installed the Win32 version of the Memcached server and built custom libraries to wrap communications with it. Finally, we created a serializable tree structure for the CMS and used it to demonstrate why configuration of the internal Memcached slab allocation can be critical to the success of the distributed cache performance. Moving along, we'll look at how to implement a custom scripting solution into the CMS using IronPython, and we'll explore both the language and the benefits it offers to us as developers.

CHAPTER 7

■ ■ ■

Scripting via IronPython

"There are two ways of constructing a software design. One way is to make it so simple that there are obviously no deficiencies. And the other way is to make it so complicated that there are no obvious deficiencies."

—C. A. R. Hoare

We've already discussed ways to extend application functionality in the CMS, primarily through reliance on the new Managed Extensibility Framework. This is an extremely effective method of modifying the behaviors and capabilities of the system but certainly doesn't represent the limit of our options. In this chapter, we'll look at how to implement a scripting engine in the CMS based on IronPython, as well as how we can leverage the language and interact with the CMS in a very fluid, natural way.

How Does the CMS Benefit from Scripting Capabilities?

There are a variety of reasons to incorporate scripting in the CMS: easier debugging of troublesome pages and content, rapid prototyping of ideas, and potentially allowing users to customize their pages at a code level come to mind immediately. Let's look at each of these possibilities in more detail.

Easier Debugging

As far as the developer experience of working with the CMS goes, we have already gained a significant amount of architecture flexibility by using the Managed Extensibility Framework to promote the use of plug-ins as opposed to changing the core CMS platform every time we need to make a change to the system.

A flexible architecture is great, but our real-time debugging abilities are still hindered somewhat by the fact that we (currently) have no way to interact with a page beyond the tracing and debugging facilities that the .NET Framework provides out of the box. We can capture memory dumps and analyze them in WinDbg (a topic covered in Chapter 8), but we're still a bit removed from a problematic event and the forensic analysis component of fixing problems.

By incorporating a scripting capability into the CMS, we effectively open to the door to interacting with the page in real time, which can be a tremendous asset while diagnosing problems that occur in a production environment. If we create not only the functionality to script the CMS, but the ability to persist those changes, we provide ourselves with the convenience of being able to hot-patch content without taking the CMS offline.

This ability to develop in real time and see the effect on the production system requires careful consideration and responsible development to ensure that it is used appropriately, but the benefits tie very closely into the next point, which is the efficiency provided with regard to rapid prototyping.

Rapid Prototyping

As we'll see, IronPython scripting allows us to operate on content in the CMS and make full use of the .NET Framework. From the developer standpoint, this has some pretty powerful implications.

It's possible to create an environment such that a developer can load a piece of content in the CMS, script entirely new controls and behaviors for that page, and persist those changes to the database to be used each time that content is loaded.

In practice, the act of creating complex controls becomes a bit trickier than that; truthfully, the best result is attained by taking a prototyped idea and executing it in a server-side control via the MEF plug-in system the CMS has established thus far. It does prove to be useful in that a developer can essentially work on CMS components from any machine with a functional Internet connection and web browser.

■ **Note** I have actually done this exact routine on a production instance of the CMS. There was an issue with a plug-in that occurred only under specific conditions, and at a very late hour I was able to eliminate the problem with an IronPython script. The following morning (and after some more rest), the problem was resolved in the plug-in, and the system was immediately updated accordingly. The combination of scripting capabilities and the MEF plug-in architecture gave me the ability to respond quickly without bringing any systems offline.

An Introduction to IronPython and Its Syntax

For the purposes of the CMS, we'll be incorporating IronPython as our scripting language of choice. Although a .NET language, IronPython is very different from C#; if you're unfamiliar with the language and its syntax, we will cover the fundamentals here before adding scripting capabilities to the CMS core later in the chapter. If you're already a well-versed Pythonista, feel free to skim or skip directly ahead to the "Building Scripting Capabilities into the CMS" section.

What Is IronPython?

The shortest answer to this question is that "IronPython is an implementation of Python that is designed to run on the .NET Dynamic Language Runtime." All the traditional Python keywords and built-in functions are present, but with the additional capability of being able to make use of the .NET Framework libraries natively. As such, you could write code in IronPython that doesn't actually use any of the framework libraries at all if you so desired. If you're already well-versed in the Python language, you'll simply be gaining .NET features rather than replacing the language syntax you've become accustomed to.

The DLR is a set of services built on top of the Common Language Runtime; these services provide a dynamic type system suitable for languages such as Python and Ruby, as well as a hosting capability. As a result, code written in a traditional .NET language such as C# is able to operate on objects created in IronPython, and vice versa. This is an extremely powerful bridge between normally separate programming languages and development styles.

■ **Note** The actual IronPython implementation is primarily written in C#; it has a very permissive Microsoft Public License, and you are free to examine the source code to IronPython at the Microsoft CodePlex site. At the time of this writing, the code can be viewed at `http://ironpython.codeplex.com/sourcecontrol/changeset/view/64033?projectName=IronPython`.

Unfortunately, because of the difficulties related to implementing full first-class language support in the Visual Studio IDE, IronPython still does not enjoy the benefits and development ease that C# and Visual Basic .NET do. This is by no means a reason to avoid using it; in fact, the more developers that pick up and enjoy the experience of working with Python and the .NET Framework combined, the more likely it is that support will continue to grow in the future.

■ **Tip** Jeff Hardy, IronPython MVP and .NET programmer, expressed the difficulty of IDE support for IronPython in his post at `http://jdhardy.blogspot.com/2009/12/how-hard-is-it-to-add-ironpython.html`. He is the author of the Visual Studio 2010 IronPython Extensions, available at `http://bitbucket.org/jdhardy/ironpython.visualstudio/`. These extensions provide some very useful features to the IDE (such as syntax highlighting).

Installing IronPython

Since IronPython is not included out of the box with Visual Studio 2010, we'll have to download it from the Microsoft CodePlex site (`http://www.codeplex.com/IronPython`). The current stable version as of this writing is 2.6.

Once you have IronPython installed, you basically have three primary options for application development: you can write IronPython code directly into the console-based interpreter, you can save source code and execute it via the interpreter, or you can host IronPython code within another application. Although we won't have time in this chapter to cover everything related to IronPython as a language, we can begin with a brief discussion to address some key points.

For the moment, we'll use the IronPython interpreter to directly execute code for the purposes of examining the syntax of the language. You'll find this under the Programs ➤ IronPython 2.6 folder as IronPython Console (or IronPython 64-bit Console if your machine is 64-bit). Figure 7–1 shows the interpreter window.

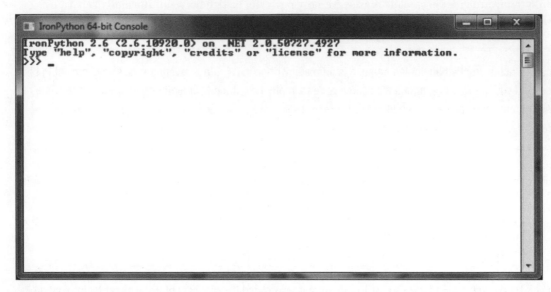

Figure 7–1. The IronPython interpreter (64-bit in this case)

The IronPython Type System

If you've never worked with a dynamic language before, the difference in programming practices can be jarring, particularly at the outset. Listing 7–1 demonstrates the nature of IronPython's type system and how the language interprets variable assignment.

Listing 7–1. IronPython Determines Variable Type Based on the Assigned Value

```
# note the lack of type information on the left side of the assignment
firstNumber = 5
secondNumber = "two"
thirdNumber = 42.0
```

IronPython Comments

IronPython single-line comments begin with a hash (#). Technically, the language doesn't support multiline comments, although it is possible to use triple-quoted strings to accomplish a similar effect.

```
class Foo:
    """
    This is technically a multiline comment.
    It is not really an appropriate method of commenting out code.
    """
```

This is not a good way to comment out blocks of code; if you were to type `Console.WriteLine("{0}",` `Foo.__doc__)`, the information we entered between the quotes would be displayed. This information is called a *docstring* and represents metadata maintained through the runtime of the application; it is somewhat similar in purpose to the C# XML documentation that has been used throughout this book (although the XML documentation is not stored within the final assembly in .NET).

```
/// <summary>
/// This information is used in a similar fashion to the IronPython docstrings.
/// </summary>
public class Foo { }
```

If we execute those commands in the interpreter and then call type( ), which is a built-in function in IronPython, on each of them, we can see that IronPython has determined each variable's type based on the inferred type of the assignment, as demonstrated in Figure 7–2. This style of programming is part of the reason that Python (and, by extension, IronPython) have become so popular among many programmers: the language is concise and lacks what is perceived to be semantic clutter. Developers with a background in C-style languages (including Java and C#) will notice that line-ending semicolons, class and method brackets, and type definitions (among other things) are all conspicuously absent from IronPython code.

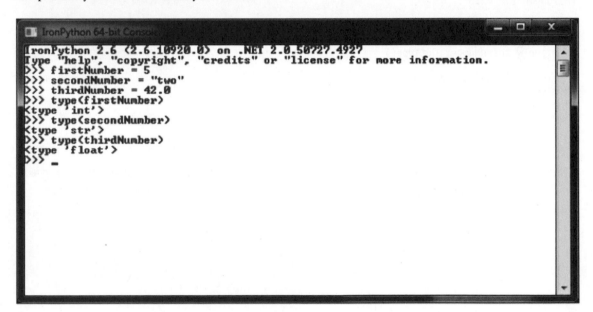

Figure 7–2. Demonstrating variable typing assignments

It's important to note that the variable types shown in Figure 7–2 are not the .NET types as defined in the `System` assembly; if so, we would expect the types returned by the interpreter to be `System.Int32`, `System.String`, and `System.Double`, respectively. IronPython is very flexible in terms of handling types between traditional Python code and the `System` types; if we make use of the CLR, we can issue the `variable.GetType()` method to examine the .NET type information for each variable, as shown in Listing 7–2 (the results are shown in Figure 7–3).

In IronPython, we can access the .NET Framework classes via the import keyword, which serves to find a particular module and initialize it if necessary. If we needed additional namespaces from within the framework, we would import the clr module and then call the AddReference() method to access the ones required (such as System.Net or System.IO).

■ **Tip** IronPython also allows you to handle referencing .NET namespaces via the import command. For example, you could pull in the entire System namespace with from System import *.

Listing 7–2. Examining the Types of Different Variables

```
import clr
clr.AddReference("System")

firstNumber = 5
secondNumber = "two"
thirdNumber = 42.0

fNumType = firstNumber.GetType()
sNumType = secondNumber.GetType()
tNumType = thirdNumber.GetType()

# print the type information to the console
fNumType
sNumType
tNumType
```

■ **Note** The clr.AddReference("System") call is not necessary in Listing 7–2; the type information is exposed simply by importing the clr module. I have included it simply as a demonstration of how to perform the step.

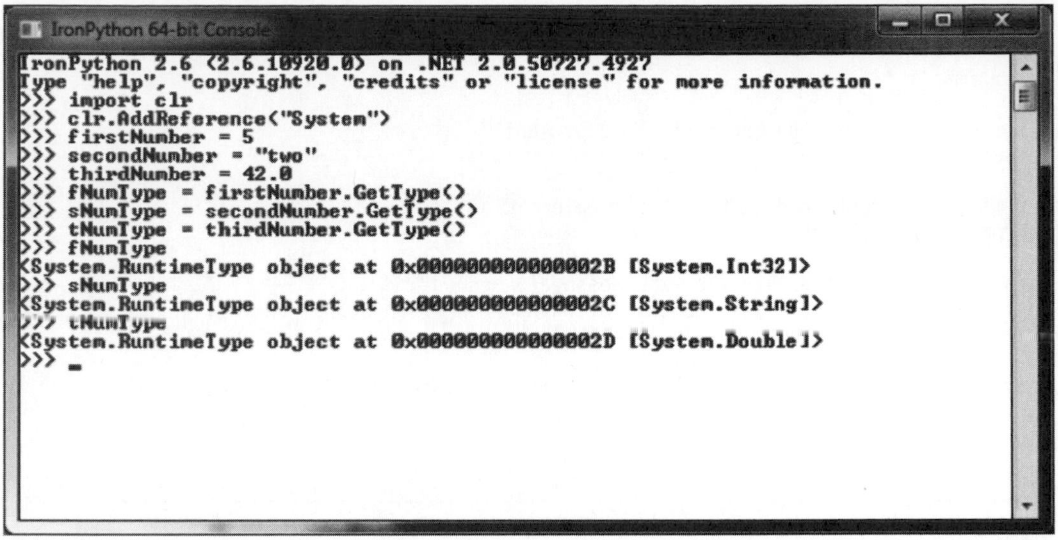

Figure 7–3. Converting to the .NET types defined in System

■ **Tip** After you've assigned these types to variables, you can run conditional checks against them or examine additional properties to make program flow decisions. Given the fNumType variable in Listing 7–2, we could state Console.WriteLine("{0}", fNumType.IsValueType), which would return "True" because Int32 is a value type in the .NET Framework. This is the foundation for very useful techniques regarding the evaluation of incoming parameters and attributes when conditional branches are required; for example, if a method passes in a System.Enum, execute one branch. If a System.Double is provided, execute a different branch.

This functionality is a direct result of the fact that all value and reference types in .NET inherit either directly or indirectly from the type Object. For more information on this topic, consult the MSDN Library entry on the Object type at http://msdn.microsoft.com/en-us/library/system.object_members%28VS.100%29.aspx.

Creating Classes and Controlling Scope

Without specific scope control characters, IronPython relies on whitespace and indentation to control the scope of classes, methods, and variables. Consider the class definition in Listing 7–3; note that the scope of the method is defined by level of indentation. The ScopeTest class represents the broadest containing scope; any methods or properties within are denoted by their indentation. The instantiation at the bottom of the listing is at the same level of indentation as the class definition; therefore, it exists outside the scope of the class itself.

Figure 7–4 demonstrates the output of Listing 7–3.

Listing 7–3. Demonstrating Scope Control via Whitespace and Indentation

```python
from System import *

# the class definition is the broadest scope present
class ScopeTest:

    # this method is contained within the ScopeTest class
    def PrintMessage(self):

        # this is contained within the PrintMessage() method
        Console.WriteLine("This is a demonstration of IronPython scope control.")


# these are at the class level and will instantiate it, then call PrintMessage()
scopeTest = ScopeTest()
scopeTest.PrintMessage()
```

■ **Note** What's the deal with the variable self being passed to the PrintMessage() method given that it's apparently not used? Hold that thought, because we will discuss the importance of self in a few pages.

Figure 7–4. The output of the scope demonstration

Adding another class at the same indentation level as the other class definition creates a separate scope for its members, as demonstrated in Listing 7–4. The output of this code is displayed in Figure 7–5.

Listing 7–4. Adding a Second Class Demonstrates the Scope of Each

```
from System import *

# the class definition is the broadest scope present
class ScopeTest:

    # this method is contained within the ScopeTest class
    def PrintMessage(self):

        # this is contained within the PrintMessage() method
        Console.WriteLine("This is a demonstration of IronPython scope control.")

# a second class definition
class NewScope:

    # this method is contained within the NewScope class
    def PrintMessage(self):

        # this is contained within the PrintMessage() method
        Console.WriteLine("This is a second class with its own scope.")

# these are at the class level and will instantiate it, then call PrintMessage()
scopeTest = ScopeTest()
scopeTest.PrintMessage()

scopeTest2 = NewScope()
scopeTest2.PrintMessage()
```

Figure 7–5. The new class has a separate scope based on indentation.

■ **Note** As this code demonstrates, IronPython instantiates classes in the form `instance = className(parameters)`. After you have assigned a class to an instance, you can use the standard dot notation familiar to C# developers to call methods in the form `instance.Method(parameters)` or assign return values in the form `variableName = instance.Method(parameters)`.

We can display the instance information about each object by simply passing the object itself as output to the console, as demonstrated in Listing 7–5. Note the output that is displayed in Figure 7–6; `scopeTest` is an instance of the `ScopeTest` class, while `scopeTest2` is an instance of the `NewScope` class.

Listing 7–5. Displaying the Instance Information About the Objects We Created

```
# displaying the types of each instance
Console.WriteLine("scopeTest instance is {0}", scopeTest)
Console.WriteLine("scopeTest2 instance is {0}", scopeTest2)
```

Figure 7–6. The instances are displayed, demonstrating the effects of scope control

Constructors as Magic Methods

IronPython supports constructors via the use of what are affectionately termed *magic methods*. Named for their ability to automatically provide object functionality simply by being called, magic methods fulfill a variety of roles; some are related to the creation of objects, some to iteration, some to comparison, and so on. Covering every magic method in IronPython is outside the scope of this chapter, but we will touch on important ones as necessary.

The first (and certainly critical) example for many developers is that of the class constructor. In C#, the constructor for a class is typically the class name with zero or more parameters supplied depending on the requirements of the class. In IronPython, constructors are magic methods, and as such are in the form __init__(self).

All IronPython's magic methods are prepended and appended with two underscore (_) characters each. Note that the constructor is a method and requires the passing of the self (a requirement we will discuss next). Listing 7–6 demonstrates creating a constructor using the __init__ magic method, and Figure 7–7 shows the output of that code.

Listing 7–6. Creating a Constructor for an IronPython Class

```
class Test:

    def __init__(self):
        print "Test class instanced."

    def Method(self):
        print "Method called."

instance = Test()
instance.Method()
```

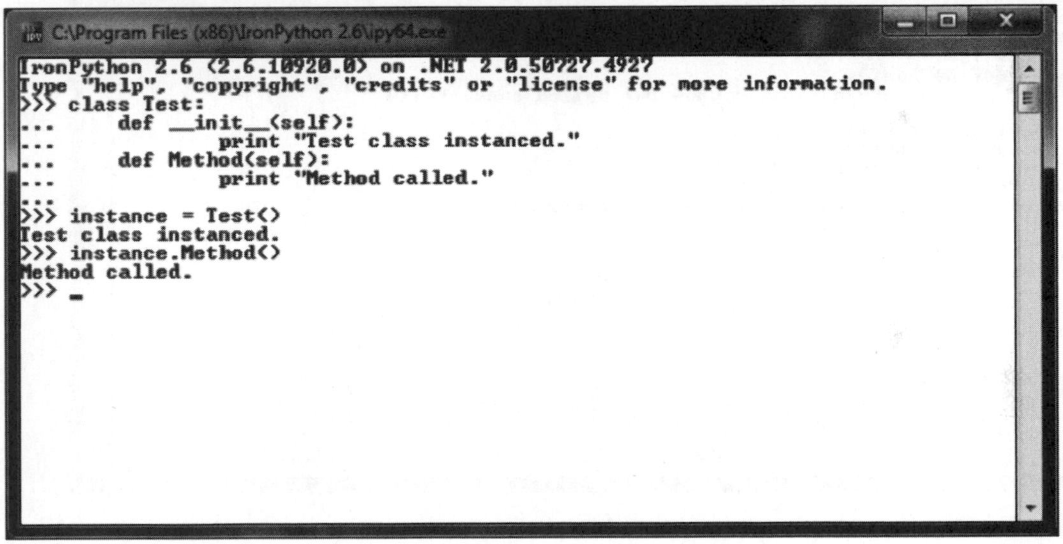

Figure 7–7. Using the constructor, which is a magic method

self

In the examples shown thus far, each method signature takes at least one variable as a parameter: self. In IronPython, all methods have to take self as the first argument in their signature. If you define a method without providing the self variable, IronPython will throw an error indicating that the method takes no arguments but 1 was provided (self is passed implicitly within the method call).

Listing 7–7 shows an example of a method that does not accept self, and Figure 7–8 demonstrates the error that the interpreter will return in such cases.

***Listing 7–7.** Attempting to Create a Method That Does Not Accept self*

```
class Test:

    def Method():
        return "This method was called successfully."

instance = Test()
instance.Method()
```

■ **Note** In IronPython, self is analogous to the C# keyword this. The difference is that the definition of the self variable is a requirement in IronPython, whereas in C# this is implicit.

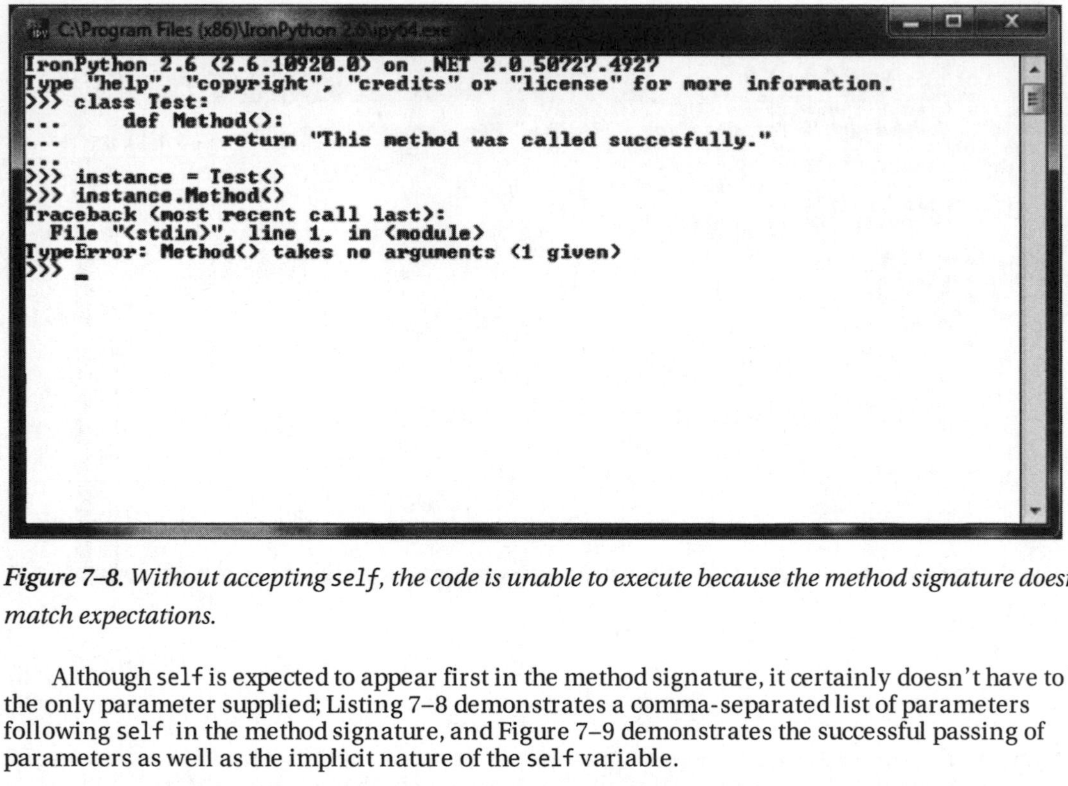

***Figure 7–8.** Without accepting self, the code is unable to execute because the method signature doesn't match expectations.*

Although self is expected to appear first in the method signature, it certainly doesn't have to be the only parameter supplied; Listing 7–8 demonstrates a comma-separated list of parameters following self in the method signature, and Figure 7–9 demonstrates the successful passing of parameters as well as the implicit nature of the self variable.

Listing 7–8. self Is Expected to Be the First, but Not Necessarily Only Parameter

```
class Test:

    def Method(self, input):
        print "You entered", input

instance = Test()
instance.Method("some text.")
```

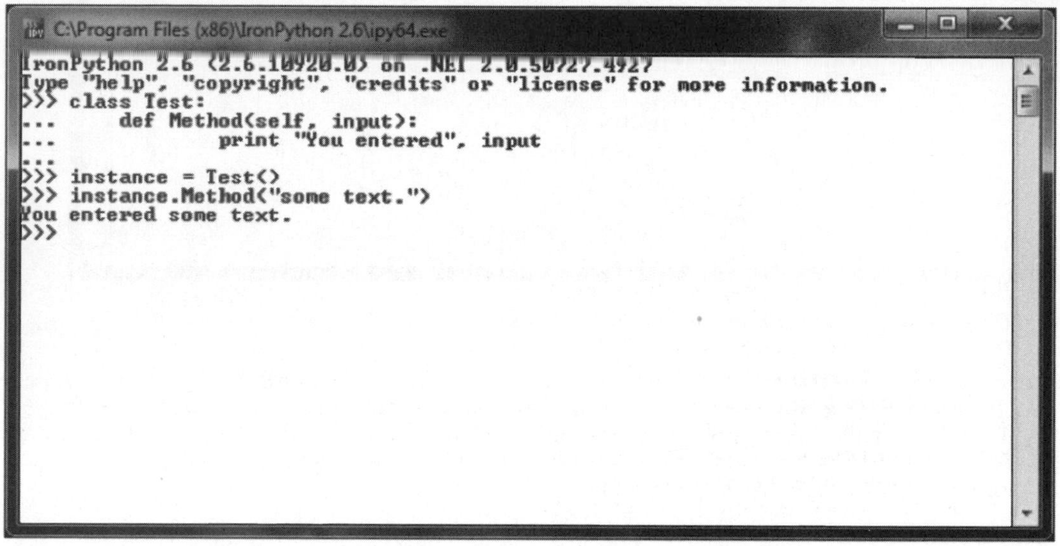

Figure 7–9. Method signatures work the same as C# but with one reserved variable position.

The self variable is also important with respect to accessing properties and methods within a particular class. For instance, if we modify the Method() section to call a new method named DoWork(), we must use the self variable to successfully reference it. Listing 7–9 uses the self variable to call the DoWork() method of the Test class (the results are shown in Figure 7–10).

Listing 7–9. We Can Access DoWork() by Relying on self

```
class Test:

    def Method(self):
        self.DoWork()

    def DoWork(self):
        print "Method() called DoWork()."

instance = Test()
instance.Method()
```

209

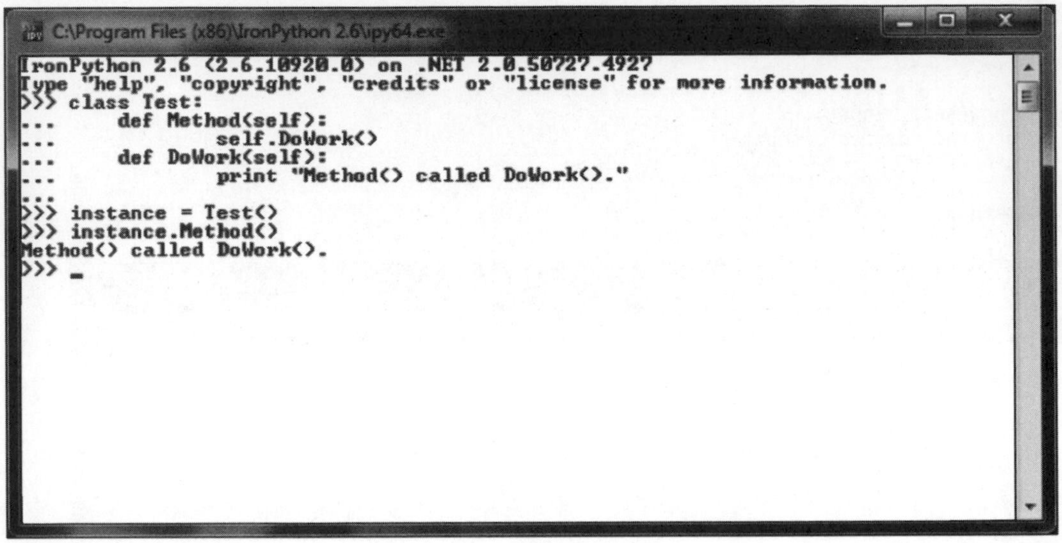

Figure 7–10. Using self to access members within the class

Finally, although the convention to use self is expected and typical among IronPython developers, you're not bound to that specific word; it is a variable that holds a reference to the instance, and the name itself holds no particular meaning. As such, you can change it to something else if desired. Listing 7–10 shows methods that use foo instead of self to achieve the same effect, at the expense of breaking convention (the results are shown in Figure 7–11).

Listing 7–10. Although Not Necessarily Recommended, You Can Use a Different Variable Name Than self

```
class Test:

    def Method(foo, input):
        foo.DoWork(input)

    def DoWork(bar, input):
        print "You entered", input

instance = Test()
instance.Method("some text.")
```

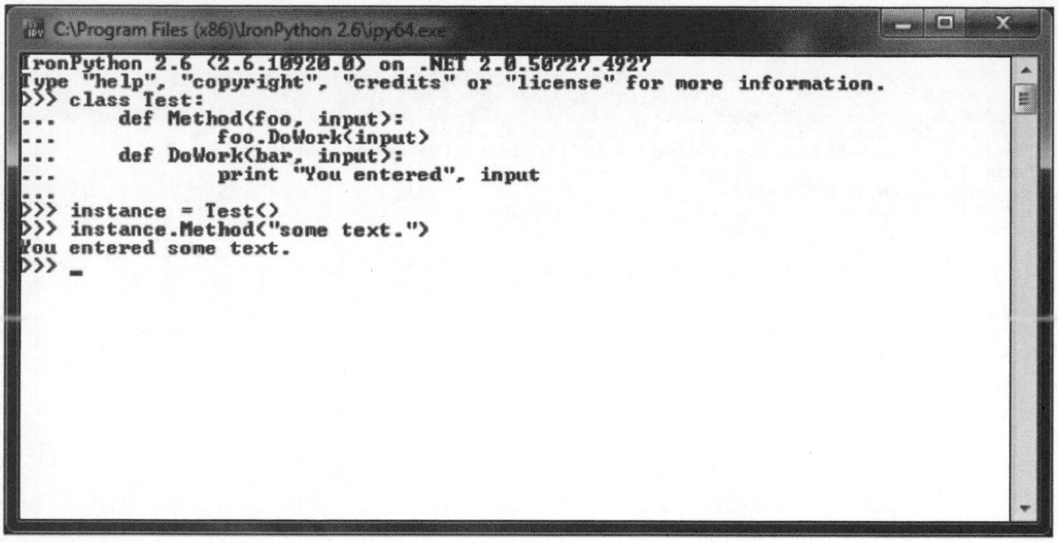

Figure 7–11. self as a variable name has no special meaning and can be changed if desired.

■ **Caution** IronPython demonstrably won't complain if you change self to some other name, but unless you have a compelling reason to do so, changing it is probably not worth the potential loss of clarity and convention.

Exception Handling

IronPython supports a try/catch approach to exception handling that will be very familiar to .NET developers. In place of the catch keyword, IronPython uses except. The try/except block is used to help manage errors that may arise during the runtime of an application.

If we attempt to divide by 0 in IronPython, we get a ZeroDivisionError exception informing us that a critical error has occurred, and the program immediately ceases execution. Wrapping this operation in a try/except block doesn't prevent the error from occurring, but it does provide an opportunity to respond without aborting the remainder of the application, as shown in Listing 7–11. You can see the results in Figure 7–12.

Listing 7–11. Wrapping a Sensitive Operation in a try/except Block

```
class Test:

    def CauseError(self):
        try:
            print 0 / 0
        except:
            print "Exception caught."
```

```
instance = Test()
instance.CauseError()
```

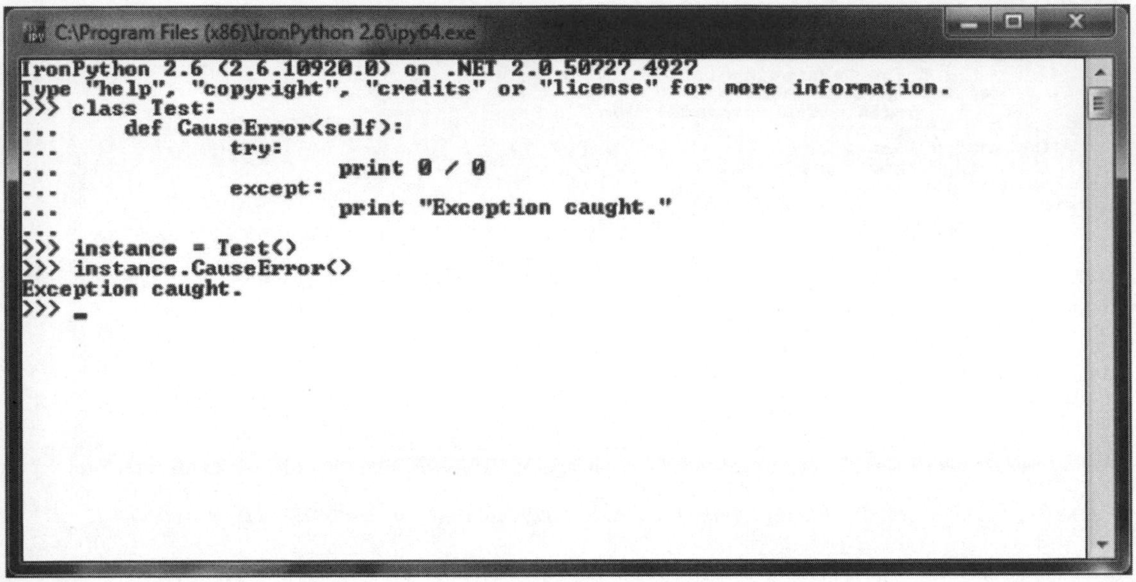

Figure 7–12. The try/except block allows response to error conditions without terminating execution.

The except block in Listing 7–11 is functional but very broad; it will catch any exception thrown by the code in the try block. The limitation with this approach is that we're not able to provide context-sensitive branches of logic based on the type of exception that was actually thrown. For example, if a ZeroDivisionError exception is thrown, we may want a different response sent to the user than other exceptions.

As in the traditional .NET languages, IronPython allows the filtering of exceptions where the most specific matching exception type hit first is used. Therefore, it is appropriate to structure the except block such that the most likely (and specific) exceptions appear first, moving toward the most generic. In Listing 7–12, the ZeroDivisionError exception appears first; if we had placed it after the generic except block, it would never be hit. Running this code results in the output shown in Figure 7–13.

Listing 7–12. Handling Specific Exception with Except Blocks

```
class Test:

    def CauseError(self):
        try:
            print 0 / 0
        except ZeroDivisionError:
            print "Unable to divide a number by zero."
        except:
            print "General exception caught."
```

```
instance = Test()
instance.CauseError()
```

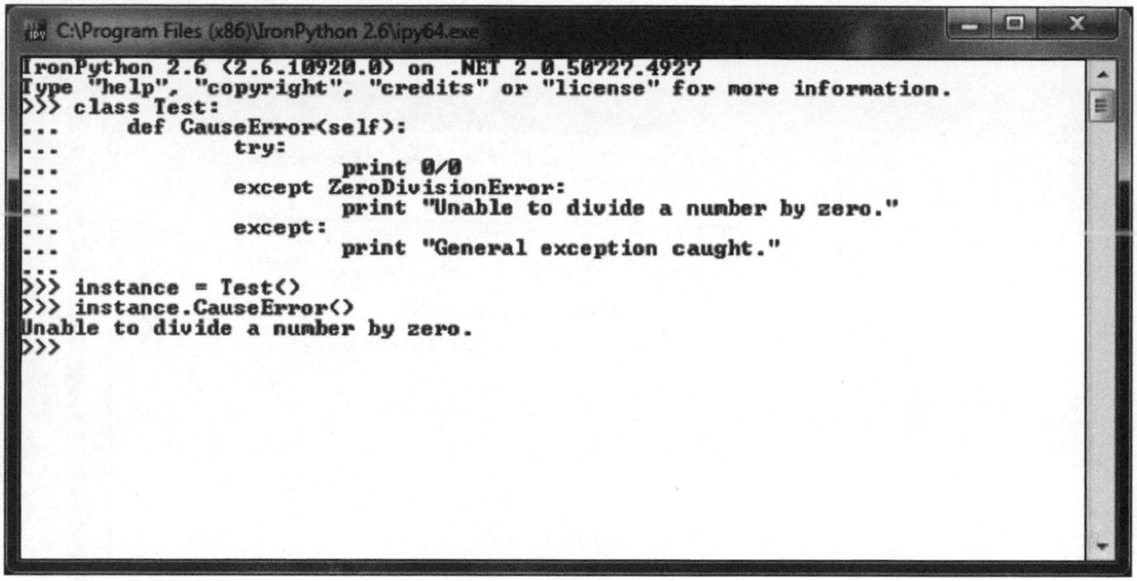

Figure 7–13. The general except block is never triggered because a more specific exception was caught.

IronPython also supports a finally block that will execute regardless of what exceptions are triggered, as shown in Listing 7–13. This is the appropriate place for (among other things) freeing resources and closing connections as you are guaranteed that code within the block will run. The results of running this code are shown in Figure 7–14.

──

■ **Note** I mention these two operations in particular because they are historically known to be application killers if not managed properly.

──

Listing 7–13. Handling Specific Exception with Except Blocks

```
class Test:

    def CauseError(self):
        try:
            print 0 / 0
        except ZeroDivisionError:
            print "Unable to divide a number by zero."
        except:
```

```
        print "General exception caught."
    finally:
        print "Executed regardless of exceptions."

instance = Test()
instance.CauseError()
```

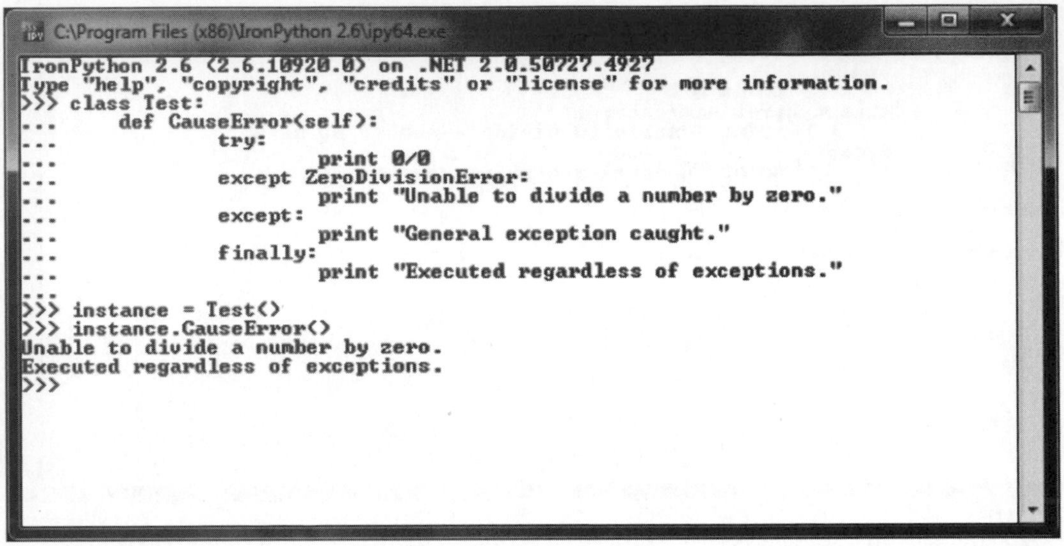

Figure 7–14. Code within a finally block is executed regardless of whether an exception is thrown.

Conditional Logic, Iterators, and Collections

In IronPython, a custom object supports iteration if it supplies a magic method called __iter__(self) that allows the return of incremental items within a set of elements. Many built-in types already provide this functionality; the code in Listing 7–14 shows a set of string objects iterated to display them in storage order (the results are shown in Figure 7–15).

■ **Tip** The .NET Framework provides an interface, IEnumerable, that can be implemented to provide iteration capabilities to custom objects.

Listing 7–14. Iterating over a Tuple of String Objects

```
class Test:

    def IterateElements(self):
        elements = ("hydrogen", "helium", "lithium", "beryllium", "boron")
```

```
    for element in elements:
        print element

instance = Test()
instance.IterateElements()
```

■ **Tip** The elements variable actually contains a tuple; in IronPython, tuples are immutable objects. They behave similarly to lists, which are in the form variableName = [element, ..., element]. A list, by contrast, is mutable. Specific examples within the language are strings and dictionaries; strings are tuples of characters and therefore immutable, while dictionaries are mutable.

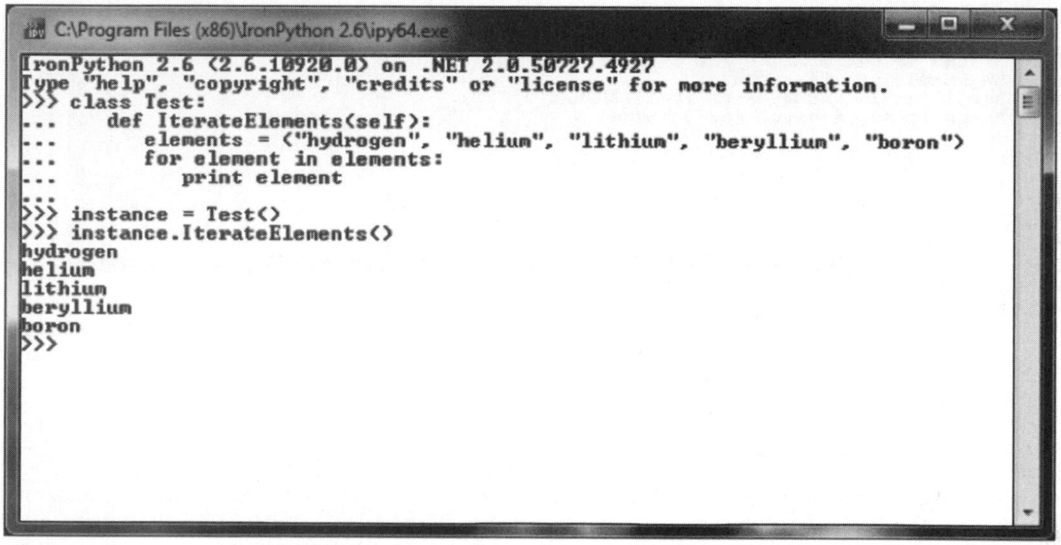

Figure 7–15. Iterating over a tuple of elements

The language also supports conditional logic in the form of the if/then/else construct (although the IronPython form is if *conditions*: ... else:), as shown in Listing 7–15. Running the code results in output shown in Figure 7–16.

Listing 7–15. Iterating Over a Tuple of String Objects with a Conditional Check for a Particular One

```
class Test:

    def IterateElements(self):
        elements = ("hydrogen", "helium", "lithium", "beryllium", "boron")
        for element in elements:
            if element == "lithium":
                print "Found lithium during iteration."
```

```
        else:
            print "Element", element, "is not a match for lithium."

instance = Test()
instance.IterateElements()
```

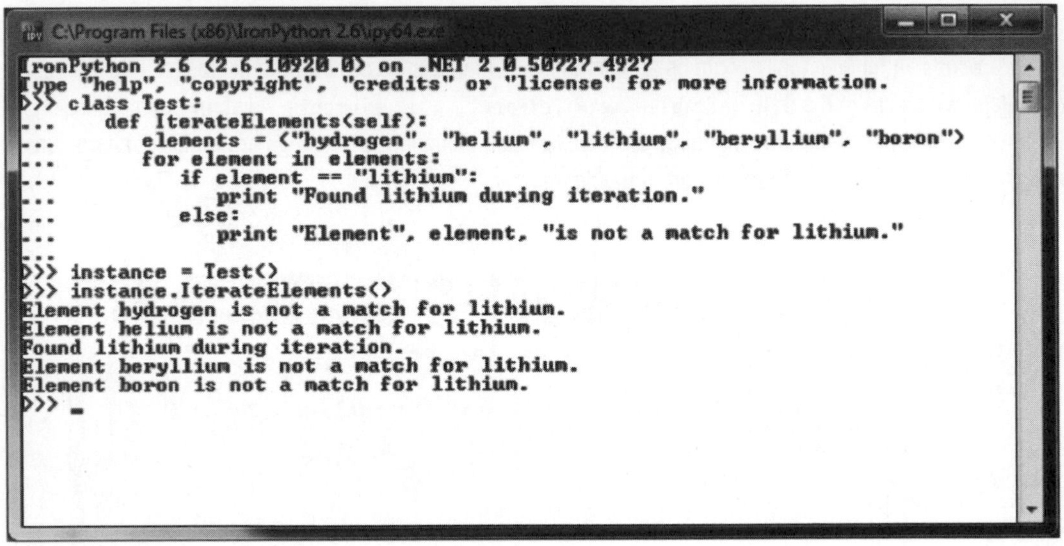

Figure 7–16. A conditional check for a particular string

Accessors and Mutators

In older versions of IronPython, properties (accessors and mutators) were implemented in the traditional Python way, which required overriding two magic methods: __getattr__ and __setattr__. There are technical issues with this route that include (but aren't limited to) performance and ease of implementation. Luckily, as the language has matured, properties have as well, resulting in a more natural syntax that should be somewhat familiar to C# developers (although a bit more verbose).

IronPython requires that we define a bit of information for properties. Specifically, we must define both the accessor and mutator methods, as well as execute assignment of an attribute that maps the methods as necessary. For example, consider the class in Listing 7–16; getName(self) and setName(self, name) are the accessor and mutator, respectively. They each operate on a variable called name, which is declared to be a property on the 6th line; it is at this point that the methods are properly mapped to the variable. The results are shown in Figure 7–17.

Listing 7–16. Defining a Set of Properties for the Test Class

```
class Test:

    def getName(self):
        return self.__name
    def setName(self, name):
        self.__name = name
    name = property(getName, setName)

instance = Test()
instance.name = "Alan" # mutator; calls the setName() method
print instance.name # accessor; calls the getName() method
```

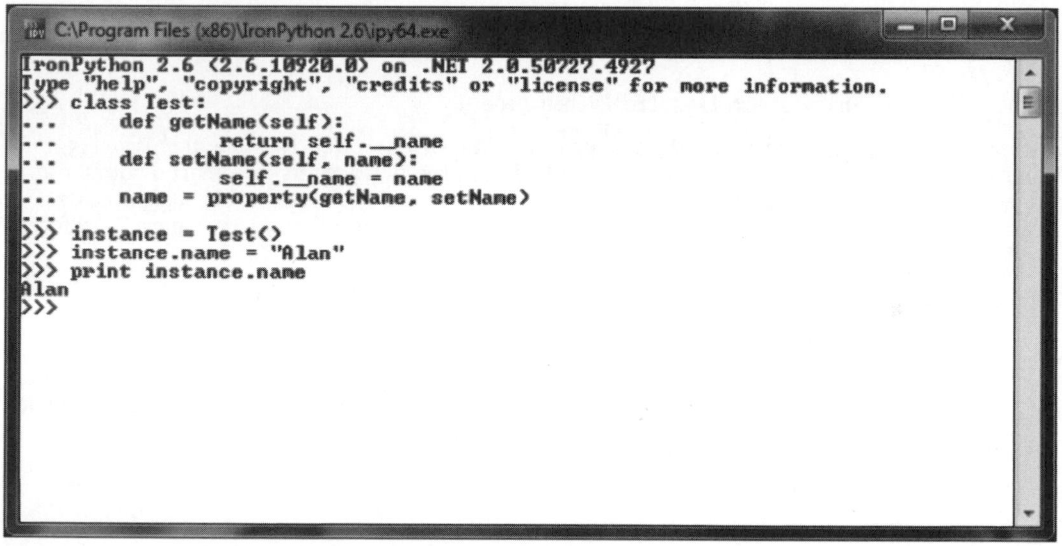

Figure 7–17. Using properties in an IronPython class

Assembly Compilation

Although we will not be focusing on distribution of code to third parties, it remains a possibility that may become a reality as you work with IronPython further. In many cases, it's neither a good idea nor permissible by your organization to distribute your source code directly to the outside world. IronPython supports compilation to either dynamic link libraries (DLLs) or to executables.

■ **Note** The DLLs and EXEs created are .NET assemblies as opposed to native code.

Compiling IronPython Code to a DLL

It is by no means a requirement to distribute your IronPython code directly as text-based script files; the IronPython interpreter provides a way for us to compile our source code to DLLs. This functionality is exposed via the clr.CompileModules() method; with it we can specify the files we want to include as well as the desired output file.

For the sake of organization, let's create a folder to store our scripts. We'll create this location separate from the CMS, in no small part to ensure a physical separation between the core project and the extensibility elements that will be applied to it. For these examples, I am assuming you have a folder called IronPython in the root of the C drive. Once you have a location, add the code in Listing 7–17 to a file within it called test.py. We will not be compiling any IronPython code in our CMS; instead, we'll simply look at how to compile from within the interpreter.

Listing 7–17. A Simple IronPython File That Will Be Compiled to a DLL

```
from System import *

def Test(self):
    Console.WriteLine("This is compiled IronPython code")
```

Now open an instance of the IronPython interpreter. You will first need to issue the import clr command to be able to use the CompileModules() method. This method accepts the desired output file, followed by parameters indicating which files to include in generating the assembly. To generate a file called test.dll, we need to issue the following command to the interpreter (see Figure 7–18 for an example of the interpreter session):

```
clr.CompileModules("C:\\IronPython\\test.dll", "C:\\IronPython\\test.py")
```

■ **Tip** For the purposes of demonstration, I used the fully qualified paths to each object in question. If you plan to do any real work along this line, modify your environment path as a time-saver.

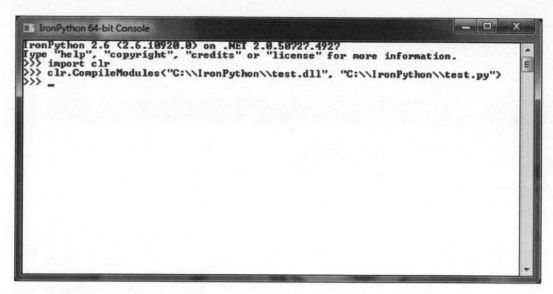

Figure 7–18. Compiling IronPython code to a DLL

At this point, we have a complete .NET assembly in the form of a DLL. If you're interested in exploring the IL that gets generated to accomplish this, run ILDASM on the test.dll file, and explore the various nodes, which are shown in Figure 7–19. It's worth noting how much IL code is required to accomplish the functionality expected with an IronPython application.

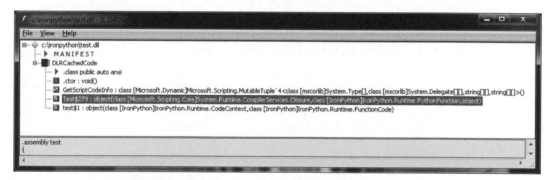

Figure 7–19. Using ILDASM to explore the IL generated by compiling IronPython code

Compiling IronPython Code to an Executable

You can compile IronPython code to a Windows executable file if desired. We won't be spending too much time on this subject because it's not something we'll use in the CMS, but it may be something you want to explore in the future.

Assuming that we have a file called test.py that defines the necessary structure of a Windows application (including an entry point and so on), we can compile it to an executable by using the pyc.py script located in the Tools/Scripts folder within the IronPython installation, as shown in Figure 7–20. The pyc.py script accepts the files involved in the compilation and allows you to define the entry point and target type.

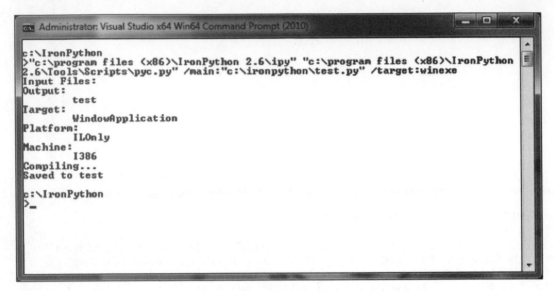

Figure 7–20. Compiling an IronPython executable is slightly more involved.

Building Scripting Capabilities into the CMS

IronPython makes an excellent option as a scripting language for the CMS. Besides being a .NET implementation of the popular (and stable) Python language, it possesses a clear, concise nature and style that lends itself well to rapid development tasks. Languages such as IronRuby exist as alternatives, but IronPython is arguably the most mature among the lot.

Although we've covered how to compile IronPython code to an assembly, the desired functionality within the CMS is that we want to be able to do limited scripting on individual pieces of content, or at the embeddable level. This may involve IronPython script files saved to the file system (which would be a task performed by system administrators and developers), or it may be accomplished through inline scripts created by end users (to whom we will provide a limited API and access to the Page object itself).

API Considerations

As we'll see in just a moment, the CMS opens the doors in a wide fashion for IronPython scripting purposes. For developers, this is great; we have access to the Page object if desired and can perform operations just as we would in C# with the same degree of flexibility and control.

The flip side to this coin is that with such an open nature, the possibility for abuse and problems rises exponentially, particularly if nondevelopers are permitted access. If an IronPython script can access the Page object, then the sky is the limit for what can be done from said script.

The issue is mitigated slightly by limiting the scope of the IronPython script, which is demonstrated in Listing 7–18. Were we to establish some form of static class or widen the scope, a script could affect multiple pages or have other unintended consequences. Even with the limited scope, there exists the possibility of abuse by providing access to the Page object.

As with any public-facing API, there are trade-offs and security considerations to be made as we are exposing the internals of our system to potentially unknown parties. For the purposes of our discussion in this chapter, we're going to give the IronPython scripts the benefit of the doubt.

There are two reasons for this: first, the code will be clearer and more focused if we don't enforce many constraints up front. Knowing that we will likely need constraints is sufficient at this point. Second, the purpose of the remaining code is to show the power and capability that can be achieved by using IronPython as a scripting language in the CMS.

Bear in mind that you'll probably want to lock things down further in your own implementations. Right now the main focus is on learning how to apply the language to achieve the functionality we desire.

To achieve this, we want to be able to execute IronPython code on the fly from within C#, which hinges directly on the ability to host the IronPython engine in your application. This engine is exposed via the ScriptEngine class and is directly paired with a ScriptScope object, which defines the scope of the variables we may want to pass back and forth to our code.

The code in Listing 7–18 is the implementation of the Scripting class in the CMS. It resides in the Business library within a folder called Scripting. The constructor sets up instances of the engine and the variable scope, and it provides methods for executing inline scripts as well as scripts that have been persisted.

Listing 7–18. A Scripting Class to Handle Execution of IronPython Scripts

```
using System;
using System.Configuration;
using Microsoft.Scripting;
using Microsoft.Scripting.Hosting;
using IronPython.Hosting;

namespace Business.Scripting
{
    public class Scripting
    {
        private ScriptEngine _engine;
```

```csharp
private ScriptScope _scope;

/// <summary>
/// Ctor; creates an instance of the ScriptEngine and ScriptScope automatically
/// </summary>
public Scripting()
{
    _engine = Python.CreateEngine();
    _scope = _engine.CreateScope();
}

/// <summary>
/// Executes an IronPython script from the web.config-dictated location.
/// </summary>
/// <param name="fileName">The name of the script file.</param>
/// <param name="className">The class to instantiate.</param>
/// <param name="methodName">The method to execute.</param>
/// <param name="parameters">
/// Any parameters the method needs to execute successfully.
/// </param>
/// <returns>
/// Dynamic; dictated by the returned information (if any) of the script.
/// </returns>
public dynamic ExecuteFile(string fileName, string className, string methodName,
                           [ParamDictionary] params dynamic[] parameters)
{
    try
    {
        _engine.ExecuteFile(ConfigurationManager.AppSettings["ScriptsFolder"] + @"\"
          + fileName, _scope);
        var classObj = _scope.GetVariable(className);
        var classInstance = _engine.Operations.Call(classObj);
        var classMethod = _engine.Operations.GetMember(classInstance, methodName);
        dynamic results;
        if (parameters != null)
        {
            results = _engine.Operations.Call(classMethod, parameters);
        }
        else
        {
            results = _engine.Operations.Call(classMethod);
        }
        return results;
    }
    catch
    {
        return null;
    }
}

/// <summary>
/// Executes an arbitrary-length IronPython script.
/// </summary>
/// <param name="script">The IronPython code itself.</param>
```

```
/// <returns>
/// Dynamic; dictated by the returned information (if any) of the script.
/// </returns>
public dynamic Execute(string script)
{
    try
    {
        return _engine.Execute(script, _scope);
    }
    catch
    {
        return null;
    }
}
}
}
```

The Execute() method accepts a script as a string object and executes it without accepting any additional parameters. The implication here is that the script is a self-contained unit of IronPython code; for example, you may include a script that performs some specific computation and returns a result to the calling class. In contrast, the ExecuteFile() method runs scripts from the file system.

There are some interesting things to note here. First, the return type for each of the script execution methods is dynamic, which (as we've discussed) is new in .NET 4. Remember that the dynamic type is effectively a placeholder for a static type that will be resolved at runtime. The benefit to using it in this fashion is that it provides extremely robust as well as brief code. You could choose to base this class around generics, as in Scripting<string> script = new Scripting<string>(). In general, although this approach is functional, the result is more code for less return compared to using the new dynamic type.

The code for handling an inline script is very different than for a specific file. In the ExecuteFile() method, we are concerned with scope, class names, methods, and parameters. The ScriptScope will be valid for the lifetime of the page and then expire; if the class were defined as static, our changes to data within the scope would impact every other user currently browsing the site. Limiting the scope to the lifetime of the page enforces some logistical walls between scripts.

Also worth noting is the expectation in this class that there will be a setting in the CMS's web.config file that defines the location of the file system-based scripts; this attribute is expected to be named ScriptsFolder. This becomes relevant when we want to open scripts directly from a folder on a drive and run it via the ExecuteFile() method.

Handling Script Files Between Tiers

As multiple tiers in the CMS will need to perform tasks based on IronPython scripts, it makes sense to create an entity called ScriptedFile in the CommonLibrary project that will define the necessary properties that go into said scripts, as shown in Listing 7–19. Note that the constructor accepts a dynamic array of parameters; we will very shortly look at the effects of passing in a reference to the current ASP.NET Page object.

Listing 7–19. An Entity in the CommonLibrary Project That Will Reference a Particular Script File

```
using System;

namespace CommonLibrary.Entities
{
```

```
public class ScriptedFile
{
    public string fileName { get; set; }
    public string className { get; set; }
    public string methodName { get; set; }
    public dynamic[] parameters { get; private set; }

    public ScriptedFile(dynamic[] parameters)
    {
        this.parameters = parameters;
    }
}
}
```

Calling Scripts for a CMS Page

The code in Listing 7–20 is fairly long and represents the code for content.aspx.cs; recall that all public CMS pages are delivered through this page. The new sections related to loading and operating on scripts have been highlight; the discussion of what has been added (and why) will follow the code itself. Note that any method in the content.aspx.cs page that did not require modification for handling IronPython scripts has been excluded from Listing 7–20.

Listing 7–20. An Entity in the CommonLibrary Project That Will Reference a Particular Script File

```
using System;
using System.Collections;
using System.Collections.Generic;
using System.Configuration;
using System.Data;
using System.Data.SqlClient;
using System.Linq;
using System.Web;
using System.Web.Security;
using System.Web.UI;
using System.Web.UI.HtmlControls;
using System.Web.UI.WebControls;
using System.Web.UI.WebControls.WebParts;
using System.Xml.Linq;
using CommonLibrary.Entities;
using Business;
using Business.Scripting;

public partial class content : System.Web.UI.Page
{
    private Scripting _scriptEngine;
    private string _script;
    private List<ScriptedFile> _scriptFiles;

    protected void Page_Load(object sender, EventArgs e)
    {
        // initialize IronPython scripts and lists of files
        _script = String.Empty;
```

```csharp
    _scriptFiles = new List<ScriptedFile>();

    if (Request.QueryString["id"] != null)
    {
        Guid id = new Guid(Request.QueryString["id"]);
        form1.Action = HttpContext.Current.Request.RawUrl.ToString().ToLower();
        LoadTemplate(id);
        LoadContent(id);
        ExecuteScripts();

        // modify page based on available plug-ins
        var business = new Business.Plugins();
        var embeddables = business.ExecuteEmbeddablePlugins(this);
        foreach (var embed in embeddables)
        {
            this.Controls.Add(embed);
        }
    }
    else
    {
        return;
    }
}

/// <summary>
/// Loads the template for a page.
/// </summary>
/// <param name="id">the ID of the page</param>
private void LoadTemplate(Guid id)
{
    List<TemplateRow> template = Business.Templates.LoadTemplate(id);
    foreach (var t in template)
    {
        LoadBuckets(t.bucketControl, t.embeddableControl);
        foreach (var script in t.scriptFiles)
        {
            _scriptFiles.Add(script);
        }
    }
}

/// <summary>
/// Loads the content for a page.
/// </summary>
/// <param name="id">the ID of the page</param>
private void LoadContent(Guid id)
{
    List<ContentRow> content = Business.Content.LoadContent(id);
    foreach (var c in content)
    {
        LoadBuckets(c.bucketControl, c.embeddableControl);
        foreach (var script in c.scriptFiles)
        {
```

```
                _scriptFiles.Add(script);
            }
        }
    }

    /// <summary>
    /// Loads an IronPython intepreter and executes IP scripts for this content.
    /// </summary>
    private void ExecuteScripts()
    {
        _scriptEngine = new Scripting();
        dynamic[] parameters = new dynamic[1];
        parameters[0] = Page;

        // iterate over any .py scripts attached to this page
        foreach (var script in _scriptFiles)
        {
            _scriptEngine.ExecuteFile(script.fileName, script.className, script.methodName,
                                      script.parameters);
        }

        // execute any inline script
        _scriptEngine.Execute(_script);
    }
```

Most of the changes should be fairly straightforward. We have defined variables to hold inline script information as well as a list of script files and their relevant information to be called. Notice that the ExecuteScripts() method is automatically configured to pass a reference to the current Page object down into any of the scripts within the system. This is a design choice that makes a great deal of sense; by passing a reference to the Page object to the script, the script now has full control over the final page and is capable of making significant modifications to it.

A Simple Scripting Example

Listing 7–21 demonstrates how simple (yet effective) the IronPython scripting experience can be; we've effectively been handed the reins and can operate on the page just as we would traditionally in C#. Listing 7–21 identifies specific buckets on the page using the FindControl() method. Recall from Chapter 2 that each bucket contains a PlaceHolder control called embeddables, which exists to house the specific embeddable subcontrols that a page might need. The script identifies this PlaceHolder within the bucket and loads a specific user control into it.

Listing 7–21. Using the Page Reference to Load Controls into the Final Hierarchy

```
class Test:
    def Method(self, page):
        header = page.FindControl("header").FindControl("embeddables")
        header.Controls.Add(page.LoadControl("~/core/embeddables/tags.ascx"))

        subnav = page.FindControl("subnav").FindControl("embeddables")
        subnav.Controls.Add(page.LoadControl("~/core/embeddables/article.ascx"))
```

For the purposes of testing, we can modify the ExecuteScripts() method in the content.aspx.cs page with a hard-coded set of values. Assuming that the code in Listing 7–21 exists in the \Plugins\Scripts folder as defined in the CMS's web.config file, the modification in Listing 7–22 will automatically execute it during the normal page life cycle.

Listing 7–22. Hard-coding a Script for Testing Purposes

```
/// <summary>
/// Loads an IronPython intepreter and executes IP scripts for this content.
/// </summary>
private void ExecuteScripts()
{
    _scriptEngine = new Scripting();
    dynamic[] parameters = new dynamic[1];
    parameters[0] = Page;

    _scriptFiles.Add(new ScriptedFile(parameters) { className = "Test", fileName = "test.py",
methodName = "Method"});

    // iterate over any .py scripts attached to this page
    foreach (var script in _scriptFiles)
    {
        _scriptEngine.ExecuteFile(script.fileName, script.className, script.methodName,
script.parameters);
    }

    // execute any inline script
    _scriptEngine.Execute(_script);
}
```

Finally, we can see the results of the script's operation in Figure 7–21. The script has effectively doubled up the controls in each bucket as expected.

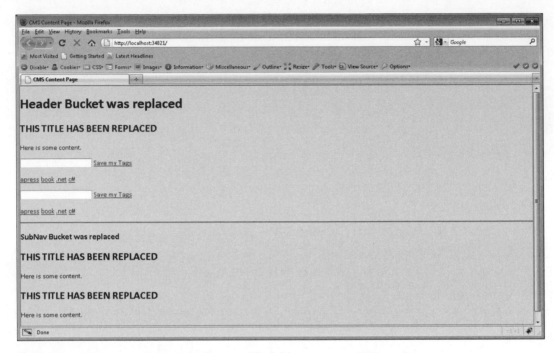

Figure 7–21. The IronPython script has modified the page control hierarchy.

Summary

Beginning with a tour of the IronPython language and syntax, we covered some of the key areas and features developers use regularly. Although an exhaustive discussion of the language as a whole is beyond the scope of a single chapter, the details covered are sufficient to begin scripting in the CMS in a meaningful and useful way. We discussed and implemented the modifications to the content.aspx.cs page such that scripts would be loaded and executed when the page is delivered to the user, and we ended the chapter by building a simple script that loads user controls into specific locations within a particular page.

■ ■ ■

## CHAPTER 8

Performance Tuning, Configuration, and Debugging

"It's easy to cry 'bug' when the truth is that you've got a complex system and sometimes it takes a while to get all the components to co-exist peacefully."

—Doug Vargas

Even though .NET 4 makes developing complex systems a simpler task, the fact remains that a CMS can be a very resource-hungry entity. The worst place to discover a performance problem is in a production environment when the web servers stop responding. In this chapter, we'll look at some ways to ensure that users are getting the best possible experience from the system, explore how to establish baseline performance metrics to see the effects of new code over time, and look at the new debugging features of Visual Studio 2010 that can make tracking down problems easier and faster.

The CMS Definition of Performance

Performance tuning is a deceptively deep and nuanced set of tasks. With regard to the CMS, we are concerned with two key factors: latency and throughput. These factors make up the performance landscape with regard to how users perceive our system and establishing the infrastructure requirements to support them.

Latency

To the end user, latency *is* performance; it is the duration of time that it takes for an operation to complete. In CMS terms, the latency is the amount of time it takes for a page in the system to be loaded and delivered to the end user.

■ **Tip** Jakob Nielsen, a well-known web usability consultant, found that for a user to consider an action to have occurred "instantly," the duration between user action and system response must be 1/10th of a second or faster. Financially, Amazon found that sales decreased 1 percent for every extra 1/10th of a second that a page took to load. You can read more about the findings at Nielsen's blog at `http://www.useit.com/alertbox/timeframes.html` and Microsoft's Experimentation Platform at `http://exp-platform.com/Documents/IEEEComputer2007` `OnlineExperiments.pdf`.

Unfortunately, this duration can be subject to many factors that are out of our hands, such as geographic location of the user compared to the server, network performance on the client side, and so on. In this way, latency can be thought of not only as the time required to complete a single task but also as the time required to complete subtasks that make up larger ones.

We can mitigate these issues to a reasonable degree by ensuring a competent mix of efficient coding, proper deallocation and release of resources, and a well-designed caching system that operates at multiple levels of the system.

Throughput

The other half of CMS performance is throughput, which is the number of successful operations the system can complete in a given unit of time.

For example, a large number of users requesting a poorly coded page that leaks resources will quickly bog the server down, reducing the number of successful page deliveries that the server can handle per second. As the throughput decreases, the latency increases, and pages arrive to clients after longer and longer durations until the site eventually crashes altogether.

Establishing Baselines

The purpose of establishing a baseline set of metrics for site performance is to evaluate changes in that performance (be they good or bad) over time; this comparison is called *benchmarking*. For this reason, it is important that the baseline remain consistent and unchanging over time.

■ **Note** In what sorts of situations would you need to reestablish a baseline? Perhaps instead of running on a single machine, the site now operates behind a load-balancer across five machines (or vice versa). Maybe a reverse proxy has been added, or the network connection has been up- or downgraded. As some fundamental conditions have changed, the baseline needs to be established again for the benchmark metrics to be meaningful.

Component vs. System Baselines

In terms of measuring latency, we've noted that the measurement can be discerned with regard to tasks or their smaller subtasks. In CMS terms, that means that we can establish baselines at the system (or page) level as well as the embeddable level, and the many shades in between.

Given that the controls that go into the creation of a CMS page can be so variable, for this chapter we will focus primarily on establishing system baselines while highlighting opportunities for testing more discrete components.

The Web Capacity Analysis Tool

Microsoft offers an excellent free tool called WCAT, short for "Web Capacity Analysis Tool." This application is designed to offer a wide variety of configuration options that can be used to simulate traffic conditions across the spectrum, from light to extreme, and provide useful (and clear) metrics that developers can use to track system performance over time.

Installing WCAT

WCAT is available from the Microsoft Download Center as part of the Internet Information Services 6.0 Resource Kit Tools. Despite the name, they will work just fine with IIS7 as well. The tools can be found at http://www.microsoft.com/downloads/details.aspx?FamilyID=56FC92EE-A71A-4C73-B628-ADE629C89499&displaylang=en.

■ **Caution** Cassini, the built-in web server that comes with Visual Studio, is not a sufficient testing platform for this type of work; set up a site in IIS with a dedicated .NET 4 application pool for the CMS.

WCAT Concepts

Logically and physically, WCAT is divided into a **controller** and one or more *clients*. The controller is responsible for communicating with the clients and instructing them that they are permitted to begin making requests, as well as for processing data regarding the performance of the site in question to deliver useful metrics back to the user.

The WCAT clients abstract the idea of connections, allowing the creation of a large number of virtual clients that can speak to the server. For example, if two WCAT instances are created that are each configured for 50 users, the server will be working with 100 concurrent connections. In this way, WCAT divides the client concept into two halves: "physical clients" are the actual WCAT client instances, and "virtual clients" are created by the physical clients. This methodology allows for significant load to be placed on a website if desired.

■ **Caution** For this chapter, I'm going to assume that you're running the CMS and WCAT from the same machine. It's possible (and preferable) to use at least two machines because the process is fairly resource-intensive, but it's also not realistic to assume that everyone has a variety of capable machines accessible. The concepts and methods are all the same, but for the numbers to be truly realistic, know that division across machines is a better solution.

Configurations

One half of the WCAT setup resides within the configuration file used for a specific test. This file is a plain-text file with settings on individual lines; it is used to define settings related to the controller and how it will behave.

Creating a configuration file for the CMS is very simple. Once the IIS 6.0 Resource Kit Tools are installed, there will be an entries for the client and controller under Start ➤ All Programs. Click WCAT Controller, which will open a command window with environmental settings for WCAT included; this is shown in Figure 8–1.

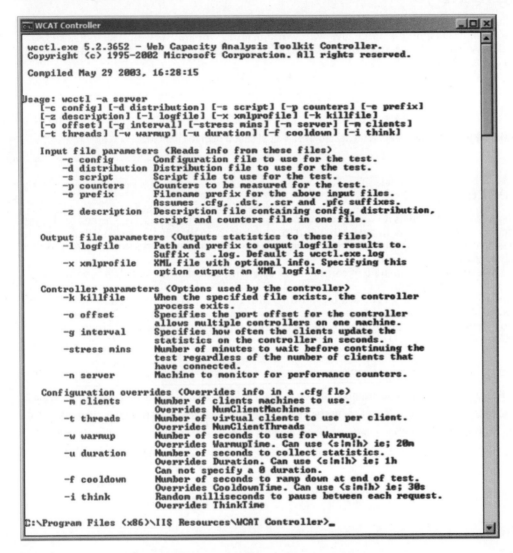

Figure 8–1. The WCAT controller command prompt

■ **Note** If you are using a 32-bit version of Windows, the path will be \Program Files\ rather than \Program Files (x86)\.

Although you can save the configuration file anywhere you like, for now let's place it in the same folder as the WCAT controller executable. Using the text editor of your preference, create a file called cms_baseline.cfg that contains what is shown in Listing 8–1.

Listing 8–1. The Sample WCAT Configuration for the CMS

```
Warmuptime 10s
Duration 60s
CooldownTime 20s
NumClientMachines 2
NumClientThreads 30
```

The parameters related to time are all specified in terms of seconds in Listing 8–1, but you are permitted to use minutes and hours if desired. For any WCAT test, there can be a warm-up period, a testing duration, and a cool-down period.

■ **Caution** Similar to the caveats around multithreading and parallelism, performance testing is very subjective and specific to the conditions of the test. You may need only 5 seconds to adequately spin up the CMS on your localhost, whereas another machine may require 15. I have provided values that worked on my machine and should leave a margin of error, but establishing a baseline may require unique settings for your particular environment.

The warm-up period gives the server an opportunity to fully initialize your application. During the warm-up period, WCAT will add virtual clients until the maximum (NumClientMachines × NumClientThreads) has been reached. Most .NET developers are familiar with the initial delay incurred by the Just-In-Time compiler as an application is loaded; this warm-up period helps to compensate. Anecdotally, 10 seconds seems to work fine on the applications I have tested.

The testing duration is exactly as it sounds; during this period, the server will be hammered with requests according to the scenario file we will create in the next step.

The cool-down period permits long-standing requests to finish executing, helping to ensure that the metrics provided are as accurate as possible. I typically allot approximately 20 seconds, which usually permits all the requests to terminate even when conditions on the server are strained.

Scenarios

The other half of the WCAT setup resides within the scenario file used for a specific test. This file is also a plain-text file with settings on individual lines; it is used to define settings related to the behavior of the WCAT clients. Examples of such settings are the page or resource being requested, the HTTP verb being used to make the request, and so on.

Open a WCAT client command prompt via the IIS resources. You should be presented with the screen shown in Figure 8–2.

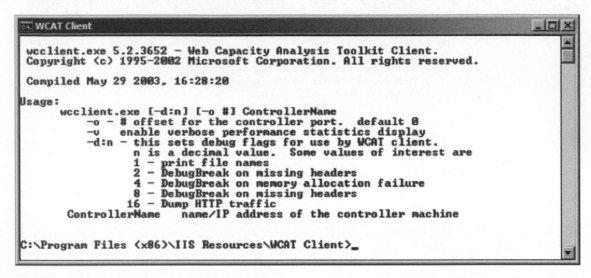

Figure 8–2. The WCAT client command prompt

In the same fashion as the configuration file, we will place the scenario file in the same folder as the WCAT controller executable. Using the text editor of your preference, create a file called cms_baseline_scenario.cfg that contains what is shown in Listing 8–2.

Listing 8–2. The Sample WCAT Scenario for the CMS

```
SET Server = "localhost"
SET Port = 80
SET Verb = "GET"
Set KeepAlive = true

NEW TRANSACTION
classId = 1
Weight = 100

NEW REQUEST HTTP
URL = "/"
```

The settings in this file should be fairly straightforward; we will be making a request to localhost on port 80 using the GET verb, and we will reuse the same TCP connections (called *persistent connection*) to send and receive HTTP communications throughout the test. This transaction is the only one for this test and makes up 100 percent of the time being used. We will be requesting the CMS home page, located at http://localhost/.

■ **Tip** In general, modern browsers support persistent HTTP connections as the creation of new ones is costly; however, they do time out automatically after a given period of inactivity to free up resources. Feel free to switch off the KeepAlive parameter to see the performance implications if a large number of clients arrive without supporting persistent connections.

Running a WCAT Test Against the CMS

With the configuration and scenario files created, we can run the test and see how the CMS performs as a baseline. From the WCAT controller window, type the following command:

```
wcctl -a localhost -c cms_baseline.cfg -s cms_baseline_scenario.cfg
```

This will spin up the WCAT controller, as shown in Figure 8–3. Note that the controller is waiting for 2 physical clients with 30 virtual clients each to establish communication before beginning the test.

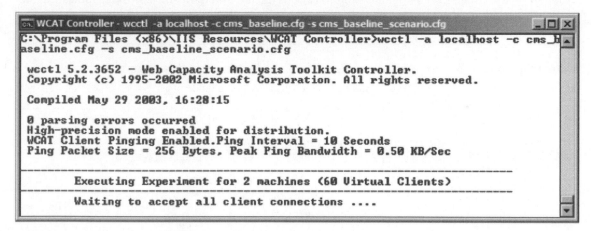

Figure 8–3. The WCAT controller is awaiting client communication.

If you do not already have two separate WCAT client command prompts open, you will need to open them. Once they are available, type the following command in each to start the clients:

```
wcclient localhost
```

■ **Note** The test will not begin until the expected number of clients have connected successfully.

The client should notify you that it is awaiting instruction from the controller, as shown in Figure 8–4.

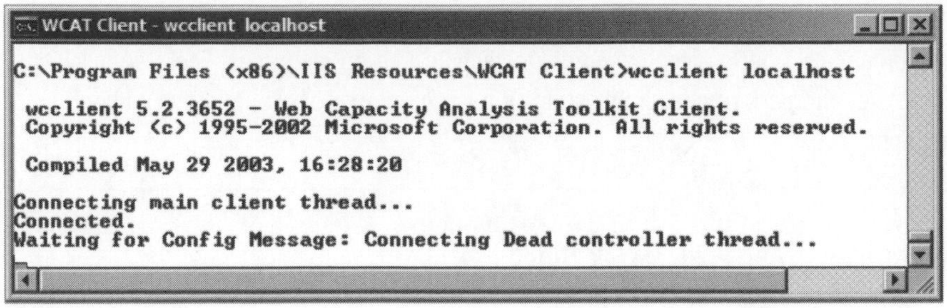

Figure 8–4. The WCAT client is connected and waiting for instruction to proceed.

Interpreting Performance Results

When the test is complete, you should see notifications in both the client and controller indicating the statistics related to each. The aggregation is present in the controller, as shown in Figure 8–5.

■ **Note** The page I tested was specifically created to have a moderate number of database-connected embeddable controls; it approximated the structure of a typical corporate home page.

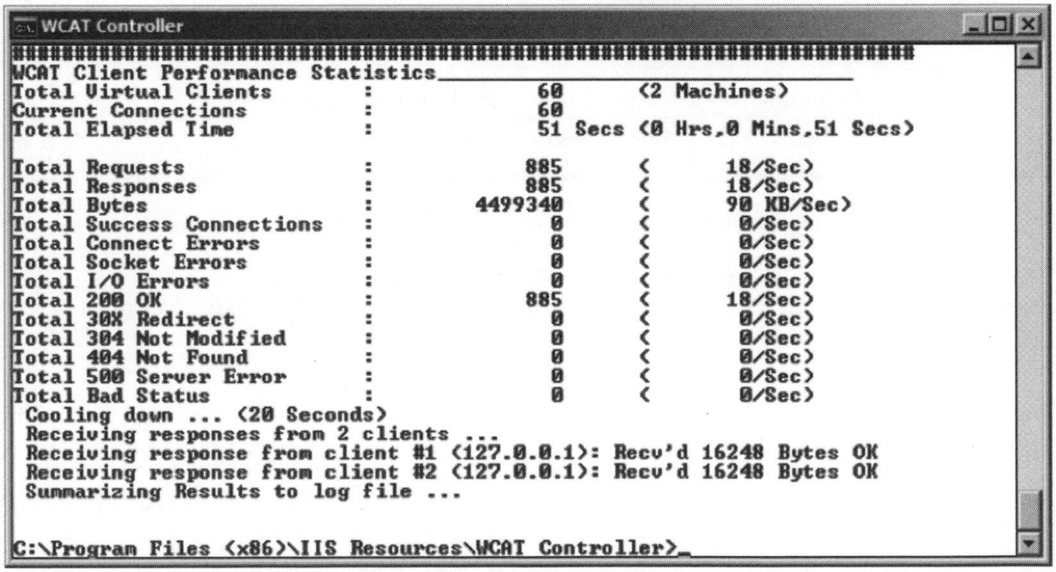

Figure 8–5. The results of the WCAT test

Based on these results, there is good news, and there is bad news. The good news is that out of 885 total requests over 60 seconds, all of them returned a response of 200 OK, indicating no server errors or other problems. The bad news is that the server was processing only 18 requests per second with a data transfer rate of approximately 90 KB per second, which is altogether terribly low.

Improving CMS Performance with Caching

There are entire books devoted solely to the task of improving the performance of web applications (even those that are static and unchanging). The potential tweaks cover every aspect of the application, from the order that JavaScript is placed on a page to how images are stored on the server. Not all of them are difficult to implement or time-consuming; caching alone can make a tremendous difference in CMS performance.

HTTP.sys and the OutputCache

One of the simplest methods of improving performance is the application of an effective caching methodology. Implementing caching too early can often hide significant performance problems, but the best coding in the world will eventually hit a performance limit based on that in a given system, tasks X, Y, and Z take a specific amount of time to complete.

Caching infrequently changing pages can make a dramatic change to both server health and user experience by simply eliminating the execution of those steps and returning the results that had been generated by a previous request. We can handle and configure this at two levels in IIS: HTTP.sys and the .NET OutputCache.

■ **Note** The use of a distributed system such as Memcached for storing CMS data differs from this type of caching in that Memcached is used to speed the retrieval of information in a request that by definition has not itself been cached. HTTP.sys and the OutputCache make up a higher level of caching that exists at the OS and server levels, respectively.

Introduced in IIS 6.0, the HTTP.sys driver is a **kernel-mode** device driver that listens for HTTP requests on the network and handles communication between IIS and the client; both IIS 6.0 and IIS 7.0 rely on this driver to process HTTP requests. Combining kernel-mode caching with .NET's OutputCache (which operates in *user mode*) results in a site that is better equipped to handle both spikes in traffic as well as consistently high load. The specific differences of kernel- vs. user-mode operation are discussed later in this chapter.

■ **Tip** Without delving into a low-level discussion of execution modes, what does it mean to maintain a cache in user mode? The user-mode cache resides directly in the worker process associated with the application and is extremely fast as a result. It is usually best to combine user-and kernel-mode caching because kernel mode by definition cannot support features such as .NET authentication that require user-mode functionality. In cases where kernel-mode caching is enabled but the feature is unsupported, the content is served without being cached.

IIS 7.0 provides an OutputCache option where both user- and kernel-mode caching can be configured. Figure 8–6 shows this window.

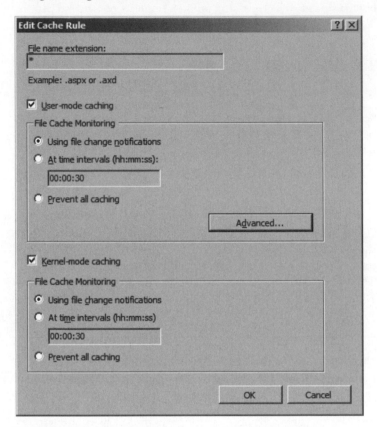

Figure 8–6. *Enabling user-mode and kernel-mode caching*

■ **Caution** In general, it's not a good idea to blindly cache everything as configured in Figure 8–6; for example, it makes little sense to devote resources to caching pages that get viewed once every few weeks. IIS 7.0 lets you customize how specific types of resources are cached at a very granular level, but for the purposes of this discussion, I want to show the two ends of the spectrum (nothing cached vs. everything cached).

Benchmarking CMS Performance

We previously established a baseline set of performance metrics for the CMS without any specific performance tweaks applied; the CMS was capable of delivering approximately 18 requests per second with a data rate of approximately 90 KB per second.

Now that we have applied a change with the intention of improving the performance of the system, we can rerun the same tests from earlier in the chapter and compare the results to learn whether the effective was positive, negative, or neutral.

Figure 8–7 shows the results of a subsequent run on the CMS.

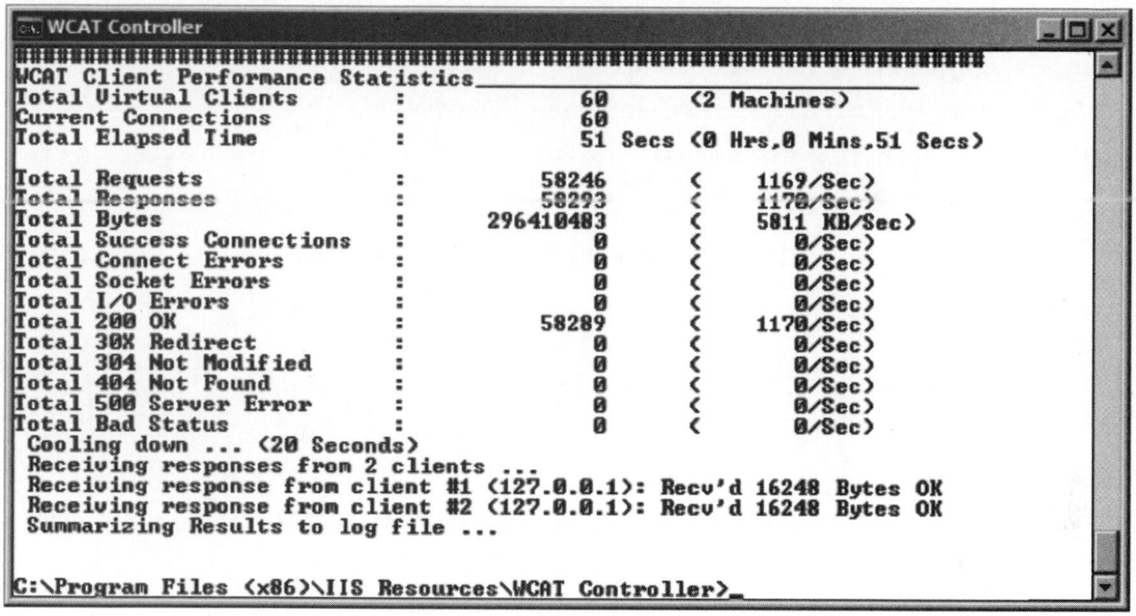

Figure 8–7. *Caching has significantly improved CMS performance.*

With one small IIS tweak, requests to localhost increased to approximately 1170 per second, with a data transfer rate of approximately 5811 KB per second. From a performance perspective, the CMS is handling 65 times more requests and data (for a total of 58,246 successful page deliveries) in the same time period as before.

Granted, it's not necessarily the case that every single page can be cached until it changes; search pages, lists of user comments, and other types of content must be capable of updating regularly. With that in mind, those pages that cannot be cached will have significantly more resources available as a result of caching the infrequently changing ones.

Configuration Considerations

Beyond the large-scale performance issues, there are additional considerations related to configuration that can crop up while deploying the CMS to a production (or even test) environment. Let's explore a few of them, why they might represent concerns, and how to quickly address them.

Enable Release Mode for Production

When a .NET application is running debug mode, the compiler will insert additional instructions into the assembly that facilitate instructional breakpoints. Debug compilation results in a larger end file size and somewhat reduced performance compared to release mode, which inserts no additional instructions (and therefore will not trigger breakpoints of any kind within the Visual Studio IDE).

Listing 8–3 shows the IL that the compiler generates for the Execute() method of the Business.Scripting class; note the IL instruction nop, which denotes "no operation." When the nop instruction is hit, execution will halt, and the address will be updated to point to the return address so that program execution may continue. This operation provides a reliable location for the debugger to halt execution and will occur before the opening and closing of scope blocks, when calling methods, when accessing properties, and similar events.

Listing 8–3. The Compiler Has Inserted nop Instructions as Placeholders

```
.method public hidebysig instance object
        Execute(string script) cil managed
{
  .param [0]
  .custom instance void [System.Core]System.Runtime.CompilerServices.DynamicAttribute::.ctor()
= ( 01 00 00 00 )
  // Code size       32 (0x20)
  .maxstack  3
  .locals init ([0] object CS$1$0000)
  IL_0000:  nop
  .try
  {
    IL_0001:  nop
    IL_0002:  ldarg.0
    IL_0003:  ldfld       class [Microsoft.Scripting]Microsoft.Scripting.Hosting.ScriptEngine
Business.Scripting.Scripting::_engine
    IL_0008:  ldarg.1
    IL_0009:  ldarg.0
    IL_000a:  ldfld       class [Microsoft.Scripting]Microsoft.Scripting.Hosting.ScriptScope
Business.Scripting.Scripting::_scope
    IL_000f:  callvirt    instance object
[Microsoft.Scripting]Microsoft.Scripting.Hosting.ScriptEngine::Execute(string,
class [Microsoft.Scripting]Microsoft.Scripting.Hosting.ScriptScope)
    IL_0014:  stloc.0
    IL_0015:  leave.s     IL_001d
  }  // end .try
  catch [mscorlib]System.Object
  {
    IL_0017:  pop
    IL_0018:  nop
    IL_0019:  ldnull
    IL_001a:  stloc.0
    IL_001b:  leave.s     IL_001d
  }  // end handler
  IL_001d:  nop
  IL_001e:  ldloc.0
  IL_001f:  ret
} // end of method Scripting::Execute
```

In general, you'll want to make sure you switch the compilation mode to release before deploying an application to production. It's surprising how many production applications I've run across that are still set to run in debug mode. Having debugging instructions in the final assembly is a definite hit to performance even in low-volume situations; wasting cycles on nop instructions certainly doesn't help when the traffic really starts to roll in.

■ **Note** The compiler will also produce additional optimizations beyond simply excluding nop instructions; the critical aspect of this is just understanding that the IL generated for debugging differs from release output.

Removing the Server, X-Powered-By, and X-AspNet-Version Headers

By default, IIS will append a variety of extra information to the HTTP response sent downstream to the client. This includes information related to the server, which version of .NET is running, and so on. Figure 8–8 shows a sample response from the CMS home page.

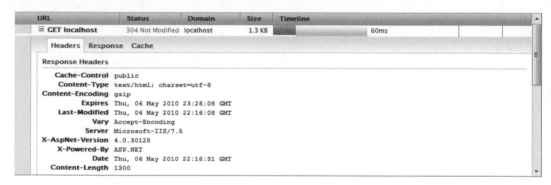

Figure 8–8. The HTTP response has additional information that could be attractive to hackers.

■ **Note** The information in Figure 8–8 (and throughout this section) was retrieved with the Firebug extension to Mozilla Firefox; this extension is available for free at http://getfirebug.com/. If you prefer a different browser (or simply to operate outside of a browser altogether), you can use an external web debugging tool such as Fiddler, available at http://www.fiddler2.com/fiddler2/.

Although removing this information isn't going to have a gigantic impact on application performance, it does help isolate the specifics of your server from prying eyes who may seek to exploit weaknesses in particular software configurations. There is a tiny performance improvement in the long term because each response will have less information; this information also doesn't directly benefit or affect the end user.

■ **Tip** In the next chapter, we'll be creating a system for friendly URLs that don't have file extensions or other system-specific materials in them. Although information such as the hidden VIEWSTATE field can still denote a site as running on IIS / .NET, every bit of security (or obscurity) helps.

Removing the X-Powered-By header is trivially simple; it resides under the HTTP Response Headers section of IIS 7.0 as shown in Figure 8–9. Simply right-click it and select Remove.

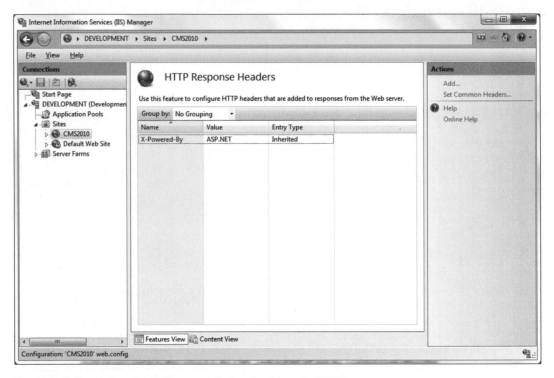

Figure 8–9. Removing the X-Powered-By header from the HTTP response

Removing the X-AspNet-Version header is also very simple; add the declaration from Listing 8–4 to the CMS web.config within the <system.web> section to do so.

Listing 8–4. Removing the X-AspNet-Version Header via the Application's web.config File

```
<httpRuntime enableVersionHeader="false" />
```

The only remaining task is to remove the Server header, which unfortunately requires the use of an HTTP module. The CMS includes one, called ObscureHeader; the code for this is shown in Listing 8–5.

Listing 8–5. Removing the Server Header via an HttpModule

```
using System;
using System.Web;

namespace ObscureHeader
{
    /// <summary>
    /// Removes the "Server" header from the HTTP response.
    /// If the CMS AppPool is running in Integrated Mode, this will run for all requests.
    /// </summary>
    public class RemoveServer : IHttpModule
    {
        public void Init(HttpApplication context)
        {
            context.PreSendRequestHeaders += RemoveServerFromHeaders;
        }

        private void RemoveServerFromHeaders(object sender, EventArgs e)
        {
            // strip the "Server" header from the current Response
            HttpContext.Current.Response.Headers.Remove("Server");
        }

        public void Dispose()
        {
            // no code necessary
        }
    }
}
```

Once registered in the <modules> section of <system.webServer> in the web.config file, as shown in Listing 8–6, this module will strip the final header from the HTTP response.

Listing 8–6. Registering the HttpModule for the CMS

```
<system.webServer>
    <modules runAllManagedModulesForAllRequests="true">
        <add name="RemoveServer" type="ObscureHeader.RemoveServer" />
    </modules>
    ...
</system.webServer>
```

If we browse to the application now, we should see significantly cleaner HTTP headers that don't display as much identifying information about the application environment to the client. Figure 8–10 shows this output.

Figure 8–10. The final, cleaned HTTP response headers

Debugging Concepts

Debuggers are a powerful weapon in the developer's arsenal. They allow dynamic analysis of an application, which refers in part to the ability to take control of the application execution. They also enable the inspection and modification of memory, the creation of breakpoints to halt the application and examine the current status, and so on. Debuggers form the backbone of legitimate development in addition to facilitating the discovery and exploitation of software flaws and vulnerabilities.

There are several different ways to divide debuggers into categories: two useful ones are *white-box* vs. *black-box* debuggers and *user-mode* vs. *kernel-mode* debuggers. We will look at each division and what defines it and then examine how .NET handles debugging in general.

White-Box vs. Black-Box Debuggers

A *white-box debugger* such as the one built into Visual Studio 2010 will have access to the source code to the application itself, and we as developers are aware of the implementation of the application at this level. The debugger therefore will have a high degree of information (and in the case of the .NET Framework, metadata) about the code itself and the environment in which it is running. White-box debuggers are common in integrated development environments and are typically fairly sophisticated because of how extensively they are wired into the IDE; for example, Visual Studio 2010's debugger actually allows you to share breakpoints with a developer on a separate machine, enabling a different developer to reproduce error conditions without being at your machine or screen sharing.

■ **Tip** This ability to share breakpoints is a very useful new feature of Visual Studio 2010, covered later in this chapter in the "Collaborative Debugging" section.

By contrast, *black-box debuggers* are attached to running processes but do not have the actual source code to the application available. This is typically the case when debugging third-party code or while attempting to reverse engineer or exploit some piece of software. The black-box debugger still provides many of the features we've discussed thus far, although more experimentation and time is typically involved in the debugging effort because we would not have insight into the implementation of the application.

In our day-to-day development, we'll typically rely primarily on white-box debuggers, although it should be noted that the tools used in this chapter can also operate in a black-box fashion on code we did not implement ourselves.

User Mode vs. Kernel Mode

An important subdivision in debugger types is whether it is operating in user mode or kernel mode. For example, suppose we spin up an ASP .NET worker process and attach a debugger instance to it. The debugger and the worker process are both operating in *user mode*, which is a fairly protected mode; applications aren't capable of accessing hardware and memory directly. Code executing in this mode is required to use the hooks provided by operating system APIs to access resources.

Kernel mode is a much lower-level of operation and debugging; this is the realm in which device drivers and other software that require machine-level access to the CPU and memory generally operate (although they're not specifically required to). Code executing in kernel mode is given the highest level of implicit trust and is capable of executing CPU instructions directly as well as referencing any memory address in the system. Although unhandled exceptions in code running in user mode generally result in the crash of the application, unhandled exceptions at the kernel mode level trigger a crash in the system itself.

■ **Tip** The `HTTP.sys` discussion earlier in the chapter noted that it was best to combine user- and kernel-mode caching because of the higher-level features that user mode provides compared to kernel-mode's low-level system access.

The x86 architecture maps these modes to a series of *rings*. Kernel mode is *ring 0*, where user mode is *ring 3*. This is a protection and isolation concept that exists to restrict levels of access to low-level resources and data; in this case, ring 0 is the lowest and most unrestricted level, while ring 3 is the highest level with the least "bare-metal" control of the hardware. Unless you're writing or debugging this type of software on a regular basis, you probably won't spend much (if any) time at this level.

■ **Tip** You can find more information about the x86 architecture as it pertains to execution modes in the Intel Architecture Software Developer's Manual at `http://download.intel.com/design/PentiumII/manuals/24319202.pdf`. Section 4.5, "Privilege Levels," addresses the specifics of the ring hierarchy (including the purposes of the remaining rings).

Debugging in Visual Studio 2010 doesn't require you to become intimately familiar with concepts such as protection rings to be productive, but understanding some of the low-level details of the debugger and the system architecture will help clarify what's happening when things go wrong.

Historical Debugging via IntelliTrace

Normally, debugging via breakpoints is a somewhat one-way operation. By that I mean we have access to the application state as it currently exists, and we can examine the value that different variables contain at the moment the breakpoint was triggered. What has been lacking thus far is a convenient way to unroll the application execution and see the steps (in their state at an arbitrary time) that led us to the breakpoint condition.

One solution is to simply write what could quickly become excessive logging code, tracking and recording the information contained in memory locations. After executing the program, you could sift through those records in the hopes of finding what you're looking for. It's not a terribly efficient use of time, and it also presumes that the necessary data will be captured properly. Alternatively, you could set a breakpoint early in the application and single-step through to a potential trouble spot, taking note of potentially relevant information along the way.

I'm sure you could think of other methods that would be better or worse, depending on the nature of the application, but it's safe to say that these options are fairly tedious on anything beyond a trivial application; if a better way exists, it makes sense to utilize it. Visual Studio 2010 introduces IntelliTrace historical debugging, literally allowing us to step backward through the execution and unwind the state to a previous point.

For example, suppose that while viewing a CMS page you notice that a certain embeddable control is missing. The issue could exist in a number of places: perhaps the database record for that content is incorrect. It's possible that the control threw an exception and was simply not loaded. Having the capability to set a breakpoint and work backward is extraordinarily powerful, allowing developers to zero in on the problem far more quickly than was previously possible.

Because the additional debugging instructions are a serious knock to performance, the full features are disabled by default in the IDE; to access them, go to Tools ➤ Options ➤ IntelliTrace and click the "IntelliTrace events and call information" radio button (Figure 8–11 shows this setting). Note that the IDE has stated that tracking this type of information can degrade performance; bear this in mind as you develop further applications, because you may believe something is performing poorer than it really would in a release environment.

Once this setting has been applied, set a breakpoint, and start the application. When the breakpoint is hit, you will notice additional choices next to the red circle to the left side of the current line of code that facilitate navigation through the application, as shown in Figure 8–12.

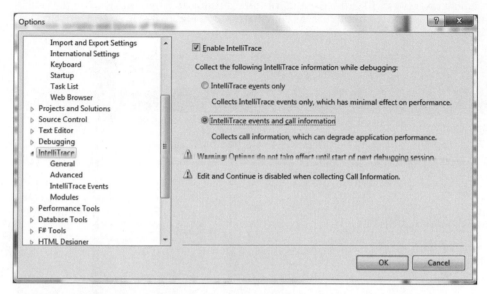

Figure 8–11. Enabling IntelliTrace in the IDE

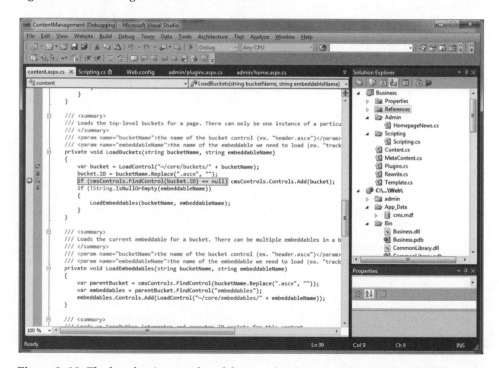

Figure 8–12. The breakpoint now has debug navigation operations to the left of the code.

Clicking the double up arrows will cause the application execution to move backward to the last valid event that IntelliTrace was able to capture, as demonstrated in Figure 8–13. The current line is highlighted in a lighter shade of maroon than the typical breakpoint.

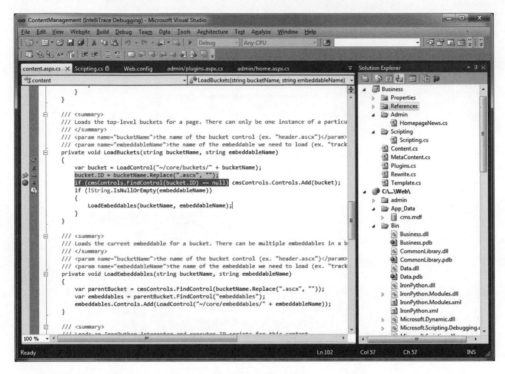

Figure 8–13. *Moving backward through the application execution*

If you select Debug ➤ IntelliTrace ➤ IntelliTrace Calls, a window will open that displays each of the calls made thus far in the application. This window is demonstrated in Figure 8–14. Key IntelliTrace calls are recorded within, and within those calls are additional operations related to that call and its scope.

Clicking any of the calls in this window expands it; the application state will automatically revert to that point in the execution history. Figure 8–15 shows the Page_Load() method as it was during this debugging session.

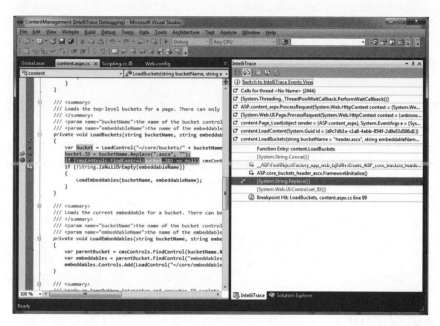

Figure 8–14. *The IntelliTrace calls view allows navigation through the application execution history.*

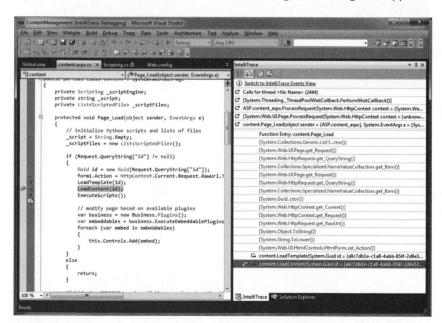

Figure 8–15. *Exploring the Page_Load() method as it was executed during this session*

That's the core of IntelliTrace debugging in Visual Studio 2010. Having the capacity to unwind the application is a tremendous boon to developers; I'm sure many can sympathize with the horror stories of hard-to-track bugs that occur only in specific conditions when the moon is just right. With the IntelliTrace information recorded, you can highlight the specific moment things went off the rails and have a better shot of not only identifying the cause but doing so in a fraction of the time compared to the traditional methods.

■ **Note** The previous iteration of the CMS had a delightful situation where IntelliTrace debugging would've been a gigantic help. When certain conditions occurred, the CMS would "lose" the site ID that helped to map content between friendly URLs and the site tree; as the object was considered to have been updated, this change was immediately stored to Memcached and dutifully retrieved, causing exceptions to be thrown every time users requested that page. Pinning the problem down involved a trek across multiple libraries with a range of conditional breakpoints set, trying to find the exact moment things went wrong. Being able to unwind from some known points would've saved a ridiculous number of hours fixing what turned out to be a simple bug that appeared only intermittently.

Collaborative Debugging

Microsoft identified room for improvement with regard to the debugging processes executed by most development teams: debugging has typically been a very solo venture—a single process debugged on a single machine by a single user only. Collaborative debugging, introduced in Visual Studio 2010, seeks to alleviate that problem.

Importing and Exporting Breakpoints

Collaborative debugging is expressed primarily through breakpoint sharing in Visual Studio 2010, and it is extremely simple to perform. First, set a breakpoint on a line; in the case of Figure 8–16, we've set it on the line that creates a new list of `ScriptedFile` objects for the `content.aspx.cs` page. For the purposes of this discussion, we'll assume there's some bug here that can be demonstrated and reproduced.

Once the breakpoint is set, right-click the line in question, and select Breakpoint ➤ Export, as shown in Figure 8–16. This will allow you to save the breakpoint information for import on another environment.

Figure 8–16. *Exporting a breakpoint*

The actual breakpoint file is simply XML that defines the code file and specific location of the breakpoint. Listing 8–7 shows the XML for the breakpoint we set on the `ScriptedFile` list assignment line; I have highlighted specific information for this condition.

Listing 8–7. *The Contents of a Typical Breakpoint XML File*

```xml
<?xml version="1.0" encoding="utf-8"?>
<BreakpointCollection xmlns:xsi="http://www.w3.org/2001/XMLSchema-instance"
xmlns:xsd="http://www.w3.org/2001/XMLSchema">
  <Breakpoints>
    <Breakpoint>
      <Version>15</Version>
      <IsEnabled>1</IsEnabled>
      <IsVisible>1</IsVisible>
      <IsEmulated>0</IsEmulated>
      <IsCondition>0</IsCondition>
      <ConditionType>WhenTrue</ConditionType>
      <LocationType>SourceLocation</LocationType>
      <TextPosition>
        <Version>4</Version>
        <FileName>.\Web\content.aspx.cs</FileName>
        <startLine>28</startLine>
        <StartColumn>8</StartColumn>
        <EndLine>28</EndLine>
        <EndColumn>48</EndColumn>
        <MarkerId>0</MarkerId>
```

```xml
            <IsLineBased>0</IsLineBased>
            <IsDocumentPathNotFound>0</IsDocumentPathNotFound>
            <ShouldUpdateTextSpan>1</ShouldUpdateTextSpan>
            <Checksum>
                <Version>1</Version>
                <Algorithm>00000000-0000-0000-0000-000000000000</Algorithm>
                <ByteCount>0</ByteCount>
                <Bytes />
            </Checksum>
        </TextPosition>
        <NamedLocationText>content.Page_Load(object sender, EventArgs e)</NamedLocationText>
        <NamedLocationLine>4</NamedLocationLine>
        <NamedLocationColumn>0</NamedLocationColumn>
        <HitCountType>NoHitCount</HitCountType>
        <HitCountTarget>1</HitCountTarget>
        <Language>3f5162f8-07c6-11d3-9053-00c04fa302a1</Language>
        <IsMapped>0</IsMapped>
        <BreakpointType>PendingBreakpoint</BreakpointType>
        <AddressLocation>
            <Version>0</Version>
            <MarkerId>0</MarkerId>
            <FunctionLine>0</FunctionLine>
            <FunctionColumn>0</FunctionColumn>
            <Language>00000000-0000-0000-0000-000000000000</Language>
        </AddressLocation>
        <DataCount>4</DataCount>
        <IsTracepointActive>0</IsTracepointActive>
        <IsBreakWhenHit>1</IsBreakWhenHit>
        <IsRunMacroWhenHit>0</IsRunMacroWhenHit>
        <UseChecksum>1</UseChecksum>
        <Labels />
        <RequestRemapped>0</RequestRemapped>
        <parentIndex>-1</parentIndex>
    </Breakpoint>
  </Breakpoints>
</BreakpointCollection>
```

In a separate environment, all that is required is for the developer to open the Breakpoints window and import the file into the IDE. Figure 8–17 demonstrates this; the import option is the red circle with the arrow on its top left quadrant (sixth from the left).

■ **Tip** You can also bring up the Breakpoints window by pressing Ctrl+Alt+B.

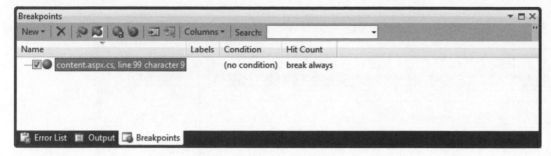

Figure 8–17. Importing a breakpoint onto it automatically in the environment.

Coupled with DataTip pinning and annotation, which we'll cover next, this permits developers to set breakpoints, note potentially troublesome areas of code, and then send that information for direct import into another environment by a different developer.

DataTip Pinning and Annotation

Sometimes during the course of debugging (or perhaps code reviews) we encounter variable names, assignments, or conditions that simply don't convey their intention clearly. Developers rely on comments to help explain tricky code segments or to clarify the business logic that goes into a specific set of operations. This is certainly a functional way to do it, but the code can quickly become cluttered if comments are the sole method of communication and conversation between developers.

Visual Studio 2010 introduces the concept of pinning DataTips to the code window, as well as annotating them. Consider Figure 8–18; here we have a breakpoint set on a particular line that for one reason or another isn't clear to us in terms of what's happening. If the mouse is hovered over the _scriptFiles variable, the DataTip we're used to seeing will appear, but it will have a pin icon to the right side. If that pin is clicked, the DataTip will attach itself to the code window for examination and annotation, as shown in the figure.

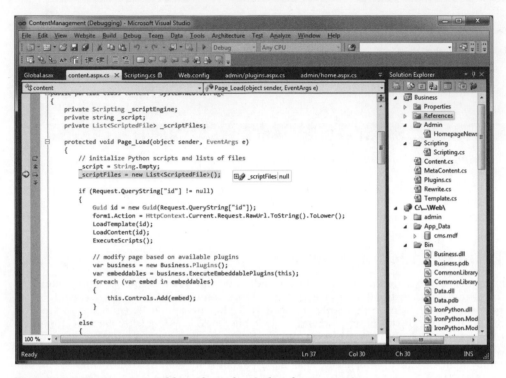

Figure 8–18. *Pinning a variable to the code window for annotation*

When the DataTip is pinned to the window, there will be a small control box to the right side of the tip itself when the mouse hovers over it. At the bottom of the box is an "Expand to see comments" option. Clicking this opens a small text box below the tip that holds the annotations, as shown in Figure 8–19.

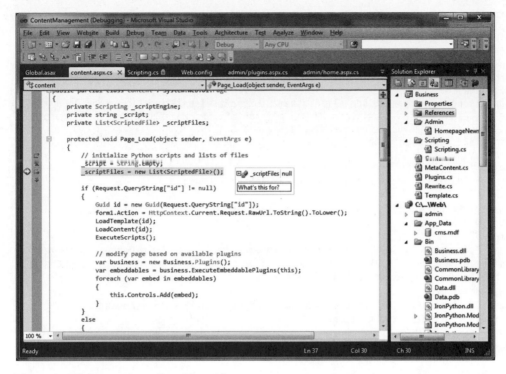

Figure 8–19. *Annotating a DataTip with comments or questions*

DataTip annotations can also be exported in a similar fashion to breakpoints. Select Debug ➤ Export DataTips to save the tips as an XML file. Listing 8–8 displays a sample DataTip file; I have again highlighted some of the information for the sake of clarity.

Listing 8–8. *An Exported DataTip XML File*

```
<SOAP-ENV:Envelope xmlns:xsi="http://www.w3.org/2001/XMLSchema-instance"
xmlns:xsd="http://www.w3.org/2001/XMLSchema" xmlns:SOAP-
ENC="http://schemas.xmlsoap.org/soap/encoding/" xmlns:SOAP-
ENV="http://schemas.xmlsoap.org/soap/envelope/"
xmlns:clr="http://schemas.microsoft.com/soap/encoding/clr/1.0" SOAP-
ENV:encodingStyle="http://schemas.xmlsoap.org/soap/encoding/">
<SOAP-ENV:Body>
<a1:PersistableTipCollection id="ref-1"
xmlns:a1="http://schemas.microsoft.com/clr/nsassem/Microsoft.VisualStudio.Debugger.DebuggerToo
lWindows.DataTips.PinnableTips.Persistence/VsDebugPresentationPackage%2C%20Version%3D10.0.0.0%
2C%20Culture%3Dneutral%2C%20PublicKeyToken%3Db03f5f7f11d50a3a">
<Tips href="#ref-3"/>
</a1:PersistableTipCollection>
<SOAP-ENC:Array id="ref-3" SOAP-ENC:arrayType="xsd:anyType[1]">
<item href="#ref-4"/>
</SOAP-ENC:Array>
```

```
<a3:PinnedTip id="ref-4"
xmlns:a3="http://schemas.microsoft.com/clr/nsassem/Microsoft.VisualStudio.Debugger.DebuggerToo
lWindows.DataTips.PinnableTips.UI/VsDebugPresentationPackage%2C%20Version%3D10.0.0.0%2C%20Cult
ure%3Dneutral%2C%20PublicKeyToken%3Db03f5f7f11d50a3a">
<unopenedState href="#ref-5"/>
<innerTip href="#ref-6"/>
</a3:PinnedTip>
<a1:UnopenedTipData id="ref-5"
xmlns:a1="http://schemas.microsoft.com/clr/nsassem/Microsoft.VisualStudio.Debugger.DebuggerToo
lWindows.DataTips.PinnableTips.Persistence/VsDebugPresentationPackage%2C%20Version%3D10.0.0.0%
2C%20Culture%3Dneutral%2C%20PublicKeyToken%3Db03f5f7f11d50a3a">
<PinnedPosition>782</PinnedPosition>
<Length>0</Length>
<XOffset>361</XOffset>
<RelativeFileName id="ref-7">Web\content.aspx.cs</RelativeFileName>
<AbsoluteFileName id="ref-
8">C:\Work\cms_2010\trunk\ContentManagement\Web\content.aspx.cs</AbsoluteFileName>
</a1:UnopenedTipData>
<a3:Tip id="ref-6"
xmlns:a3="http://schemas.microsoft.com/clr/nsassem/Microsoft.VisualStudio.Debugger.DebuggerToo
lWindows.DataTips.PinnableTips.UI/VsDebugPresentationPackage%2C%20Version%3D10.0.0.0%2C%20Cult
ure%3Dneutral%2C%20PublicKeyToken%3Db03f5f7f11d50a3a">
<identity.Moniker id="ref-
9">C:\Work\cms_2010\trunk\ContentManagement\Web\content.aspx.cs</identity.Moniker>
<identity.Position>790</identity.Position>
<watchItemCount>1</watchItemCount>
<watchItem0 id="ref-10">_scriptFiles</watchItem0>
<comments id="ref-11">What&#39;s this for?</comments>
<showingComments>true</showingComments>
<uniqueIdentity id="ref-12">{a160d366-698f-41af-9e4e-f7cd50027a23}</uniqueIdentity>
</a3:Tip>
</SOAP-ENV:Body>
</SOAP-ENV:Envelope>
```

■ **Note** Pinned DataTips are visible only while the application is being debugged. They will disappear when not debugging and reflect the value of the variable based on the last time (if any) it was modified.

Summary

The performance of a system has a very real set of implications for user behavior and potentially revenue, depending on the application of that system. As such, having firm data as well as a response plan for troublesome situations is critical to the success of our system. We covered the key terms of performance and how they related to the CMS, explored WCAT and the establishment of baseline metrics, cleaned the HTTP responses delivered to the client, and looked at ways that Visual Studio 2010 improves the debugging experience to ease the identification and resolution of problems when they do occur. As we move into the final chapter, we'll look beyond metrics and into the realm of search engine optimization.

■ ■ ■

## CHAPTER 9

Search Engine Optimization and Accessibility

"Google only loves you when everyone else loves you first."

—Wendy Piersall

In this chapter, we'll look at the concepts behind search engine optimization and how they apply to a content management system. We will touch on some usability concepts that will make your site more accessible to disabled users. We'll also discuss ways to facilitate your users arriving at URLs that are memorable, friendly, and easily shared; this concept is as useful to a search engine as it is to a human user. Although we'll discuss the broader concepts of SEO first, we will spend the majority of our time developing a system for handling friendlier URLs, because this requires a greater amount of specific coding to implement.

■ **Note** The search engine ecosystem is complex, and there are entire cottage industries built around helping people improve their site rankings; some are legitimate, and some are pure snake oil of the worst kind. This chapter does not aim to perform the task of SEO analysis because each site and organization's needs are unique and distinct. The purpose is to introduce some key concepts, put SEO into context for developer concerns, and show how to make the CMS a bit more user-friendly than it would be otherwise.

An Introduction to Search Engine Optimization

Engaging in search engine optimization is to attempt to increase the visibility of and traffic to a particular site by improving the rank associated with it by a given search engine. In plain English, you want people to frequently visit the site you worked so hard on, and a component of that desired success is the need for search engines to rank you as not only of high quality but as high relevance to the topics being investigated by users.

At a high level, a search engine performs the tasks that used to be handled manually by systems administrators. As new web servers came online in the early 1990s, public lists were updated to reflect new web presences and help those early adopters find one another. It's not hard to imagine how this sort of tracking becomes impossible, especially given the history of the Internet and how quickly it exploded into the massive ecosystem that it has become today. Search engines began to pop up in the mid-90s, indexing pages and helping to identify content that existed on the Web. This is something of an oversimplification of the history; search engines are now backed by complex algorithms that determine the relevance (or rank) of content, weighing one piece of content against many others to help users find the most appropriate information based on their search criteria.

With that in mind, how does a search engine go about making these decisions? What makes page A stand out from the crowd of pages B, C, and D? It used to be the case that engines relied heavily on HTML <meta> tags (such as the description and keyword values) to make decisions about what was on a page and whether it was relevant to a given search; this evolved somewhat into an analysis of *keyword density* within a page. These proved to be heavily flawed implementations because each of these factors are easily manipulated by anyone with access to the markup of a page. I could easily hide the words *auto loan* throughout the markup of a page that was about donating money to charity; my page may not have anything to do with auto loans, but users searching for those keywords would theoretically be more likely to arrive at my page anyway.

■ **Note** Keyword density refers to the number of times a particular word or phrase appears within a piece of content.

Science or Dark Art?

Depending on which side of the fence you sit on, search engine optimization could be one or the other. In reality, it's both. Part of the vagueness arises because there is no singular search engine (even though Google and Yahoo are fairly synonymous with Internet searches at this point, and Bing is making headway), and the specific algorithms that go into the sorting and ranking of pages are essentially trade secrets for each individual company. Without a standard, it can be difficult to precisely anticipate the expectations of individual engines; it's also the reason why a search for a term in Google will return something potentially very different than Yahoo, or than Bing, and so on.

The fun doesn't stop there, however. It's fairly common among the search engine heavyweights to allow users to create accounts for themselves that uniquely identify them within the particular site; as users search and browse content, the search engine is able to better offer personalized results.

Not only are you contending with a given search engine's algorithms, you also have to consider the individual search history and needs of particular users and how that impacts their specific search results. It can all seem fairly daunting; Bruce Clay, a well-known SEO consultant and speaker, famously declared in 1998 that "ranking is dead" because of personalized user search results.

General Guidelines

It may seem like SEO is something of a moving target. Search engine manufacturers change their algorithms frequently, for reasons ranging from staying current to reducing the ability of malicious parties to game their systems and influence results in unintended ways. Although the exact algorithms and processes are proprietary, SEO can (for our purposes) be boiled down to a few key points:

- Clean, clear markup is easier to parse and interpret.

- Sites that have been around for a while are regarded with a somewhat higher level of trust.

- Although titles and meta tags are a bit less important these days, their relation is considered helpful.

- JavaScript should enhance the site features, but a site should not rely on it for functionality.

- Provide alt text for images to aid users who are disabled.

- Choose color schemes that permit color-deficient users to navigate and read comfortably.

- Offer user-friendly URLs that make use of relevant keywords.

- Handle redirects (permanent versus temporary) appropriately.

Not all of this can be influenced by good coding practices, but what can be influenced is fairly easy to do. In essence, the search engines are simply looking for clean, well-organized web sites that make use of best practices rather than kludges and trickery.

The bullet points regarding alt text and color schemes are listed with SEO but serve what are arguably more accurately described as usability purposes. There is a direct correlation to SEO, however, because search engines place heavy emphasis on both the number of inbound links to your site from other web presences, as well as the number of users who click through to your site from search engine results. A site that is usable to a wide audience in addition to offering quality content is one that will be ranked favorably compared to inaccessible ones.

■ **Note** Google offers an excellent primer in SEO topics and tips it considers most helpful to developers at http://www.google.com/webmasters/docs/search-engine-optimization-starter-guide.pdf.

Establishing Clear Markup

If browsers do one thing very well, it's managing to competently and adequately render the massive amounts of *tag soup* on the Internet today. Tag soup refers to the tangled mess of HTML that results from sloppy web design; browsers may encounter malformed tags, tags that are nested improperly, and unescaped characters. Unfortunately, although browsers *can* render the nest of vipers that is a semantically poor page, search engines don't look upon the practice quite so kindly.

For example, the markup in Listing 9–1 is incorrect; the tags are nested improperly. In semantically valid HTML, tags can be thought of as a stack (a "last in, first out" data structure): when you push tags onto the stack by opening them, they must be popped off in reverse order.

Listing 9–1. Semantically Incorrect HTML

```
<p>
   <div>
      <strong><em>This</strong></em> is some markup. It's fun!
   </p>
</div>
```

This is an excellent example of tag soup. Although the application of CSS style attributes to this will likely result in some interesting display characteristics, the browser *will* dutifully render it. Bearing in mind that the tags could be viewed as a stack, let's clean the markup appropriately (see Listing 9–2).

Listing 9–2. Semantically Valid HTML

```
<div>
   <p>
      <strong><em>This</em></strong> is some markup. It&apos;s fun!
   </p>
</div>
```

Note the operations present in Listing 9–2; the `<div>` is opened, then the `<p>`, then the `<strong>`, and finally the `<em>`. They are then closed in reverse order; first the `<em>`, then the `<strong>`, then the `<p>`, and finally the `<div>`. We have also escaped the apostrophe using the `&apos;` value, which the browser will interpret as an apostrophe and insert it accordingly. The motivation for escaping characters is simply that certain character elements are sensitive for security or encoding purposes; encoding them ensures that the behavior of the page is consistent, secure, and as expected.

A variety of standards exist that enforce different levels of structural and semantic requirements, as well as validators that examine the markup of a page and identify problems based on the standard being tested against. The World Wide Web Consortium (W3C) is the authoring body of these standards and also provides a very useful validator for both HTML and CSS, available at `http://validator.w3.org`.

HTML Metadata the .NET 4 Way

Although page titles and metadata used to be regarded highly in terms of search engine optimization, they have fallen out of favor in recent years because of abuse. It was an all-too-common practice to stuff these fields with keywords that were not necessarily related to the content in an attempt to drive traffic from unrelated searches to a particular piece of content.

They do still have a place in the search engine world in search engine results pages (SERPs). For example, use Google to do a search on the word *Target*. In the results, the web site for Target.com should be the first link available. Note the information for this link as displayed in Figure 9–1.

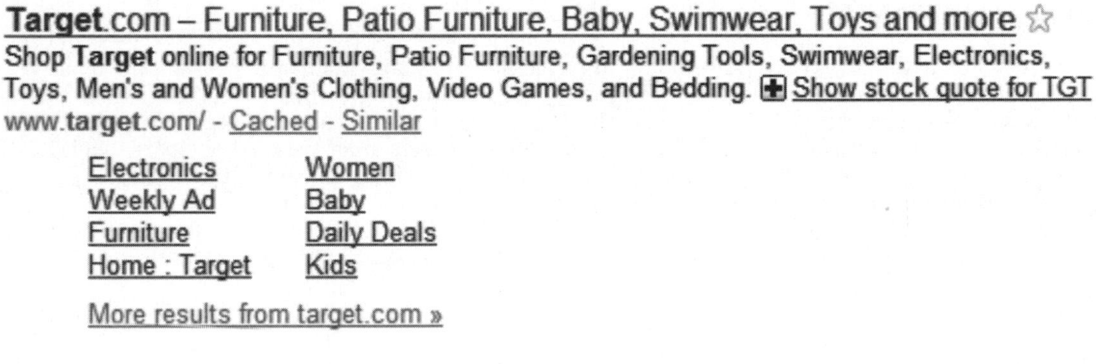

Figure 9–1. The SERP information for Target's company web site

If you view the source to the http://www.target.com page, you should see the information in Listing 9–3 toward the top. Note the usage of the <title> tag to establish the link title and the <meta name="description"> tag to create the text immediately below the link title; the <meta name="keywords"> tag defines potential areas of interest that the site supplies but isn't visibly used in the SERPs.

Listing 9–3. The http://www.target.com Title and Metadata Information

```
<title>Target.com - Furniture, Patio Furniture, Baby, Swimwear, Toys and more</title>

<meta name="description" content="Shop Target online for Furniture, Patio Furniture, Gardening
Tools, Swimwear, Electronics, Toys, Men's and Women's Clothing, Video Games, and Bedding.
Expect More. Pay less." />

<meta name="keywords" content="patio furniture, furniture, gardening tools, swimwear, baby,
electronics, toys, bedding, shoes, home décor, sporting goods, shop online" />
```

In previous iterations of .NET, you had to create the meta tags manually, meaning you had to structure the markup accordingly and insert them into the Page object before being rendered to the client. Microsoft now provides convenience methods for performing this task in the form of the Page.MetaKeywords() and Page.MetaDescription() methods. Listing 9–4 demonstrates how we would add the meta tags to the Target home page in .NET 4.

Listing 9–4. Setting the Page Keywords and Description

```
protected void Page_Load(object sender, EventArgs e)
{
    Page.MetaDescription = "Shop Target online for Furniture, Patio Furniture, Gardening Tools,
Swimwear, Electronics, Toys, Men's and Women's Clothing, Video Games, and Bedding.  Expect
More. Pay less.";

    Page.MetaKeywords = "patio furniture, furniture, gardening tools, swimwear, baby,
electronics, toys, bedding, shoes, home décor, sporting goods, shop online";
}
```

Graceful JavaScript Degradation

Search engines used to have a devil of a time handling pages that were heavy JavaScript users; to a degree, this is still true. Developers are encouraged to use JavaScript on noncritical parts of pages to enhance the experience rather than create it.

Examine Listing 9–5; in it, we've chosen to create navigation for our site that is heavily reliant on JavaScript for functionality.

■ **Note** The typical application of JavaScript for navigation is usually to aid in drop-down animations and similar features; demonstrating that fully would require additional CSS and JavaScript that would clutter the conversation. With that said, I will testify that I have actually seen this done in a production site, so perhaps it's worth demonstrating if only as a cautionary tale of woe.

Listing 9–5. JavaScript-Based Navigation

```
<ul id="navigation">
    <li><a href="#" onclick="window.location='http://mysite.com/home';">Home</a></li>
    <li><a href="#" onclick="window.location='http://mysite.com/services';">Services</a></li>
    <!-- additional pages… -->
</ul>
```

In Listing 9–5, the JavaScript *makes* the experience; without it, the user is simply not able to navigate the site in any fashion. If a user without JavaScript enabled (or available in their browser of choice) can't navigate the site, it's safe to assume that a search engine won't be able to either, and the results of your efforts will be greatly diminished.

A quick way to get a sense of how a search engine will browse your page is to run it through a text-based browser such as Lynx. This has the added benefit of showing you how your page will look to users that are disabled; the output of a text-based browser is highly comparable to screen readers as well as search engines. There is a free service available at http://cgi.w3.org/cgi-bin/html2txt that will convert a given page to its text-based equivalency. Figure 9–2 shows the text-browser output of the Best Buy home page.

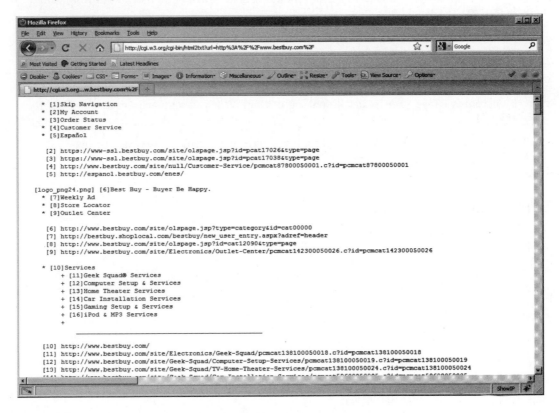

Figure 9–2. The text rendering of the Best Buy home page

Providing alt Text for Images

This point is more of an accessibility issue than a search engine one, but it's something that validators will flag as important (and it is). Images on a web page should possess alt text attributes for two reasons:

- First, if an image fails to load, the text will be present in its place.

- Second, users with text-based browsers will by definition not see any of the images on your page (instead seeing the alt text, if present).

Also, although the focus is on accessibility for disabled users, search engines *do* look at alt text to help identify what is contained in a particular image.

Listing 9–6 shows the markup for an image that has an alt attribute applied. If for some reason the browser cannot retrieve the image resource or the user is on a text-based browser, the words "Login error" will appear in place of the image; depending on the image and what its relation to the content is, this can be an absolutely critical step for users of your site.

Listing 9–6. Supplying alt Text for Images

```
<div id="loginFailed">
    <img src="error.png" alt="Login error" />
    <p>Your login credentials could not be authenticated. Please try again.</p>
</div>
```

■ **Note** The Google webmaster blog provides a video on alt text, providing alt keywords, and further accessibility issues at http://googlewebmastercentral.blogspot.com/2007/12/using-alt-attributes-smartly.html.

Color Scheme Sensitivity

Developing an effective color scheme that accommodates the various color deficiencies users may possess is a unique challenge to be tackled on a site-by-site basis. Validators will sometimes flag color issues (such as using a light gray color for both the foreground and background in a style sheet) but in general, it's best to rely on tools designed to identify and aid in determining color issues specifically.

■ **Tip** Adobe has a great online tool for generating color schemes called Kuler; it's available for free from http://kuler.adobe.com/. There are already a great deal of community-submitted color schemes, and generating color schemes of your own is trivial. When designing the color content of your sites, it's an excellent idea to combine the color output of Kuler schemes with the results of the Color Contrast Comparison tool described next.

One such tool for determining the accessibility of a set of colors is Joseph Dolson's Color Contrast Comparison site, available at http://www.joedolson.com/color-contrast-compare.php. You can enter two hexadecimal color codes, and the site will evaluate them against Web Content Accessibility Guideline (WCAG) standards and give a pass/fail return value.

In Figure 9–3, I have used the tool to evaluate the contrast between two fairly close shades of red. The site has indicated that they fail the WCAG accessibility test as the level of contrast between the two colors is insufficient for easy readability. I chose the two variants of red, #FF0000 and #FF6666, because they (or some similar combination) appear quite frequently in so-called Web 2.0 dialog boxes, particularly in the form of confirmation, warning, and error boxes. Noting that color selection can play a huge role in site usability is important to hammer home and often overlooked.

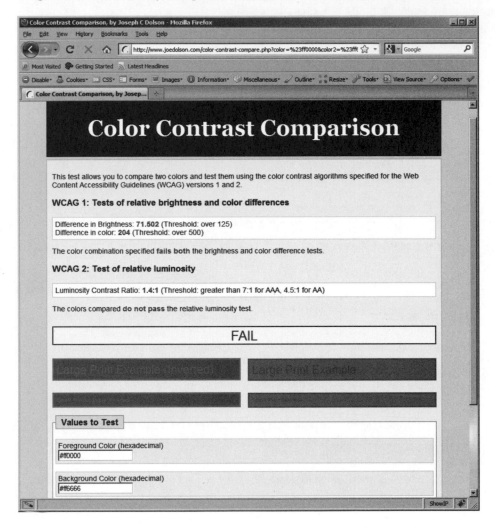

Figure 9–3. Joseph Dolson's color contrast evaluator

Friendly URLs

One thing that dynamic sites are frequently not good at is the implementation of URLs in a fashion that gels with the expectations of users. It's easy as a developer to think in terms of GUIDs or other system details (such as "the home page lives at contentID 18003214"); this has context and purpose that is obvious to someone who understands the underlying code. To search engines (and users), this is meaningless. When designing a system that is intended to (or potentially might) face the generic public, it's wise to hide these sorts of low-level system implementation details that provide nothing of value to the user. It's more meaningful and comfortable to have a URL like /about-us/.

In addition to the usage benefits, search engines themselves have evolved over the years. Search engines used to take issue with dynamic URLs (such as those provided by a CMS). For example, to a search engine, the following URLs are all unique and distinct:

- `/content.aspx?id=5730299`

- `/content.aspx?page=about-us`

- `/content/about-us/`

- `/about-us/`

For various reasons, it makes sense to have /about-us/ be the desired (and indexed) location so that users have the capacity to arrive from the others if necessary but directed to the *canonical link* immediately. Search engines should index just the canonical link, ensuring that most users arrive via the route you prefer.

■ **Tip** Canonical links were created by Google as a way to indicate to the search engine which URL a given page preferred to have indexed as the true location. It's a hint to the search engine, not a directive; Google seems to respect it consistently in my experience, and other major search providers have picked up on it and are respecting it in their own results. You can find more information at `http://googlewebmastercentral.blogspot.com/2009/02/specify-your-canonical.html`.

Data Requirements for Friendly URLs

IIS7 now has an optional add-on for URL rewriting, mapping one URL to another. It requires more maintenance than we can really expect for the potential growth that a CMS contains; it's quite easy to balloon up in content very quickly, and no one wants to maintain this sort of list by hand. As such, we will design a custom solution that will allow us to map URLs from an ugly, system-usable form to something that users and search engines prefer; our solution will parse incoming HTTP requests directed to the application using our idealized URLs and (behind the scenes) serve markup to the client that has been rendered by the content.aspx page.

Why Not Use the Microsoft.Web.Administration Classes?

You *can* modify the URL rewrite module configuration using the `Microsoft.Web.Administration` classes, but this doesn't currently support any form of database storage; the rewrite mappings are all stored in configuration files on disk within the site itself. Writing to the configuration files (which must be done when a URL is added, deleted, or updated) results in an application restart, which is not desirable in a production environment.

There are also hosting considerations in that scenario; sites hosted behind a load-balancer will have to either use a shared configuration method or roll the changes across each box. Either way, the application restart will impact every box in the environment at the same time, resulting in your site effectively being "down" as far as users are concerned.

I have worked on a system that supported more than 100 distinct sites with more than 100,000 pages within, all situated behind a load balancer on 3 Windows Server machines; it's very detrimental to performance to write to the configuration files in this type of scenario, whereas database access is cheap by comparison. For smaller systems or systems that won't add or update URLs frequently, the `Microsoft.Web.Administration` classes provide an excellent way to accomplish the same result without investing time in developing a lot of code by hand.

The data requirements for a friendly URL are much simpler than the actual code that drives them, so we'll begin there. What exactly do we need to have for a friendly URL to function properly?

- The content ID for a particular page; this should be unique (one entry per ID allowed)

- The friendly URL

We should decide on an important design consideration right now: do we want to support aliases for a friendly URL? By alias, I am referring to /aboutus/ and /about/ referring to and automatically redirecting the user to the canonical /about-us/. Although we may not need the functionality now, let's design an alias system as well. An alias would need the following:

- The content ID for a particular page; not unique (many entries per ID)

- The alias URL

Now we can start the business of designing tables to support these systems. Let's begin with a table called `FriendlyURLs`. The T-SQL to create this table is defined in Listing 9–7.

Listing 9–7. The T-SQL to Create the FriendlyURLs Table

```
SET ANSI_NULLS ON
GO

SET QUOTED_IDENTIFIER ON
GO

CREATE TABLE [dbo].[FriendlyURLs](
    [contentID] [int] NOT NULL,
    [url] [nvarchar](200) COLLATE SQL_Latin1_General_CP1_CI_AS NOT NULL,
```

```
 CONSTRAINT [PK_FriendlyURLs] PRIMARY KEY CLUSTERED
(
[contentID] ASC
)
WITH (
    PAD_INDEX = OFF,
    IGNORE_DUP_KEY = OFF) ON [PRIMARY]
) ON [PRIMARY]
```

As before, we can add a bit of sample data to the table for use as we develop code to support these URLs. Figure 9–4 shows the sample.

contentID	url
1	/homepage-test/

Figure 9–4. A friendly URL for the home page content we've created

Next, we'll create the AliasURLs table that will allow us to provide alternative ways of reaching this content if desired. Listing 9–8 defines the T-SQL to create this table.

Listing 9–8. The T-SQL to Create the FriendlyURLs Table

```
SET ANSI_NULLS ON
GO

SET QUOTED_IDENTIFIER ON
GO

CREATE TABLE [dbo].[AliasURLs](
        [contentID] [int] NOT NULL,
        [url] [nvarchar](200) COLLATE SQL_Latin1_General_CP1_CI_AS NOT NULL
) ON [PRIMARY]
```

Note that we didn't apply any primary key constraints; we do intend for multiple URLs to be available for accessing a particular piece of content. There can be only one primary URL, but many aliases. Let's create a few aliases for use in a bit, as shown in Figure 9–5.

contentID	url
1	/homepage/
1	/home/
1	/default/

Figure 9–5. Several aliases that will direct the user to the primary URL

Stored Procedures for Friendly URLs

We need to create a few stored procedures that will allow us to get the information we need when retrieving content data. First, let's create the GetContentIDByPrimaryURL procedure that will return the content ID for a given friendly URL (shown in Listing 9–9).

Listing 9–9. The T-SQL to Create the GetContentIDByPrimaryURL Stored Procedure

```
SET ANSI_NULLS ON
GO

SET QUOTED_IDENTIFIER ON
GO

CREATE PROCEDURE [dbo].[GetContentIDByPrimaryURL]
        @url nvarchar(200)
AS
BEGIN
        SELECT contentID FROM FriendlyURLs WHERE url=@url
END
```

Next, we need a stored procedure that will determine the correct primary URL when an alias is the method of arriving at the CMS. GetPrimaryURLByAlias, as shown in Listing 9–10.

Listing 9–10. The T-SQL to Create the GetPrimaryURLByAlias Stored Procedure

```
SET ANSI_NULLS ON
GO

SET QUOTED_IDENTIFIER ON
GO

CREATE PROCEDURE [dbo].[GetPrimaryURLByAlias]
    @aliasURL nvarchar(200)
AS
BEGIN
    SELECT url FROM FriendlyURLs WHERE contentID =
      (SELECT contentID FROM AliasURLs WHERE url = @aliasURL)
END
GO
```

Earlier, when we supplied test data we said that the primary (or canonical, if you prefer to think in Google-speak) URL for content ID 1 was /homepage-test/. Let's run the GetPrimaryURLByAlias stored procedure with the alias /home/ provided and ensure we're getting the correct result, which is shown in Figure 9–6.

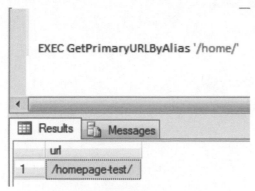

Figure 9–6. The expected output of the stored procedure is the primary URL.

If a user arrives at our site via one of the aliases, say /home/, the CMS will examine the alias data first. If a suitable alias is found, the URL will be returned, and the CMS will redirect the user to that new page. If an alias is not found, then the primary URL table will be checked for a matching URL. If a match is not found in the primary table, then the CMS should return a friendly Page Not Found.

Exploiting the Page Life Cycle

To handle something like extensionless URLs, we've got to dig into the life cycle of a typical page in .NET. Although I'm not going to break down every event here, I will highlight the one that we need to focus on: Application_BeginRequest.

You can work with page events in the Global.asax file in the root of your application. Right-click the Web project and click Add New Item. Select Global Application Class, and add it to the project. Once added, you'll see that a variety of methods have already been provided for you. Remove everything between the script tags, and add the Application_BeginRequest method, as shown in Listing 9–11.

Listing 9–11. The Clean Global.asax File with Application_BeginRequest Added

```
<%@ Application Language="C#" %>

<script runat="server">

    void Application_BeginRequest(object sender, EventArgs e)
    {

    }

</script>
```

This event fires when a user requests a page from your application. We will use this event as a point at which we can interrupt the normal processing of a request and handle things our own way. We can perform a simple experiment first to see how effective this method really is. Modify the Global.asax file so that it looks like Listing 9–12.

Listing 9–12. Catching Requests and Passing Them to a Predetermined URL

```
<%@ Application Language="C#" %>

<script runat="server">

    void Application_BeginRequest(object sender, EventArgs e)
    {
        HttpContext.Current.RewritePath("content.aspx?id=1", false);
    }

</script>
```

Run the application again; try navigating to /Web/not-a-real-page, and you should see the output as displayed in Figure 9–7.

■ **Tip** You'll notice that the style sheet we created earlier is no longer applied to the page. This is because we have interrupted the normal processing of a page, and all requests get routed to the content.aspx per our instructions. We will fix this issue shortly; for now, just note that it is both normal and not unexpected at this stage.

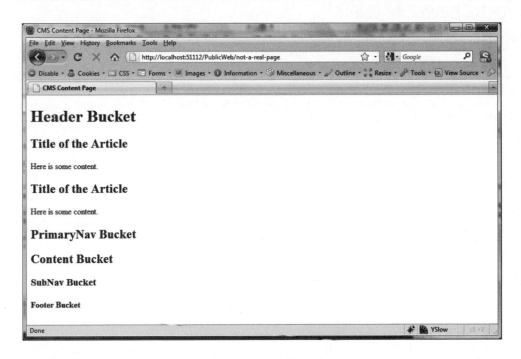

Figure 9–7. The Application_BeginRequest method is routing our pages to a specific location.

I hope it's clear that you now have what amounts to absolute control over URL processing for these pages. Essentially any input can be handled, so long as the web server is capable of processing the request and sending it to your application.

Request Exclusion

Now we can go ahead and exclude certain types of requests from the pipeline immediately, which will allow us to restore our style sheet. We'll begin by writing code in the Global.asax file and fleshing out the other libraries as needed.

At this point, we could come up with a list of media files and exclude them from the request pipeline in the Application_BeginRequest method, but that's not a clean solution. A better way would be to instantiate our Business library and let it handle this type of task, as shown in Listing 9–13.

Listing 9 13. Setting Up Code to Exclude Certain Requests

```
<%@ Application Language="C#" %>

<script runat="server">

    void Application_BeginRequest(object sender, EventArgs e)
    {
        var request = HttpContext.Current.Request.RawUrl.ToString().ToLower();

        // all excluded types should signal an exit from the rewrite pipeline
        if (Business.Rewrite.IsExcludedRequest(request)) return;

        HttpContext.Current.RewritePath("content.aspx?id=1", false);
    }

</script>
```

So, the question becomes, what types of requests do we want to exclude? Based on experience, here is the list that covers most common requests in a CMS:

- .css
- .js
- .png
- .gif
- .bmp
- .jpg/.jpeg
- .mov
- .ashx
- .asmx

Open the Business project, and create a new class file called Rewrite. This class will serve as the overall manager of the request pipeline moving forward. Listing 9–14 shows the code for the Rewrite class.

Listing 9–14. The Code to Exclude Certain Types of Requests

```csharp
using System;
using System.Collections.Generic;
using System.Linq;
using System.Text;

namespace Business
{
    public static class Rewrite
    {
        /// <summary>
        /// Checks incoming request against a list of excluded types
        /// </summary>
        /// <param name="request">the incoming request</param>
        /// <returns>true if the current request should be excluded</returns>
        public static bool IsExcludedRequest(string request)
        {
            if (request.Contains(".css") ||
                request.Contains(".js") ||
                request.Contains(".png") ||
                request.Contains(".gif") ||
                request.Contains(".bmp") ||
                request.Contains(".jpg") ||
                request.Contains(".jpeg") ||
                request.Contains(".mov") ||
                request.Contains(".ashx") ||
                request.Contains(".asmx"))
            {
                return true;
            }
            return false;
        }
    }
}
```

Running the application again shows that our code was successful in identifying that the .css file request was processed by the .NET pipeline and intercepted by our own rewrite pipeline (see Figure 9–8).

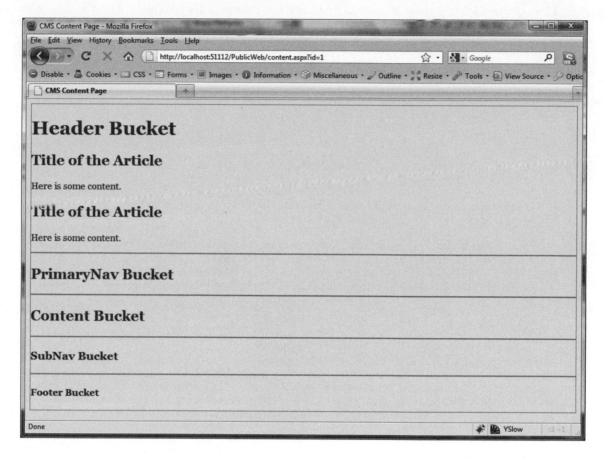

Figure 9–8. The CMS page again has the proper style sheet applied.

■ **Note** If you browse to /Web/, you'll see a directory listing; the content.aspx file is never hit. The default page in the Visual Studio server is Default.aspx. This problem can be solved when run through IIS by adding content.aspx as a default content page.

Retrieving Friendly URLs

We have established what the CMS needs to ignore on a request-by-request basis; now we can turn our attention to retrieving content based on friendly URLs.

Although the CMS will check alias URLs first, we'll build the primary URL feature first, as shown in Listing 9–15. (It's redundant to check primary URLs first; if an alias is the correct match, the code would have to check the primary, the alias, and then the primary again after a redirection.)

Listing 9–15. Checking Primary URLs for a Matching Request

```
<%@ Application Language="C#" %>

<script runat="server">

    void Application_BeginRequest(object sender, EventArgs e)
    {
        var request = HttpContext.Current.Request.RawUrl.ToString().ToLower();
        int? contentID = null;

        // all excluded types should signal an exit from the rewrite pipeline
        if (Business.Rewrite.IsExcludedRequest(request)) return;

        // attempt to pull up a content ID by checking the primary URLs
        contentID = Business.Rewrite.GetIDByPrimaryURL(request);

        if (contentID != null) HttpContext.Current.RewritePath("content.aspx?id=" + contentID,
false);
    }

</script>
```

We have a nullable content ID, in case no proper value can be found after we check the database. The Business library's Rewrite class needs a GetIDByPrimaryURL method that should return an integer value for the content ID (or null if no value is found). If the contentID value is not null, we'll rewrite the execution path to the correct ID and retrieve content for that particular value.

Let's modify the Rewrite class in Business with our desired result, as shown in Listing 9–16.

Listing 9–16. The Rewrite Class Calls Down to the Data Tier for the Necessary Information

```
using System;
using System.Collections.Generic;
using System.Linq;
using System.Text;

namespace Business
{
    public static class Rewrite
    {
        /// <summary>
        /// Checks incoming request against a list of excluded types
        /// </summary>
        /// <param name="request">the incoming request</param>
        /// <returns>true if the current request should be excluded</returns>
        public static bool IsExcludedRequest(string request)
        {
            if (request.Contains(".css") ||
                request.Contains(".js") ||
```

```
                    request.Contains(".png") ||
                    request.Contains(".gif") ||
                    request.Contains(".bmp") ||
                    request.Contains(".jpg") ||
                    request.Contains(".jpeg") ||
                    request.Contains(".mov") ||
                    request.Contains(".ashx") ||
                    request.Contains(".asmx"))
            {
                return true;
            }
            return false;
        }

        /// <summary>
        /// Attempts to pull up a content ID for an incoming friendly URL
        /// </summary>
        /// <param name="request">the incoming request</param>
        /// <returns>a nullable integer for the content ID if available</returns>
        public int? GetIDByPrimaryUrl(string request)
        {
            return Data.Rewrite.GetIDByPrimaryUrl(request);
        }
    }
}
```

Since we've already performed the leg-work of writing the stored procedure for retrieving primary URLs, it's a pretty simple task of writing the necessary data access code. Add a Rewrite class to the Data project with the content from Listing 9–17.

Listing 9–17. The Data Access code for Retrieving Primary URLs

```
using System;
using System.Data;
using System.Data.SqlClient;
using System.Collections.Generic;
using System.Linq;
using System.Text;

namespace Data
{
    public static class Rewrite
    {
        /// <summary>
        /// Returns a content ID for a particular request
        /// </summary>
        /// <param name="request">the incoming request</param>
        /// <returns>a nullable content ID for the content if available</returns>
        public static int? GetIDByPrimaryUrl(string request)
        {
            int? contentID = null;

            using (var conn = Factory.GetConnection())
```

```
        {
            var comm = Factory.GetCommand("GetContentIDByPrimaryURL");
            comm.CommandType = CommandType.StoredProcedure;
            comm.Parameters.AddWithValue("@url", request);

            try
            {
                conn.Open();
                var reader = comm.ExecuteReader();
                if (reader.Read())
                {
                    contentID = reader.GetInt32(0);
                }
                conn.Close();
            }
            finally
            {
                conn.Close();
            }
        }

        return contentID;
    }
}
}
```

While we're on the subject of cleaning URLs, there's no real reason for users to see the /Web/ segment of the URL that we've displayed so far. To remove it, click the Web project, and in the Properties tab below the Solution Explorer, change the Virtual path property from /Web to just /. Figure 9–9 shows this particular property.

Figure 9–9. The Virtual path property has been changed to a single slash.

Because we changed the Virtual path property of the project, we need to make one more small tweak to the Global.asax file so that the content.aspx file is at the expected path, as shown in Listing 9–18.

Listing 9–18. A Minor Tweak to the content.aspx Path

```
<%@ Application Language="C#" %>

<script runat="server">

    void Application_BeginRequest(object sender, EventArgs e)
    {
        var request = HttpContext.Current.Request.RawUrl.ToString().ToLower();
        int? contentID = null;

        // all excluded types should signal an exit from the rewrite pipeline
        if (Business.Rewrite.IsExcludedRequest(request)) return;

        // attempt to pull up a content ID by checking the primary URLs
        contentID = Business.Rewrite.GetIDByPrimaryUrl(request);

        if (contentID != null) HttpContext.Current.RewritePath("/content.aspx?id=" +
contentID, false);
    }

</script>
```

Now you can run the application again; try browsing to any URL that isn't defined in the FriendlyURLs table. You should be presented with a stark 404 error indicating that the particular page couldn't be loaded, as shown in Figure 9–10. We will provide a more friendly 404 page at the end of this chapter.

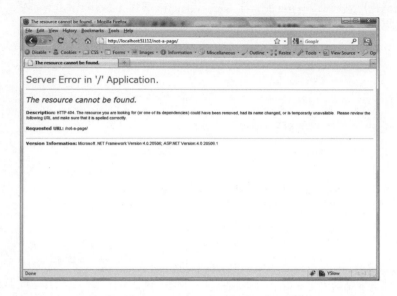

Figure 9–10. Browsing to unknown URLs brings up a decidely unfriendly 404 page.

Now try browsing to /homepage-test/; you should find that content ID 1 loads properly, and all the buckets, embeddable, and style sheet information is functional, as shown in Figure 9–11.

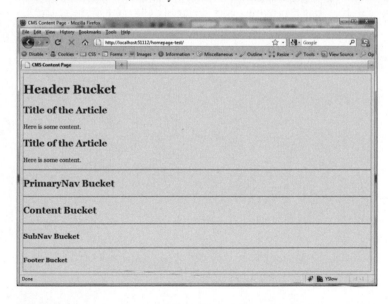

Figure 9–11. Browsing to the /homepage-test/ URL brings up content ID 1 without exposing implementation details.

Retrieving Alias URLs and Response.RedirectPermanent()

Now that we have the necessary functionality to support primary URLs, we can turn our attention toward alias URLs. We've already created the stored procedure for returning the primary URL based on an incoming alias URL, so let's jump right into designing our code in Global.asax, which is shown in Listing 9–19.

Listing 9–19. Accounting for Alias URLs and Their Redirections

```csharp
<%@ Application Language="C#" %>

<script runat="server">

    void Application_BeginRequest(object sender, EventArgs e)
    {
        var request = HttpContext.Current.Request.RawUrl.ToString().ToLower();
        int? contentID = null;
        string foundPrimaryViaAlias = String.Empty;

        // all excluded types should signal an exit from the rewrite pipeline
        if (Business.Rewrite.IsExcludedRequest(request)) return;

        // attempt to pull up a primary URL by checking aliases
        foundPrimaryViaAlias = Business.Rewrite.GetPrimaryUrlByAlias(request);

        // if we found a primary, indicating this was an alias, redirect to the primary
        if (!String.IsNullOrEmpty(foundPrimaryViaAlias))
        {
            Response.RedirectPermanent(foundPrimaryViaAlias);
        }

        // attempt to pull up a content ID by checking the primary URLs
        contentID = Business.Rewrite.GetIDByPrimaryUrl(request);

        if (contentID != null) HttpContext.Current.RewritePath("/content.aspx?id=" +
contentID, false);
    }

</script>
```

■ **Note** Response.RedirectPermanent is a new addition to .NET in version 4. Most developers are familiar with the older Response.Redirect, which issued a temporary redirect (302) to new content. Although functional, it's not accurate in the eyes of search engines under some conditions. For example, our alias is an available method of arriving at content, but it's not the permanent home for it; a 302 redirect would indicate that the alias only temporarily points to the parent content. The RedirectPermanent method allows for 301 redirects ("Moved Permanently"), which is more accurate information for a search engine. To the end user, there is no difference in experience while using the site.

This code calls the Business library's Rewrite class and attempts to get a primary URL as a result. If it is able to do so, then the class must have been able to find an alias, so therefore the request should be permanently redirected to the primary URL. Let's make some changes to the Rewrite class in the Business library to support this code, as shown in Listing 9–20.

Listing 9–20. A Business Tier Pass-Through for the Data Tier

```csharp
using System;
using System.Collections.Generic;
using System.Linq;
using System.Text;

namespace Business
{
    public static class Rewrite
    {
        /// <summary>
        /// Checks incoming request against a list of excluded types
        /// </summary>
        /// <param name="request">the incoming request</param>
        /// <returns>true if the current request should be excluded</returns>
        public static bool IsExcludedRequest(string request)
        {
            if (request.Contains(".css") ||
                request.Contains(".js") ||
                request.Contains(".png") ||
                request.Contains(".gif") ||
                request.Contains(".bmp") ||
                request.Contains(".jpg") ||
                request.Contains(".jpeg") ||
                request.Contains(".mov") ||
                request.Contains(".ashx") ||
                request.Contains(".asmx"))
            {
                return true;
            }
            return false;
        }

        /// <summary>
        /// Attempts to pull up a content ID for an incoming friendly URL
        /// </summary>
        /// <param name="request">the incoming request</param>
        /// <returns>a nullable integer for the content ID if available</returns>
        public static int? GetIDByPrimaryUrl(string request)
        {
            return Data.Rewrite.GetIDByPrimaryUrl(request);
        }

        /// <summary>
        ///  Attempts to pull up a primary URL based on an incoming alias
        /// </summary>
        /// <param name="request">the incoming request</param>
```

```
        /// <returns>a primary URL string, if available</returns>
        public static string GetPrimaryUrlByAlias(string request)
        {
            return Data.Rewrite.GetPrimaryUrlByAlias(request);
        }
    }
}
```

Simple enough. Now we only need to add code in the Data tier to call our stored procedure and return a primary URL if one can be found. Open the Rewrite class, and make the modifications shown in Listing 9–21.

Listing 9–21. The Rewrite Class in the Data Tier, Modified to Return Primary URLs

```
using System;
using System.Data;
using System.Data.SqlClient;
using System.Collections.Generic;
using System.Linq;
using System.Text;

namespace Data
{
    public static class Rewrite
    {
        /// <summary>
        /// Returns a content ID for a particular request
        /// </summary>
        /// <param name="request">the incoming request</param>
        /// <returns>a nullable content ID for the content if available</returns>
        public static int? GetIDByPrimaryUrl(string request)
        {
            int? contentID = null;

            using (var conn = Factory.GetConnection())
            {
                var comm = Factory.GetCommand("GetContentIDByPrimaryURL");
                comm.CommandType = CommandType.StoredProcedure;
                comm.Parameters.AddWithValue("@url", request);

                try
                {
                    conn.Open();
                    var reader = comm.ExecuteReader();
                    if (reader.Read())
                    {
                        contentID = reader.GetInt32(0);
                    }
                    conn.Close();
                }
                finally
                {
```

```csharp
                conn.Close();
            }
        }

        return contentID;
    }

    /// <summary>
    ///  Attempts to pull up a primary URL based on an incoming alias
    /// </summary>
    /// <param name="request">the incoming request</param>
    /// <returns>a primary URL string, if available</returns>
    public static string GetPrimaryUrlByAlias(string request)
    {
        string primaryURL = String.Empty;

        using (var conn = Factory.GetConnection())
        {
            var comm = Factory.GetCommand("GetPrimaryURLByAlias");
            comm.CommandType = CommandType.StoredProcedure;
            comm.Parameters.AddWithValue("@aliasUrl", request);

            try
            {
                conn.Open();
                var reader = comm.ExecuteReader();
                if (reader.Read())
                {
                    primaryURL = reader.GetString(0);
                }
                conn.Close();
            }
            finally
            {
                conn.Close();
            }
        }

        return primaryURL;
    }
}
}
```

Now run the application, and browse to /home/. You should immediately be redirected to the primary URL, which is /homepage-test/, as shown in Figure 9–12. Feel free to experiment with the other aliases and ensure that everything is working properly.

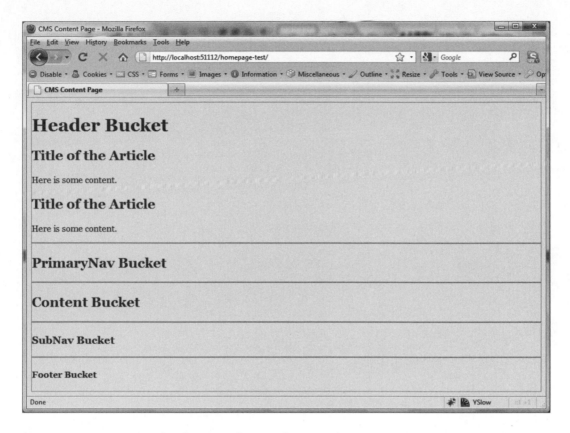

Figure 9–12. Browsing to the alias URL /home/ redirects to the primary URL /homepage-test/.

Summary

This wraps up the discussion of how to implement a content management system, as well as the book itself. In this chapter, we explored some key SEO concepts and went over some guidelines to follow when carrying out SEO. We then saw where these concepts and guidelines fit in the context of the CMS as a whole. We implemented a custom system for mapping URLs between unfriendly and friendly types and made use of .NET 4's new RedirectPermament method to improve the accuracy of how search engines view content within the site.

Building a CMS that is both extensible and high-performance is a complex task at best, but .NET 4.0 has a lot of technology behind it to make the process easier, if not outright enjoyable. As such, I recommend again that you grab a copy of the source code from the Apress site, because it contains a lot of additional code and examples that simply wouldn't all fit into the book.

I hope that the CMS serves as a good starting point for your future endeavors; maybe we will meet again for .NET 5.0.

Index

■■■

■ N

You Need the Companion eBook

Your purchase of this book entitles you to buy the companion PDF-version eBook for only $10. Take the weightless companion with you anywhere.

We believe this Apress title will prove so indispensable that you'll want to carry it with you everywhere, which is why we are offering the companion eBook (in PDF format) for $10 to customers who purchase this book now. Convenient and fully searchable, the PDF version of any content-rich, page-heavy Apress book makes a valuable addition to your programming library. You can easily find and copy code—or perform examples by quickly toggling between instructions and the application. Even simultaneously tackling a donut, diet soda, and complex code becomes simplified with hands-free eBooks!

Once you purchase your book, getting the $10 companion eBook is simple:

1. Visit **www.apress.com/promo/tendollars/**.

2. Complete a basic registration form to receive a randomly generated question about this title.

3. Answer the question correctly in 60 seconds, and you will receive a promotional code to redeem for the $10.00 eBook.

233 Spring Street, New York, NY 10013

Offer valid through 11/10.